Nationalism and Globalism in Design   Hugh Aldersey-Williams

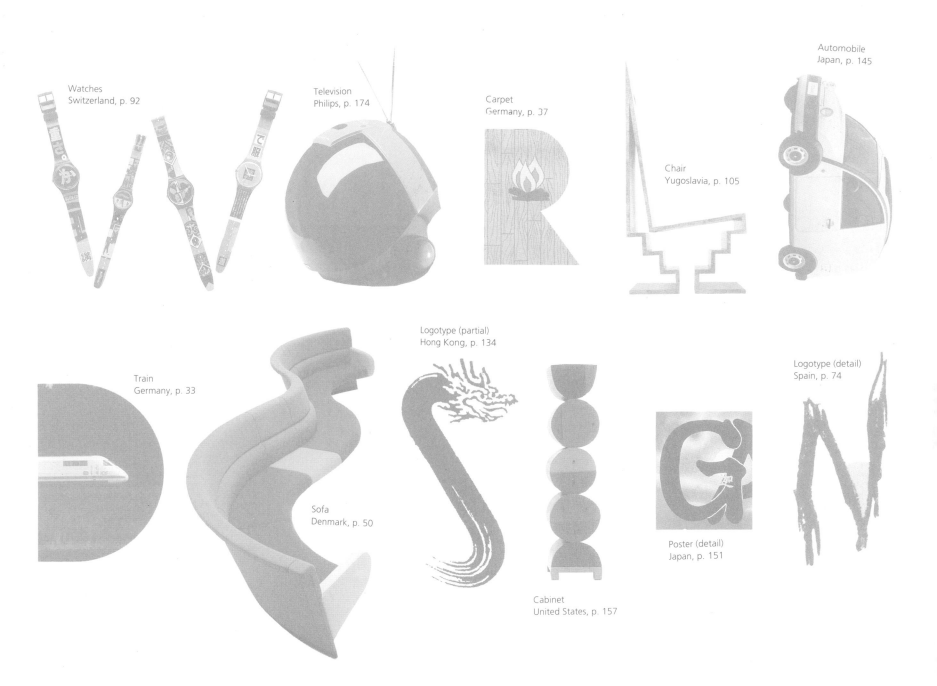

Watches
Switzerland, p. 92

Television
Philips, p. 174

Carpet
Germany, p. 37

Chair
Yugoslavia, p. 105

Automobile
Japan, p. 145

Train
Germany, p. 33

Logotype (partial)
Hong Kong, p. 134

Logotype (detail)
Spain, p. 74

Sofa
Denmark, p. 50

Poster (detail)
Japan, p. 151

Cabinet
United States, p. 157

In memory of my American grandparents,
Hosmer and Elinor Redfield

First published in the United States of America in 1992 by
Rizzoli International Publications, Inc.
300 Park Avenue South, New York, NY 10010

Library of Congress Cataloging-in-Publication Data

Aldersey-Williams, Hugh.
    World Design : nationalism and globalism in design /
Hugh Aldersey-Williams.
        p.   cm.
    Includes bibliographical references and index.
    ISBN 0-8478-1461-0
    1. Design—History—20th century. I. Title.
NK1390.A43   1992
745.4'442—dc20   91-25674
                                                CIP

World Design

Nationalism and Globalism in Design

Hugh Aldersey-Williams

RIZZOLI
NEW YORK

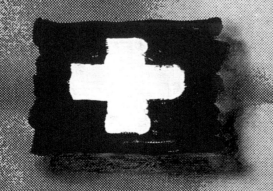

MY OWN CULTURE

Contents

Poster
Frédéric Metz
Bretelle, Université du Québec à
Montréal, 1986

I am an Anglo-American. On my American side I am mostly English, but also one-quarter German, a fraction French, and after that I lose track. I am a simple composite compared to many. Increasingly we are, as the labels on honey jars proclaim of their contents, the "produce of more than one country."

Born and brought up in Britain, I was drawn nevertheless to the United States. While I was there, I wrote a book called *New American Design,* conscious that it was my status as a privileged visitor, as an outsider looking in, that gave me if not the percipience then at least the gall to attempt such a project. Among the principals of the twenty-one firms featured in the book, I counted first-generation immigrants to the United States from nine different countries. Yet these were new *American* designers. Such is the nature of nationality in the United States.

When people set out to work in the modern world the collage of nations gets rapidly more complex. One need look no further than this book. In addition to its Anglo-American author, it has a designer of Cuban-Irish origin and an editor of Armenian descent. It is printed in Japan by an American publisher with Italian ties.

None of this complexity, typical in so many commercial processes, in any way diminishes the importance of the nation or of national identity, however. Indeed, consciousness of nationhood has grown more than anyone could have imagined during the time that this book was being written. Nations are being created (Germany, Quebec? Lithuania?) and dissolved (The Soviet Union? Yugoslavia?) at a greater rate than at any time since the Second World War. Nations remain central to the calculation of political, economic, and cultural actions.

Members of the design profession are as interested as anybody in the question of national identity in the modern world. As delegates from the worlds of commerce and culture, designers are in a better position than most to put theory into practice. In this book I have tried to show how designers are thinking about their cultural identity and how this can or could alter the way they work and the nature of the objects they create.

Of course, this concern is not shared by all designers, probably not even by a majority. Many appear to believe that they can design things that are somehow "culture-free." In searching out the minority of objects that clearly express some aspect of their national character or in listening to the comments of those few designers who seek such expression, I risk being accused of the unscholarly act of selecting only those facts that fit my theory. What about all those products that do not show these characteristics? It would indeed be easier to publish a book with a selection of designs thought devoid of national character to suggest that, as some already believe, globalism has already triumphed. But that is not the point. By stating—sometimes perhaps overstating—the case for national design and by pointing out examples, I hope to offer encouragement to designers who are concerned with the threat posed by globalization to national design identities and who wish to combat that threat in their work.

The national case studies presented here include countries of many types: old and new, large and small, rich and poor, united and fractious. I have not been able to visit all countries worthy of exploration, and no offense is intended to the many that have been omitted.

Often on my travels, I was met with disavowals. One or two people clearly thought I was crazy. More often, designers denied any cultural identity in their own work yet were happy to describe it in the local songs, literature, or architecture. Many felt they could readily identify national styles of design in other countries but not in their own country or in their own work. Such unselfconsciousness on the part of designers is encouraging. It suggests not that national characteristics do not exist but that they are deep-rooted and subliminal. They elude capture and dissection.

One designer warned me that "trying to define, then foster, a nation's aesthetics is like trying to catch an endangered species and save it from extinction by keeping it in a zoo." Perhaps so, but is this a worthless pursuit? In the modern world, where else do most of us see animals but in zoos and on television? More important, endangered species are kept in zoos to breed in order that they may one day be returned to the wild. Perhaps national design identities need a similar period of protection and nurture before they grow sufficiently robust to survive in the wild, where they will become prey to the forces of technological change and international trade.

Certainly, traveling through this global jungle, it was at times almost possible to lose one's sense of purpose. Each glimpse of a globalist conquest, each airplane interior, each snatch of piped Andrew Lloyd Webber music, each Benetton store brought new doubts. Fortunately, the dispiriting process of travel was always relieved upon arrival when each new meeting with a designer would revive my enthusiasm for my task.

Hugh Aldersey-Williams
London
February 1991

Acknowledgments

I am fortunate in that the Internationales Forum für Gestaltung (International Forum for Design) Ulm chose to organize a conference and workshop on "Design and Cultural Identity" at a crucial point during the gestation of this book, and I am grateful to the forum for its support in enabling me to attend this meeting.

Many designers around the world gave their time generously in interviews and conversations or by putting pen to paper to record their comments. In addition to those whose remarks are quoted or whose work is illustrated in the text, there were some designers and many other friends who provided exceptional intelligence, sustenance, and shelter while I was traveling. Their names are listed below. I am indebted to them all.

Finally, I should like to thank my wife, Moira, who endured both my absence and my presence during the two years that it took to bring this book to fruition and who provided inestimable support at all times.

Germany:
Shakwy Abd El-Hafez
Reinhard Komar, IFG Ulm, Stuttgart
Ingrid Lempp, Value Design, Hamburg
Annette Musiolek, *Form und Zweck,* Berlin
Alexander and Gudrun Neumeister, Neumeister Design, Munich
Jörg Ratzlaff, Thomas Gerlach, Frogdesign, Altensteig
Angela Schönberger, IDZ, Berlin
Erik Spiekermann, MetaDesign, Berlin
Dagmar Steffen
Theres Weishappel, Gabriel Kornreich, Büro für Gestaltung, Berlin
Brigitte Wolf, Rat für Formgebung, Frankfurt

The Netherlands:
Robert Blaich, Philips, Eindhoven
Ada Lopes Cardozo, PTT Nederland, Den Haag
Gert Dumbar, Studio Dumbar, Den Haag
René Kemna, Van Holsteijn en Kemna, Delft
Rick Vermeulen, Gerard Hadders, Hard Werken, Rotterdam

Denmark:
Jens Bernsen, Danish Design Centre, Copenhagen
Niels Peter Flint, O2, Copenhagen

Great Britain:
Hassan Bakheit, Dashclever, Canterbury
Steve Braidwood
Robert Brown, Brunel Institute of Bioengineering, Uxbridge
Brigitte Burnett
Jan Burney

Emma Dent Coad
Willy De Mayo
Danny Green
Eric Hobsbawm
Geoff Hollington, Hollington Associates, London
John Chris Jones
Lois Love, Wolff Olins, London
Catherine McDermott, Kingston Polytechnic, Kingston-on-Thames
Hamish Muir, 8vo, London
Jeremy Myerson
Peter Popham, *The Independent*, London
Matthew Rhodes, Schiang UK, London
Winfried Scheuer, Xeno Design, London
John Stoddard, Moggridge Associates, London
James Woudhuysen, Fitch RichardsonSmith, London

France:
Liz Davis, Les Ateliers, Paris
Diane Hill
Margo Rouard, Agence pour la Promotion de la Création Industrielle, Paris

Spain:
Fernando Amat, Vinçon, Barcelona
Mai Felip Hösselbarth, Fundación BCD, Barcelona
Pati Núñez, Associate Designers, Barcelona

Italy:
Nicholas Bewick, Studio De Lucchi, Milan
Clare Brass
Silvio Caputo
Marco Cavallotti, Triennale di Milano, Milan
Tom and Didi Di Palma, DP Foreign Press Service, Milan
Claudia Donà
Isao Hosoe, Ann Marinelli, Isao Hosoe Design, Milan
Perry King, Santiago Miranda, King-Miranda Associati, Milan
Helen Rainey, International Design Agency, Milan

Switzerland:
Uwe Bahnsen, Virginia Pepper, Art Center Europe, La Tour-de-Peilz
Carol Chisholm

Hungary:
András Mengyán, Hungarian Academy of Crafts and Design, Budapest
Anna Velkey, Karakter Studio, Budapest

Yugoslavia:
Oleg Hržić
Janez Suhadolc

Russia
Andrew Maschaninov, Studio MAD, Leningrad
Irina Pribinova, Soviet Society of Designers, Leningrad
Tatiana Samoilova
Yuri Soloviev, Soviet Society of Designers, Moscow

Egypt:
Ahmed Ata, Gamal Aboud, Faculty of Applied Arts, Helwan University, Cairo
Julian Metcalfe
Badran Mohamed Badran, Industrial Design Development Center, Cairo

India:
Uday Athavankar, Industrial Design Center, Bombay
David da Silva
VK Jagannathan, Jags Design Research Centre, Bombay
Preeti Khandelwal, *Interiors Annual*, Bombay
Jogi Panghaal
Shyla and Naushad Patel
Gita Piramal
Vikas Satwalekar, MP Ranjan, Dhimant Panchal, National Institute of Design, Ahmedabad

Singapore:
Jonathan Bonsey, Addison Design Consultants
Gregory Foster, Philips Singapore
Peter Lawton, Yeo Chung Sun, Irène Colhag-Yeo, Lawton and Yeo Design Associates

Hong Kong:
Alan Chan, Alan Chan Design Company
Ji-Ping Chang, Patrick Bruce, Christopher Law, RSCG Conran Design
Choi Kai-Yan, Design Ideal
Christopher Chow, Hong Kong Trade Development Council
Lyn Pepall, Eastern Electronics Company
Matthew and Irene Turner
Sue and Duncan Wilkinson

South Korea:
Chang Sea Young, Kyung S. Min, Space Group of Korea, Seoul
Choi Kil-Yull, Lee Sung-Man, Min Myung-Suk, *Design Journal*, Seoul
John Ridding, *Financial Times*, Seoul

Japan:
Azby Brown
Kiyoharu Fujimoto, GK, Tokyo
Shin Fukushima, Keiko Ihara, GK Institute of Doguology, Tokyo
Naomi and Elizabeth Ichihara
Tadanori Nagasawa, Design Analysis International, Tokyo

United States:
Véronique Aptekman-Silver and Stu Silver
Constantin Boym, Red Square, New York
Yoshiko Ebihara, Gallery 91, New York
Annetta Hanna, Chee Pearlman, Nick Backlund, *International Design*, New York
Haig Khachatoorian, North Carolina State University, Raleigh
Herbert Pfeifer, Frogdesign, Campbell, California
Earl Powell, Design Management Institute, Boston
Gene Reshanov, Polivka Logan Designers, Minneapolis
Jeff Smith, Gerard Furbershaw, Bill Evans, Lunar Design, Palo Alto, California
Tucker Viemeister, Smart Design, New York
Cooper Woodring, Better Mousetraps, Plandome, New York

Canada:
François Dallegret, Artorium, Montreal
Tom McFall, University of Alberta, Edmonton

Globalism, nationalism, and design

Advertisement
Oliviero Toscani
Benetton, 1990

Benetton has been one of the few global corporations to capitalize on a higher ideal of universalism.

Handycam video camera
Sony

In electronic products, everybody regards miniaturization as a benefit. The Japanese have proven themselves best in this field, and so global electronic products are almost always Japanese-made.

1. "Europe Resists Global Brands," *DesignWeek* (September 21, 1990): 6.

2. Michael E. Porter, *The Competitive Advantage of Nations* (Free Press, 1990).

3. "The State of the Nation-State," *The Economist* (December 22, 1990): 73.

4. Paul Ricoeur, "From Nation to Humanity: Task of Christians" in *Political and Social Essays by Paul Ricoeur,* David Stewart and Joseph Bien, eds. (Ohio University Press, 1974).

5. ———, *History and Truth,* trans. Charles A. Kelbley (Northwestern University Press, 1965).

6. "National Characteristics of Design" exhibition catalog, Boilerhouse Project (London: Victoria and Albert Museum, 1985).

Ask designers what they think "global design" is, and the impulsive answer often comes back in a torrent of familiar brand names, with the likes of McDonald's and Coca-Cola high on the list. These brands are indeed global in their reach: Coca-Cola topped the 1990 "ImagePower" survey conducted by the San Francisco-based corporate identity consultants, Landor Associates. McDonald's ranked eighth and Pepsi tenth in this measurement of the recognition of international brands.[1]

Yet their products are not "designed." Despite the fact that they are prepared in many localities, their appearance and the appearance of the companies that make them are effective in suggesting their American origins. The products of The Walt Disney Company, which ranked fifth in the Landor league table, not only reflect their American origins but are also generally made in America. This, then, is not global design but global distribution of a national product.

The other companies on the Landor list of global brands manufacture consumer durables. Sony, Daimler-Benz (the maker of Mercedes-Benz automobiles), Kodak, Toyota, and IBM placed second, third, fourth, seventh, and ninth, respectively. Some of them call themselves globalists. But once again, their products often provide strong hints as to the originating company's root nationality.

Most global products reflect nothing more profound than the power of their manufacturers. Global food and drink is American food and drink. Global movies are Hollywood movies, despite the fact that the environment and behavior they portray is patently alien to much of their audience. Global electronics goods are Japanese electronics goods. The world's luxury items are French luxury items, and so on. According to Michael Porter of Harvard Business School: "Nascent global industry leaders always begin with some advantage created at home, whether it be a preferred product design, a higher level of product quality, a new marketing concept, or a factor cost advantage."[2] American fast-food and mass-entertainment industries grew apparently insuperable because they learned to satisfy the world's largest domestic market before turning their attention overseas. The success of Sony and Panasonic accords with the Japanese preoccupation with miniaturization and to some extent was gained with the help of government assistance to the then-fledgling national consumer-electronics industry.

It is small wonder that globalism and globalization have become an obsession in business and culture alike. Since the Second World War, our lives have been transformed in many ways that appear to diminish the importance of national borders. Trade between nations has multiplied by a factor of thir-

teen since 1950.[3] The effect of technologies—not least the technology of war—has served to bring communities closer together. Nuclear annihilation threatens us all. The media have an ever-greater reach. People are more mobile. Capital is held internationally and, as a consequence, economic and political events in one country affect those in another more than ever before. The French essayist Paul Ricoeur coined the term "mondialization" to reflect this growing interdependence, observing that "the foreign policy of every country has become the domestic policy of humanity."[4]

There is a moral argument in favor of globalization, although this aspect of the matter does not appear to have detained the globalists of the business world. Throughout modern history there have been utopian thinkers who have wished for the dissolution of national boundaries. For their part, designers are often people of a liberal cast of mind who are inclined to believe that national borders are invidious things. Their dilemma is that they do not wish to abet the emergence of narrow political nationalism through design that celebrates national cultures, but neither have they seen much to inspire them in the only apparent alternative of global design. Ricoeur states the paradox succinctly in his essay "Universal Civilization and National Cultures": "The phenomenon of universalization, while being an advancement of mankind, at the same time constitutes a sort of subtle destruction, not only of traditional cultures, which might not be an irreparable wrong, but also of . . . the creative nucleus of great cultures."[5]

The designers' dilemma becomes more pressing as it becomes more apparent that global design will not sweep all before it. The supposition made in the 1970s by Theodore Levitt and other business theorists that national tastes and cultures would converge, does not appear to be coming true. People's habits of eating, drinking, washing, working, and playing remain distinct. Thus, the products that help them do these things will and should continue to reflect the different ways they do them from country to country, even if many manufacturers would rather they did not. According to the catalog from the "National Characteristics of Design" exhibition held at the Victoria and Albert Museum's Boilerhouse in 1985: "What might be true is that the differences between the way products from different countries look have become more subtle. In fact there is every indication that the way they look will become increasingly variegated."[6]

National or regional character will certainly not be eradicated in the forseeable future. Globalist corporations are jumping the gun by pretending that regional differences do not exist in their multination-

Versailles line wristwatch
Swatch, 1990

Products that are highly fashionable are often more globally acceptable.

Scanman scanner
Frogdesign
Logitech, 1989

My First Sony children's audio equipment
Sony, 1989

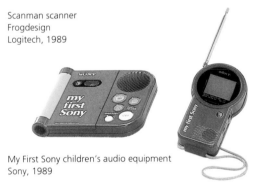

Faucet
Plan Créatif
Porcher

It can sometimes seem that "global design" entails little more than simple forms, large radii, and a splash of color.

7. *Webster's Ninth New Collegiate Dictionary* (Merriam-Webster, 1986).

8. Kenichi Ohmae, *The Borderless World* (Harper Business, 1990).

9. Ibid.

al markets. In so doing, they are implicitly attempting to unify or homogenize mankind (according to one's view of whether this is a positive or a negative goal). So-called global products are undoubtedly less than ideal for many users, but because of the power of these corporations and the related enfeeblement of local manufacturers, the choice for the user is often that between the global product and no product at all. The result is an erosion of cultural identity as it has historically been expressed in the form of useful, locally made artifacts.

It is often assumed that global products are predominantly plastic and mass produced. The concomitant assumption is that local, regional, or national design can best be expressed—perhaps can only be expressed—through the use of indigenous materials and the employment of traditional skills. There is a wedge now being driven between globalism, artificiality, and mass production on the one hand and regionalism, naturalism, and craft on the other. Those who oppose globalism and favor regional design must resist this divergence and seek out, instead, the potential for current materials and technologies to augment meaningful local cultural content in future design. They must draw the distinction between *extrinsic* and *intrinsic* descriptors of regional styles of design.

Webster's Dictionary defines globalism as "a national policy of treating the whole world as a proper sphere for political influence," before inviting comparison with "imperialism" and "internationalism."[7] Framed in terms familiar to trading companies, the definition might become "a corporate policy of treating the whole world as a market."

This definition does not stipulate whether that world comprises a single market or many different ones. The room for ambiguity is hinted at in Webster's referral to entries under "imperialism" and "internationalism," terms that represent the negative and positive extremes of globalist behavior in trade as in politics. In the former camp are those who wish to market the same goods to the greatest number of people and who see global brands as the way forward; in the latter are those who are interested in ensuring their competitiveness by accommodating the wishes of consumers in regional segments within their world market. Different approaches suit different product types. IBM, for example, has taken a global approach with a monolithic design language. Swatch and Sony are global more because of the fashion appeal of their products. On the other hand, many large automobile manufacturers go to some lengths to specify versions of their basic models that they believe will appeal to particular regional markets.

Among design companies, Frogdesign is per-

haps the best pretender to the globalist title. It has offices in Germany, Tokyo, and California from which it entertains the romantic idea of reaching a universal audience through products that make a simple appeal to the emotions. Frogdesign's cofounder, Hartmut Esslinger, is much taken with the theories of Kenichi Ohmae, the Japan managing director of the McKinsey management consultancy, put forward in his book *Triad Power,* and rationalizes the existence of Frogdesign offices in each of the three "triad centers"—Europe, the United States, and Japan—on this basis. The Japanese group, GK, is the only other design firm with this triple foothold, but its attitude to global design is more ambivalent than that of Frogdesign.

Although "global design" has its adherents and its detractors, little thought appears to have been given to a working definition of the phrase. It is not clear what it means in terms of either function or style. The protagonists of global design cited here produce work that is solidly rooted in the tradition of the Bauhaus and Ulm schools. Platonic geometry dominates the form. The function is generally transparent. Decoration is kept to a minimum, although colors are bright. The use of simple shapes rounded off with large radii is well suited to the process by which molded plastic parts are produced in large numbers. It would seem that in stylistic terms global design is nothing more than good old-fashioned functionalism decked out in softer shapes and brighter colors.

Ostensibly, globalists are more sensitive than centralized multinationals to local requirements. According to Ohmae: "A global corporation today is fundamentally different from the colonial-style multinationals of the 1960s and 1970s. It serves its customers in all key markets with equal dedication."[8] This statement is disingenuous, and many people in those markets would disagree with it. Just because the dedication is "equal" does not mean it is absolute or sufficient for all customers in all markets or even for most customers in any market.

Ohmae describes five stages through which a corporation evolves to become "genuinely global." Stages one and two involve the export of its products, first through local distributors and then through its own agencies. In stage three, the company also begins to locate some manufacturing, marketing, and sales activity in the countries to which it exports. By stage four, the company has become an insider, undertaking local research and development, design, and engineering, which allows it "to replicate in a new environment the hardware, systems and operational approaches that have worked so well at home."[9] In stage five, companies must devolve all operations, relying on a network of local managers

Train à Grande Vitesse
Atlantique
Roger Tallon, ADSA Design
Programme
SNCF, 1989
Photograph by Lafontant

The TGV has become an expression of France's technological culture. Later arrivals, such as the German ICE train, strive to look different.

Inter-City Express high-speed
train
Neumeister Design and others
Deutsche Bundesbahn

Flying Object desk
Elixir
Narbur, 1990

Corporate identity
Michael Peters Group
Conservative Party, 1987

Very different government-inspired design revolutions in France and Britain have led respectively to distinctive new vocabularies in furniture and in graphic design.

10. Ohmae, *The Borderless World*.

sharing the same corporate culture. Says Ohmae: "Moving to stage five is another matter entirely. What is called for is what Akio Morita of Sony has termed global localization, a new orientation that looks in both directions. At base the problem is psychological, a question of values.

"Before national identity, before local affiliation, before German ego or Italian ego or Japanese ego, comes the commitment to a single, unified global mission."[10] In practice, most corporations espousing global design, including Sony, have not yet progressed beyond stage three or four, although Philips and IBM are two examples of companies that are beginning to implement a design management policy based on a stage-five structure.

Despite the rise of global businesses, globalism is not a concept that attracts ordinary consumers. Far more powerful in people's minds is the idea of the nation. Nationalism is as topical now as it has been at any time since the Second World War. The future of nations and of national character provide compelling subjects for speculation. There are presently good reasons for this interest in many parts of the world.

At the end of 1992 the twelve countries of the European Community will abolish their internal national barriers to the free movement of goods, services, people, and capital. Designers and businesses need to know if the European Community of 1992 will really become the "single market" that is frequently touted or will remain twelve subtly different ones. If, as is likely, the single market will apply for certain types of products and services, while national (or regional) distinctions will remain important in others, they need guidance on which applies when.

Early impressions are that national character will survive in design as in many other areas of cultural endeavor. Recent European experience has highlighted dramatically different design directions in many countries, notwithstanding the unifying power that the European Community exerts over its members. France and Spain have enjoyed a burst of activity in many disciplines, most clearly seen in furniture design. This has taken place at the expense of Italy, which dominated postwar furniture design. Spain is being energized by the emergence of designers who have been educated and have gone into business during the fifteen years of democracy and cultural revival since the fall of General Franco. France has benefited from a government that has taken a paternal interest in the promulgation of a certain sort of design. Britain's very different government has promoted a very different design revolution, pioneering the introduction of a style-led, postindustrial service economy at the expense of product innovation and design.

The idea of pan-European brands aimed at the mythical Euroconsumer that many initially envisaged has receded, except in those areas such as luxury and duty-free goods, where global brands already exist. Articles on design, advertising, and marketing in Europe now warn, instead, of the pitfalls of naïve attempts to impose a uniform taste on discrete markets. Such homogeneity would be not only impractical but boring. Italian advertising would have to lose its bawdiness because it would offend buttoned-down northern tastes. Puns would have to go from British commercials because no one else would understand them. Everybody would be the poorer.

Even within the European Community, the question of cultural identity is not simply a choice between being nationalist or being *communautaire*. The Community and Europe in general are quilted with regions that treasure their own cultural identities—Catalonia, Scotland, Brittany, Bavaria, and so on. With Europe's nation-states weakened by confederation into the Community, these would-be nations see their chance for greater autonomy. They will want to express that autonomy, and design could be one of the best ways to do it.

In the Soviet Union of President Mikhail Gorbachev, perestroika means economic reconstruction. It is still uncertain how this gradual acceptance of capitalist principles will make itself apparent in Soviet design. Will the Soviets imitate European styles or will they look to their own traditions? Will reconstruction lead to a Reconstructivist style, as some avant-garde designers propose?

Many Soviet republics seek secession from the Union or greater autonomy within it. Led by the Baltic republics, these regions are looking westward to the countries with which they have historical ties. Lithuania follows developments in Poland; Latvia and Estonia look to Finland and Scandinavia. Within Yugoslavia, too, individual republics are fissile. Slovenia is especially keen to dissolve old ties and is creating new ones with Italy and Austria that are stronger than at any time since the fall of the Austro-Hungarian empire.

The more economically liberal Eastern bloc countries claim to have had reconstruction before the Soviets. Larger political dynamics condition how these nations' design will develop. Many Eastern European countries aspire to European Community membership. Full membership is a long way off, but the fact that they too are looking westward provides clues as to how their material cultures will evolve.

During the 1980s the Pacific overtook the Atlantic as the ocean over which most of the world's trade makes its passage. The rise of the Pacific Rim countries and the strengthening of links between them have been astonishing. Yet the world's mea-

"Ascent axis"
Yuri Avvakumov/Sergey
Podyomshchikov
1990

*Theoretical projects by
young designers in the
Soviet republics indicate
that perestroika may be
expressed in the emergence
of a "Reconstructivist" style.*

Multiple-media
information terminal
Kozo Design Studio
1984

*After a period of
emulating, then surpassing,
Western design standards,
the Japanese are beginning
to articulate their own
style.*

Paper showroom
Shigeru Uchida
Aoyama Mihoncho, 1989
Photograph by Nacasa &
Partners

11. "Design and Cultural Identity," Internationales Forum für
Gestaltung, Hochschule für Gestaltung, Ulm, Germany, September
1989.

12. Jane Holtz Kay, "Analyzing Success Stories of Products," *The
New York Times* (October 26, 1989).

13. H. G. J. Duijker and N. H. Frijda, *National Character and National
Stereotypes* (North-Holland Publishing Company, 1960).

14. "Designing for Product Success: Essays and Case Studies from
the TRIAD Design Project Exhibit," (Boston: Design Management
Institute, 1989).

sure of design quality remains anomalously
Eurocentric. Because the Asian economies grew by
imitating Western products, these countries' own
product cultures have been largely discarded.

Japan is the senior member of this group.
Having reached maturity as a manufacturing power,
it can no longer imitate American and European
design, relying upon a low wage base to undercut
similar products made in their home markets. Japan's
gross national product per head is now higher than
that in the United States or in most European countries. It now finds itself needing to compete effectively against the emerging manufacturing nations of
South and Southeast Asia, which enjoy much lower
manufacturing costs. One way to do this would be to
rediscover a distinctive culture of design. Japan is
now led to consider what constitutes Japanese style.

Japan's new rivals, the so-called Four Tigers of
the Orient—Korea, Taiwan, Hong Kong, and
Singapore—will also, in due course, face the need to
innovate rather than imitate as they too find they can
no longer compete by undercutting labor costs as
the next wave of developing countries—China, India,
Thailand, Malaysia, and the Philippines—starts snap-
ping at their heels.

There is no doubt that design that pays closer
heed to national cultural identity is growing in importance as designers begin to voice their concern that
global design is not all to the good. The Internationales Forum für Gestaltung Ulm—a foundation
that seeks to revive the spirit of the city's famous
design school—held a conference and workshop on
the subject in September 1989. The unspoken aim
was to reconcile the conflicting views on the importance of, and prospects for, the expression of cultural
identity in design of the peripatetic capitalists of the
international design community on the one hand
and the sandaled saviors of the culturally oppressed
on the other. It came as no great surprise that little
common ground had been established by the end of
the seminar. For the latter camp, Erskine Childers, a
director of the United Nations Development
Program, set the tone in a keynote address that set
out the aims of the UNESCO Decade for Cultural
Development (1988–97), one of which is the "affirmation of cultural identities." Worryingly, Childers
appeared to advocate a kind of protectionism for vul-
nerable cultures, but he also recognized that cultural
renewal can and must happen in the context of the
overlapping and cross-pollinating network of cultures
that has arisen from growth in media and personal
mobility. With regard to this second, and more significant, process of cultural affirmation, Childers
issued a call to arms: "The designer emerges as having a far more pivotal role than has generally been
realized. If we look along the entire sequence of

effort involved in modern living, it is in fact the
design profession that provides the essential links in
the chain."[11]

The power of the designer to affirm cultural
identity is an unknown quantity. Many designers are
confused both about the nature of cultural identity
and about whether and how to express it in their
work. Some clearly believe there is no such thing.
Interviewed on the occasion of the "Triad Design
Project" exhibition of the Design Management
Institute, for example, Arnold Wasserman, vice president of industrial design at Unisys, listed some design
stereotypes: "If you want rigor, you go to German
designers. If you want flair, you go to Italians. If you
want Zen intuitions about people's needs and
desires, it's the Japanese. For tail fins, go to
American designers." But he added, "These stereotypes are absolutely wrong."[12]

Although these stereotypes may be of little
interest to Unisys, the one thing they are not is absolutely wrong. The design globalists, including
Wasserman and the Design Management Institute,
may wish that stereotypes did not exist because they
disrupt their commercial world order, but by definition they are never absolutely wrong.

On the contrary, some scholars believe that
"stereotypes are often imputations of character
traits," although their reduction to a list of adjectives
should be treated with skepticism. "So, if the French
are said to be frivolous, it is not difficult to find con-
firmation for this opinion in the behaviour of
Frenchmen; but if one looks for indications of seriousness in the French, one finds them also."[13]

Several of the products featured as case studies
in the catalog of the "Triad Design Project" exhibition did, in fact, betray some evidence of peculiarly
national preoccupations. The range of Braun cof-
feemakers displayed the characteristic style of the
company, a formalism widespread in Germany that
stems from a doctrine that products should have a
certain functional look. (Their makers describe them
as functional, but it is often the appearance of functionality rather than functionality itself that is important.) And it was not by chance that the ergonomic
screwdriver that constituted another case study came
from a Swedish company, Bahco.[14] Ergonomics is a
driving factor in the Scandinavian countries, where
Lutheranism and a harsh climate help to ensure that
things could hardly be otherwise. Except for one
example, the Sony WM-109 Walkman, which explicitly claimed inspiration from local cultural tradition,
the cultural dimension in these products' genesis and
subsequent success was conveniently ignored.

Even in more extreme cases, where the investment required to design and manufacture a product
is so great that it can seldom be entertained solely by

Land-Rover Discovery
RSCG Conran Design
Austin-Rover, 1989

Although modern in materials and styling, the Land-Rover Discovery was promoted with the help of traditional images of the British landed gentry.

Afghan carpets, 1991
Courtesy R and Y Ambalo,
London

In order to thrive, cultures must renew themselves by remaining open to outside influences. A dramatic example of this was seen in Afghanistan after the Soviet invasion when weavers incorporated the outlines of the machinery of war into their carpets. At first ingenuously done, the carpets were soon produced in large quantities to satisfy tourists and collectors.

15. Interview with the author, March 1990.

16. A. Inkeles and D. J. Levinson, "National Character: The Study of Modal Personality and Sociocultural Systems" in Handbook of Social Psychology, Volume II, G. Lindzey, ed. (Addison-Wesley, 1954), quoted in Duijker and Frijda, *National Character and National Stereotypes.*

17. John Breuilly, *Nationalism and the State* (Manchester University Press, 1985).

18. Eric Hobsbawm and Terence Ranger, eds., *The Invention of Tradition* (Cambridge University Press, 1983).

a national company, and where it would seem that a design really is global, there is frequently evidence of the national culture of the nominal manufacturer. Automobiles, for example, frequently reflect national characteristics despite the fact that the network of factory ownership, parts supply, and distribution is a fine international mesh. French cars are comfortable in a luxurious, sloppy way; German cars are comfortable, but only if you sit in their harder, bucket seats in the ergonomically correct manner. Even gear ratios are sometimes set so as to suggest quiet performance from a German car but noisy bravura from its Latin competitors.

Uwe Bahnsen, the former vice president of design at Ford of Europe, believes the scope for differentiation according to cultural criteria will increase in the industry: "Uniformity has taken over to a very large extent, but national differences haven't entirely eroded. Some regional characteristics will become stronger again. The variety of products needed to meet the aspirations of smaller groups of customers will create the need to find ways to combine or retain a high level of economy of scale but create a level of flexibility to respond to different segments."[15]

Elsewhere, designers are beginning to take more overt steps to test their ability to affirm their cultural identity through their work. A recent study project at the International Studio of the Les Ateliers design school in Paris set students the task of designing "French" products. Students and alumni of the Cranbrook Academy of Art have been attempting to do the same for the United States. In Britain the Scottish Development Agency, a government organization, is trying to put its finger on what is "Scottishness" in design.

The puzzle is not a simple one. Design that evinces national character cannot be described according to a foolproof list of color preferences and template shapes. If *global design* is a term that eludes easy definition, then so is *national* or *nationalist design*. One possibility is to start with the character of a nation's people. If one accepts the suggestion that "national character refers to relatively enduring personality characteristics and patterns that are modal among adult members of a society,"[16] then national character in design should be as apparent from the range of products made by a society as personal national character is in its people. Special difficulties arise, however, in attempting this type of definition. The products of a culture are created by a small, essentially self-selected and self-aware group of people. These people, the designers, have the power, to some extent, to impose a national character by virtue of their unique position. What they do both individually and as a professional group can shape a national design character.

In *Nationalism and the State,* the historian John Breuilly states, "Nationalism clearly builds upon some sense of cultural identity, even if it is the major creator of that sense . . . cultural identity becomes whatever nationalists say it is."[17] This means that where traditions have been eradicated, new ones may be invented that are equally eligible to be called "national." This knowledge is vital both to designers in countries that are industrializing rapidly and where traditions are under threat and to those in developed countries where similar traditions have long since disappeared. Both must work with what they have in order to devise something new. They should not try to shut out present influences in order to preserve an obsolete vernacular, for, as the historian Eric Hobsbawm says, "Such movements, common among intellectuals since the Romantics, can never develop or even preserve a living past . . . but must become 'invented tradition.'"[18]

It is also worth pausing to consider why national character should be seen as more important than the character of either smaller or larger communities. After all, regions that are larger than individual countries, such as the European Community or the Arab world, are sometimes more useful in describing matters of economics and commerce, and regions that are smaller than individual countries, such as Catalonia or the North American Pacific coastal strip, often contribute disproportionately to the image of the country of which they are part.

Nevertheless, it is the nation—and in the context of design and other commercial activities, this means the nation-state—that remains the principal designator of cultural character. Although the existence of a national border is not a sufficient proof of the presence of a nation (how did that border come to be drawn?), the facts of political, economic, and commercial life often give that border a disproportionate weight. Regions are effectively transformed into nations (Lombardy, the economic powerhouse around Milan, represents Italy as a whole, for example) and nations into regions (the Benelux countries; Canada as a province of the United States). When a nation's design industry is located almost entirely within a region, as is the case in Catalonia and Lombardy, it is already hard to say whether its output is a fairer reflection of national character or of that region's character, which becomes the national character by default.

The nation-state seems likely to persist despite the ever-greater integration and interdependence of national economies. Indeed, its importance may be growing as pan-national political ideologies such as communism go into decline. As *The Economist* points out, "Unless the nation-state fails to satisfy its other purposes as well—defence, social identifica-

Falstaf cooking pans
Alessandro Mendini and others
Alessi, 1990

*Alessi briefed four
internationally known designers
to design knobs for the lids of
Mendini's pans that would
reflect national character. Arata
Isozaki (left) and Philippe Starck
(center-right) produced quirky,
asymmetric designs. Michael
Graves (center left) and Yuri
Soloviev (right) reflected
superpower seriousness with
neoclassical shapes.*

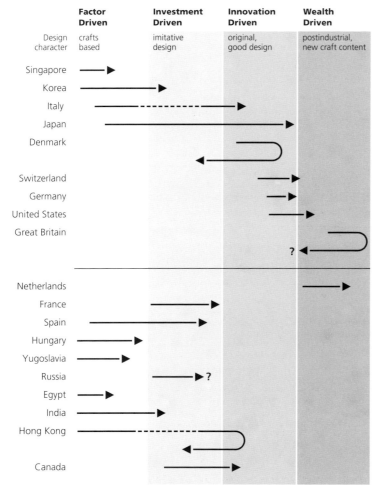

	Factor Driven	Investment Driven	Innovation Driven	Wealth Driven
Design character	crafts based	imitative design	original, good design	postindustrial, new craft content

Table 1. Estimated evolution of national competitive development since 1945 (from Porter). The table has been adapted to suggest the character of design that emerges from each manufacturing regime. The entries above the horizontal rule are as Porter. Entries for other countries are added.

19. "The State of the Nation-State," *The Economist* (December 22, 1990): 73.

tion, rule-making—the global economy will not be in a position to pronounce its obituary."[19] And if the nation-state survives because it can offer these securities, national identity will doubtless continue to be more important than the identity either of larger regions invented for economic convenience or of small subnational communities. In addition, design has been more closely linked with the nation-state than other creative pursuits. Design is promoted by national organizations, and in exhibitions and published works it is frequently pigeonholed by nation.

Although it is the nation-state upon which cultural identity in design centers, all nation-states are not equal. Some small or strongly focused nations (the Netherlands, France, Japan, for example) display a relatively cohesive national identity through their design. Others, too large, too diffuse, or too divided (the United States, India, the Soviet Union, Yugoslavia) cannot. The problem of defining and exploiting a national design character varies greatly among the more homogeneous nations (Japan, Korea, Denmark), the melting pots (the United States, the Netherlands, Great Britain), the multicultural societies (Canada, India), and the city-states (Singapore, Hong Kong). (See Table 1.)

A further obstacle to the promotion of national design is its unavoidable association with political nationalism. The link or potential link between cultural identity (virtually unquestioned as "a good thing") in design and the resurgence of nationalism in many corners of the world ("a bad thing") cannot be denied. In this regard, it might be said that designers believe in nations but not in the borders that separate them.

Nationalism per se need not be a bad thing, however. In the first half of the nineteenth century, nationalism had a positive connotation at a time of free-trade mercantilism. It was only in the twentieth century that trade suffered in proportion to the rise of more dangerous forms of nationalism accompanied by protectionism and a resistance to progress and modernity.

It is conceivable that the expression of national cultural identities by design could prove instrumental to the emergence of benign new nationalisms. This is not to say that a national style (or styles) would be applicable to all products or even to most products, but it could renew and enrich national cultures if applied to some types of product. Such nationalisms would have to be compatible with technological progress and with free-trade practices. They could encourage product diversity, stimulate market demand, and perhaps even do a little to improve mutual understanding among the peoples of different nations and cultures. They would not be incompatible with the "mondialization" in other realms of

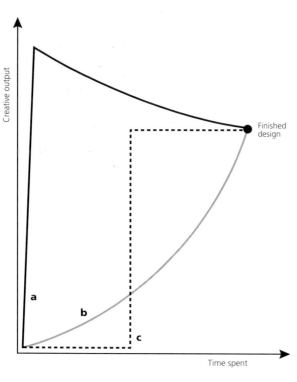

Creative output

Finished design

a

b

c

Time spent

The Milan-based Japanese designer Isao Hosoe, only partly tongue-in-cheek, has drawn graphs of creative output over time for three regional types: a) Latin; b) German; and c) Anglo-American. Type A produces an immediate response but then a rapid decrease of creative effort. Hosoe places the Italians, French, and Japanese in this category. Type B is a slow but cumulative effort yielding a gestalt. Type C shows a delay for accurate observation before the answer emerges suddenly and completely.

20. Ernest Gellner, *Nations and Nationalism* (Blackwell, 1983).

21. Eric Hobsbawm, *Nations and Nationalism Since 1780* (Cambridge University Press, 1990).

22. Porter, *The Competitive Advantage*.

23. "Porter v Ohmae," *The Economist* (August 4, 1990): 59.

modern life. In his book, *Nations and Nationalism,* Ernest Gellner writes, "The nationalist principle can be asserted in an ethical, 'universalistic' spirit. There could be, and on occasion there have been, nationalists-in-the-abstract, unbiased in favor of any special nationality of their own, and generously preaching the doctrine for all nations alike: let all nations have their own political roofs, and let all of them also refrain from including non-nationals under it. There is no formal contradiction in asserting such non-egoistic nationalism. As a doctrine it can be supported by some good arguments, such as the desirability of preserving cultural diversity, of a pluralistic international political system, and of the diminution of internal strains within states. . . . Late industrial society (if mankind is spared long enough to enjoy it) can be expected to be one in which nationalism persists, but in a muted, less virulent form."[20]

Hobsbawm believes that nationalism, for all its prominence, is of less historical importance now than it has been in the past: "It is no longer, as it were, a global political programme, as it may be said to have been in the nineteenth and earlier twentieth centuries. It is at most a complicating factor, or a catalyst for other developments." He illustrates his argument with reference to the Catalans, whose "culture flourishes, but on the tacit assumption that it is Catalans who will communicate with the rest of the world through Spanish and English, since few non-residents in Catalonia will be able to communicate in the local language."[21]

Such nationalism may no longer serve much political purpose, but it could contribute materially to company performance. Against the tide of multinational commerce and global business talk, the concern of a few designers to protect their national styles could seem romantic and forlorn. Reassurance that such thinking is not merely nostalgic comes from Michael Porter in his book *The Competitive Advantage of Nations:* "The globalization of industries and the internationalization of companies leaves us with a paradox. It is tempting to conclude that the nation has lost its role in the international success of its firms. Companies, at first glance, seem to have transcended countries. Yet . . . differences in national economic structures, values, cultures, institutions, and histories contribute profoundly to competitive success."[22]

Though there is little explicit mention in his book of design or broader cultural matters, Porter's message is that national attributes of products and services are, often unwittingly, being used in certain industries as a trade advantage. A corporation's competitive profile is built up from many factors that are shaped by the home nation—location, its early history with local customers, the pool from which its staff

is drawn, the education of its staff and customers, and legislation.

Porter's careful question is not "Why do some nations succeed and others fail in international competition?" but "Why does a nation become the home base for successful international competitors in an industry?" The difference is vital even today. Although a company may call itself "global" and its market may be worldwide, it may still be well advised to locate a particular production process—innovation, design, engineering, manufacturing—in a particular country with a proven strength, for whatever reason, in that field.

Porter is, in effect, reinforcing stereotypes, or at least digging out their underlying truths. Yes, he proclaims unashamedly, there are reasons why Japan has taken the lead in consumer electronics and why Hollywood creates successful movies. Even Swiss chocolate and Dutch tulips are not Swiss and Dutch by chance. The secrets of success are not always directly related to the availability of resources. Intrinsic factors are more important than extrinsic ones: the Dutch climate is not ideal for flower growing; Switzerland is not known for its cocoa plantations.

Reviewing Porter's book and Ohmae's *The Borderless World* together, *The Economist* answers its own question: "Who is right? Mr Ohmae's view is essentially futurology, an idea of how things should and perhaps will be, as global forces gather strength; it is also a rallying cry, exaggerated for effect. Yet books have marvelled about the coming global shopping centre, stateless corporations and so on for at least two decades; progress towards that goal is slow. Firms like IBM, Sony or Nestlé have their tentacles spread throughout the world and gain plenty from such non-domestic suckers, but the firms' character and competitiveness remain American, Japanese and Swiss. World citizenship remains science fiction. Unless the world is about to change, the verdict goes to Porter, on points."[23]

What is true of the role of the nation in the dry matters of business must surely be truer still where the cultural ingredient is stronger. There are or have been at various times strong regional and national identities in music and architecture, for example. Design is where culture and commerce meet. If these other arts and those businesses that Porter describes can continue to show national and regional characteristics—and, in the global village, to trade upon them—then surely design can too.

It might be said that this is nationalism as sideshow. Stripped of its political purpose, can this nationalism serve any purpose other than to provide trading companies with a spurious means of differentiating themselves from their competitors? At

Rover chair
Ron Arad
One-Off, 1981

Et La Guillotine Rata Les Pieds
Louis XVI chair
Christian Duc
VIA, 1989

*Designers who have immigrated
have often produced work in
homage to their adopted
cultures. The Israeli Ron
Arad works in London, the
Vietnamese Christian Duc
in Paris.*

24. "Design and Cultural Identity."

25. Porter, *The Competitive Advantage*.

worst, the expression of national character could become no more profound than the nation-themed village sets at Disneyworld. But it has a more worthy potential. If pursued with sufficient skill and vigor, national design could begin to restore to artifacts some of the meaning they have lost as societies have become more secular, more industrialized, and more intertwined.

It is in the context of these developments, for example, that Loek van der Sande of Global Design in the Netherlands, a former president of the International Council of Societies for Industrial Design, is able to remark that "culture is the world commodity of the twenty-first century."[24] In the seventeenth and eighteenth centuries, he argues, wealth was determined by access to natural resources, and in the nineteenth and twentieth centuries it came through the ability to manufacture goods and control the money and credit supply. In the future, he believes, national character will become a tradeable resource. Although his comment sounds cynical at first, it quickly becomes apparent that there is no other course. Cultures do not grow in a vacuum. For the expression of cultural identity to survive in any valid sense, it must acknowledge, and indeed swim with, the powerful tides that engulf it. As Porter notes: "National differences in character and culture, far from being threatened by global competition, prove integral to success in it."[25]

The view of culture as a commodity gains credibility upon closer consideration of what a designer is called upon to do. Different sets of factors bear on work done in different creative fields. The composer of music has a fairly free hand in determining the character of his or her work. An architect, on the other hand, has less creative autonomy and is bound by factors of teamwork, raw materials, and a building's context. In design, the character of the individual is important at one level, as it is in all creative acts. National character may be important, too. But for a designer, other factors are often present, such as the collective character or house style of the company where he or she works and the character or "corporate culture" of clients. It would be foolish to say that a given design was 20 percent individual, 50 percent corporate, and 30 percent national, but clearly an immigrant designer working as part of a multinational team in close cooperation with a foreign client's engineering department to create, say, a piece of medical equipment is subject to a very different mix of cultural ingredients from a single designer collaborating with a local craftsperson on a glass vase.

Central to this issue is the question of how much of each design may be the product of an individual's creative psyche and how much is the result

EXAMPLE	NATION OF DESIGNER	STUDIO	CLIENT	MARKET
Studio Dumbar for Dutch post office, Sony WM-109	a	a	a	a
Dieter Rams for Braun, Mario Bellini for Olivetti	a	a	a	a-z
Geoff Hollington for Herman Miller	a	a	b	b
King and Miranda for Spanish clients	a	b	a	a
King and Miranda for Italian clients	a	b	b	b
Luigi Colani for Canon	a	b	c	c
Bořek Sípek for Driade	a	b	c	a-z

Table 2. Global/local matrix for product origination and distribution. Single countries represented by letters a, b, c; global market by a-z.

When King and Miranda Associates designed the Vuelta tables for Spanish client Akaba, the culture of designer, client, and target market were the same although the designers' studio was in Milan (type a, b, a, a).

The Czech émigré Bořek Sípek designed these chairs for an Italian client but not only for the Italian market (type a, b, c, a-z).

Studio Dumbar's corporate identity for the Dutch post and telecommunications company is an example of design by and for one culture (type a, a, a, a).

German-born Luigi Colani maintains his studio in Switzerland and works for Japanese clients. His studies of cameras for Canon duly influenced the entire Japanese market (type a, b, c, c).

of education, working and living environment, peers, magazines, and all the other unavoidable clutter of national and international influences. One possible clue as to the balance between the personal and the contextual is provided by an examination of the few works published on design exclusively by women. It is difficult to discern any consistent quality of these designs that distinguishes them from designs by men. All other things being equal, one would surely expect more difference between women's and men's design than between the design of country X and country Y. If no difference is discernible in this case, one might conclude that circumstantial and traditional factors in design creativity are powerful in relation to individual temperament.

Matters are further complicated because national, corporate, studio, and individual identities are not mutually exclusive. They overlap and distort one another. A good studio will influence a designer's individual technique; a powerful client will, to some extent, determine the character of the work of the studio it employs. Nationality bears on the character of client, studio, and individual alike.

The traditional pattern, which predates the establishment of the design profession, is that of a local artisan creating a product for local use. Many designers today still frequently work for local clients who will sell their products primarily on the domestic market. However, the patchwork nature of cultural identities in the modern world is making more complex patterns commonplace. Increasingly, more than one nationality is involved in the design process. There are many levels of simulation and dissimulation (see Table 2). The client may be based in country A, selling mainly to country B, but employing a firm in country C with a project designer from country D. Good designers can emulate or simulate particular national characters on demand to the apparent satisfaction of all concerned.

Designers sometimes choose to settle in a country more conducive to their professional development than the one of their birth; they frequently find clients in countries other than their own. In the latter case, they may be called upon to design in their own idiom if that is what it is thought would appeal to the target market, or they may be obliged to adopt some of the characteristics of the nation where the client and its market are based.

But to what degree should designers act as chameleons, adopting regional or national style characteristics other than their own simply for the gratification of themselves or their clients? The apparent deceptiveness of some examples of national design need not detract from their validity. Composers have proved adept at writing music in the style of countries other than their own. The execution of contex-

GUARDIAN

Corporate identity
Plan Créatif
Guardian Royal Exchange, 1989

Designers are often called upon to be cultural chameleons. Plan Créatif designed the logotype for the French arm of the British Guardian Royal Exchange insurance company to look British, echoing the colors and forms used on London buses. The American Landor Associates used the art of Joan Miró for the logotype of a Catalan bank. A Briton, David Lewis, has designed many of Bang and Olufsen's quintessentially Danish products.

Bank logotype
Landor Associates
La Caixa, 1982

Audio equipment
David Lewis
Bang and Olufsen

tual and new vernacular architecture is not restricted to local architects. In design, one need look no further than to the Frenchman Raymond Loewy, who created some of America's most distinctive icons, or to David Lewis, the Englishman who has helped make Bang and Olufsen a paragon of Danish design. As Hobsbawm points out, "more often than not the discovery of popular tradition and its transformation into the 'national tradition' of some peasant people forgotten by history was the work of enthusiasts from the (foreign) ruling class or elite, such as the Baltic Germans or the Finnish Swedes."[26]

Examples such as these show the leeway that is available in the interpretation of cultural tradition. The core of this book aims to draw brief portraits of the state and quality of national design character in a number of countries as seen by their leading designers. These are counterpointed with profiles of the globalist policies of some leading corporations and design firms.

The consciousness and perception of cultural identity vary greatly from country to country, as does the perceived need to reinforce or reinvent that identity. In many cases, designers are uncertain of the degree to which national character can be manipulated in their work. From the foregoing introduction and the following section, which examines the experience of architects and composers in coming to terms with regionalism and nationalism in their fields, it is hoped that designers might discover that aspects of national character may be explored with more ease and delight than they had imagined.

26. Hobsbawm, *Nations and Nationalism.*

The example of other arts

The assertion of regional (often, in effect, national) identity has been attempted in fields of cultural endeavor other than design. In these fields, practical constraints concerning the manufacture and distribution of the finished article are either absent or are less of an obstacle to realization in the form desired by the creator.

This assertion has not been necessary on a conscious level in the language-based arts, which have their own protection against the homogenizing force of the global media. And it has not been a general concern in painting and sculpture, fields of creativity that have become increasingly self-referential. (Fine art once grew from roots more clearly than it does now. Representational art was more or less obliged to reflect its surroundings, but abstract painters and sculptors, such as the Dutchman Piet Mondrian and the Briton Barbara Hepworth, also drew inspiration from the landscapes with which they were familiar.)

Architecture is the best example of an art in which regional character is always relevant. A building cannot escape its context, whether that context takes the form of other buildings, and hence of a region's architectural history, or simply of a stretch of terrain. Regionalism has been a particular concern of architects at various times over the past two centuries, since the time when "natural" regional character was seen to be threatened by industrialization and the more efficient exchange between countries of architects, architectural ideas, and building materials.

A more contrived regionalism is seen in music. With no physical context for their work, composers are not bound to write music that responds to its locality. However, musical regionalism became widespread among certain composers who wished to oppose the growing "universalism" of German compositional technique during the nineteenth century. In this case, regionalism was more often than not nationalism. In the twentieth century, thanks to radio and recording media, all music—"national" and "universal" alike—has become an international commodity, distributed with the ease of small products.

A designer is much like an architect in the sense that he or she must give three-dimensional form to an object that must serve a useful purpose. Like a house, a product must accommodate itself to a context: it must suit the way in which it will be used as well as the place where it will be put. The problem of regional expression is similar in design and architecture, although it is undoubtedly more difficult in the former, with its mass-produced parts and standard materials, than in the latter which, but for the grandest edifices, is a less industrialized process, with most building parts produced locally and in small batches.

But products are not rooted to the spot like buildings, and a designer ultimately has little control over the context in which his or her creation will be seen and used. In this respect, a designer is like a composer, creating something that will be multiplied and distributed for use in a variety of ways and circumstances.

The pursuit of regional character in these two arts offers lessons for designers. Architects and musicians have been articulating a debate about the merit of and potential for such character in their work for longer than designers have. They have been doing so with greater clarity and candor. They can point to works that are generally agreed to exhibit a positive regional or national character, that avoid political propaganda on the one hand and pastiche on the other, and that have won critical and popular acclaim.

Regionalism in Architecture

House
Breganzona, Ticino, Switzerland
Mario Botta, 1988

*Botta's architecture does not
"fit in" with its surroundings but
is seen as regionalist
nevertheless.*

House
Giza, Egypt
Hassan Fat'hy, 1938

*Fat'hy imported ideas from the
Nubian desert for houses for
wealthy clients in the Cairo
suburbs.*

1. Kenneth Frampton, "Towards a Critical Regionalism: Six Points for an Architecture of Resistance" in *The Anti-Aesthetic,* ed. Hal Foster (Bay Press, 1983).

2. Juhani Pallasmaa, "Tradition and Modernity: The Feasibility of Regional Architecture in a Postmodern Society," *Architectural Review* (May 1988): 26.

3. Brian Brace Taylor, "Perspectives and Limits on Regionalism and Architectural Identity," *Mimar* 19 (January–March 1986).

4. Kenneth Frampton, "Place-Form and Cultural Identity" in *Design after Modernism,* ed. John Thackara (Thames and Hudson, 1988).

Regionalism has been a recurrent preoccupation among architects of a thoughtful turn of mind. In the last decades of the nineteenth century and early years of the twentieth, architects adapted the prevailing styles in ways seen only in their localities. Antoni Gaudí wrought his variations on Art Nouveau in Catalonia, which were very different from those of Charles Rennie Mackintosh, who was working in Scotland at the same time. Jože Plečnik had learned his trade in Vienna under Otto Wagner but he adapted the Jugendstil architecture that he practiced in his native Slovenia to reflect his interest in Slovene nationalism. In the United States, Henry Hobson Richardson and his younger employee, Charles McKim, later of McKim, Mead & White, pared back the excesses of their Beaux-Arts training and mixed in other influences to establish a robust classicism suited to the America of the time.

This wave of architectural regionalism coincided with the rise of European nationalisms and the consolidation of the United States after the Civil War. Today there is renewed interest in regionalism, not as a way of giving expression to political values but simply as a means of re-creating an architecture that has a sense of place, as a resistance to the homogenizing force of international commercial development and the availability of commodity building materials.

Because of this shift of emphasis, the term *regionalism* alone no longer suffices. The critic Kenneth Frampton uses the phrase *critical regionalism* to describe an approach that sets itself in opposition to the forces of technological progress but that is also concerned to amount to more than the nostalgic re-creation of past styles.[1] The term *critical regionalism* is not intended to describe a style or a vernacular revival but rather a force that pushes local culture in opposition to the prevailing trend. Other critics, such as Juhani Pallasmaa, are equally concerned not to convey the wrong idea of regional architecture through careless nomenclature. Pallasmaa notes that "an architecture capable of supporting our identity has to be situationally, culturally and symbolically articulated. I am disturbed by the notion of regionalism because of its geographic and ethnological connotations. I would rather speak of situational or culture-specific architecture."[2]

The caution over what to call this architecture is symptomatic of a certain self-consciousness felt by its proponents. The architects themselves are reluctant to confess; it is not their business to affix labels. As one practitioner has said, "Few architects (I know of none personally) would ever qualify themselves as 'regionalist' in their perceptions or their approach to design. Most architects conceive of their role within a more localised realm, or on the contrary, a wider framework."[3]

There is, however, a general consensus among the critics, even if it is not admitted by the architects themselves, as to who are the regionalists today. Pallasmaa describes how Luis Barragan incorporates features—he cites the presence of death—of Mexican culture in his work and how the Portuguese Alvaro Siza abstracts elements from the social and building traditions in Porto, the city where he practices. He adds to his list the rather different Imre Makovecz, a Hungarian architect who explicitly evokes local folkloric themes in his work. Other acclaimed regionalists of recent decades include Rafael Moneo in Spain, Hassan Fat'hy in Egypt, and Mario Botta in the Ticino canton of Switzerland. Frampton generally avoids naming names, but he implies that regionalist architecture stands the best chance of emerging from locations of a certain size and texture—"Zurich, Lugano, Udine, Athens, Venice, Porto, Helsinki, Stockholm, Copenhagen, Madrid, Barcelona, Amsterdam, New Delhi, or Mexico City,"[4] but not, he implies, London, Paris, New York, Los Angeles, or Tokyo.

Shortcomings and contradictions quickly become apparent when one considers the different individuals' interpretations of architectural regionalism. Makovecz's story-telling literalism is perhaps too blatant—originality verging on weirdness is not regionalism simply because it is practiced in one place. Botta's Ticinese houses are highly modern in appearance and bear little immediate resemblance to existing buildings in the area. What is clear is that Botta's best work has a presence that is somehow seen to legitimize its territorial claim. (The work of his imitators, christened the "Bottinis," does not.) Foreign observers have admired the projects of Fat'hy and other Egyptian regionalists such as Abdel Wahed El Wakil and Gamal Bakry as reinterpretations of Egyptian vernacular. Locals point out, however, that the Cairo-based Fat'hy appropriated elements of Nubian desert architecture from some hundreds of miles to the south of the capital city and employed them in houses for wealthy clients in the Cairene suburbs.

Sincere regionalism, then, is no simple matter. It is not a birthright, and above all it is not *obvious*. Nor is it simply a matter of blending in. It is not the architecture condoned by well-meaning city authorities, such as those in Santa Fe, New Mexico, or Bath, England, which seek to encourage conformity to a local "style" and yet which, by often employing mediocre architects, succeed only in producing embarrassing banalities.

In the current debate, it is also important to put distance between the "positive" architecture of "critical regionalism" and what Frampton calls "populist or historicist regionalism" of the sort that can be

Egerstrom house
San Cristobal, Mexico
Luís Barragan, 1968

*Paradoxically, some of the
architects most strongly
associated with international
Modernism have produced
some of the best regional
buildings.*

House
Ahmedabad, India
Le Corbusier, 1956

5. Leon van Schaik, "Against Regionalism," *Architecture in South Africa* 3/4 (1986): 19.

6. Frampton, "Towards a Critical Regionalism."

7. Frampton, "Place–Form and Cultural Identity."

8. Alan Colquhoun, "Regionalismi e Tecnologie," *Casabella* (May 1983): 24.

9. Peter Buchanan, "With Due Respect: Regionalism," *Architectural Review* (May 1983): 14.

used to manipulate people's feelings. This latter is found in the architecture of the Third Reich, which deliberately echoed the Romantic Classicism of the Prussian Karl Friedrich Schinkel, and in the false vernacular theme parks and retail environments seen more recently in Western Europe and North America. Some find in this architecture a sufficient argument against any form of conscious regionalism today: "Obviously one can point to healthy regionalism . . . ; but one can equally . . . point to unhealthy regionalism such as that espoused by Albert Speer and his patron, in which folksy cottages redolent with references to the regional folk history replaced what Nazism saw as unhealthy internationalism. Ask yourself then into whose hands the argument of 'regionalism' play[s] in [the Republic of South Africa] in 1986, and consider carefully how such arguments play into the self-delusions of the governing class."[5]

Its political implications aside, critical regionalism, with its implicit resistance to technological realities, is perhaps of limited relevance to those seeking a model for regionalist product design, just as it must be of little help to architects in the large cities of northern Europe, North America, and Japan. The value of critical regionalism lies in the sheer directness of the prescriptive elements it recommends as starting points for creative thought. According to Frampton: "It may find its governing inspiration in such things as the range and quality of the local light, or in a *tectonic* derived from a peculiar structural mode, or in the topography of a given site."[6]

Frampton continues: "More than any other art form, building and architecture have an interactive relationship with nature. Nature is not only the topography and the site itself but also climate and light, to which architecture is ultimately responsive to a far greater degree than any other art. Built form is necessarily susceptible to an intense interaction with those two elements, and hence with time, in its diurnal and seasonal aspects.

"All of this seems so self-evident as hardly to require restating, and yet we tend to forget how universal civilization, that is, universal technology, . . . tends towards the elimination of exactly those features which would otherwise relate the outer membrane of a given fabric to a particular place and a specific culture."[7]

As Alan Colquhoun points out in criticizing both Frampton's proposition and that of the architect Robert Stern, who has advocated an American regionalism that draws upon the traditions of cultural minorities, both arguments rely for their strength on the perception of technology as an ogre: "Like the regionalist philosophies which sprang up from within the ideology of modernism in the 1930s and the 1950s, the new regionalist doctrines are all based on

the idea of a return (whether reducible to the rhetorical modes of the comic or the ironic) to an artisanal architecture which somehow symbolises a cultural 'essence' smothered by universal technology."[8]

Despite the overall tenor of Frampton's argument, it is worth noting that none of the parameters that he prescribes as a starting point for the generation of regional architecture is predicated on the rejection of technological change. For designers, who are in still less of a position to turn their backs on the facts of modern industrial life than any architect, the value of Frampton's argument is that it demonstrates the potential mutual independence of cultural and technological factors—not that there is necessarily an inverse relation between them.

Another red herring is that regionalism necessarily acts in opposition to international Modernism. It is not uncommon for regionalist partisans to scorn Modernism for its romantic and naïve image of "New Universal Man"[9] who has presumably shrugged off all national character and regional qualities. There is, however, abundant evidence to refute the supposed incompatibility of Modernism and regionalism. It appears today that it is precisely those figures accused of holding universalist Modernist ideals—architects such as Le Corbusier, Louis Kahn, Alvar Aalto, Luis Barragan, Oscar Niemeyer, Charles Correa, Alvaro Siza, and Oriol Bohigas—who have, on occasion, turned out to be the most sensitive and convincing regionalists.

A case can also be made for regionalism of more recent Modernist architecture that makes no explicit claim to such character. Some commentators see the so-called high-tech style that is particularly prevalent in Britain and France as particular to those countries, echoing their nineteenth-century engineering bravura. Although they would certainly shun the label "regionalist," Jean Nouvel in France and Norman Foster and Richard Rogers in Britain often cite the Eiffel Tower and Paxton's Crystal Palace in London as works they admire. Certainly, this species of architecture is less favored in neighboring Germany, Holland, and Scandinavia, where new buildings tend to be more humanistic and less mechanistic.

With a slightly greater leap of the imagination, it is possible to believe that the postmodern classicism of Michael Graves and Robert Stern is no less American than the buildings of the Greek Revival two hundred years earlier. Both are reinterpretations of classical architectural themes, and in one form or another classicism has been seen as appropriate in a country that makes much of its democratic ideal. In Japan the otherwise up-to-the-minute architecture of Tadao Ando and Fumihiko Maki has a Zen Buddhist quality both in the choice and detailing of the build-

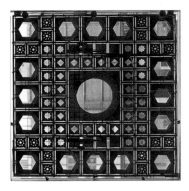

Institut du Monde Arabe
Paris, France
Jean Nouvel, 1988

The French architect Jean Nouvel appropriated many Arabic motifs for the Institut du Monde Arabe, but by providing a technological Western interpretation of them he avoided producing a pastiche.

Barnsdall house
Hollywood, California, USA
Frank Lloyd Wright, 1920

Wright shows better than most how regional character can be created by bringing together apparently unrelated source material.

10. William J. R. Curtis, "Towards an Authentic Regionalism," *Mimar* 19 (January–March 1986).

11. Peter Buchanan, "Only Connect," *Architectural Review* (October 1984): 22.

12. Pallasmaa, "Tradition and Modernity."

13. Suzanne Stephens, "Regionalism and the Vernacular Tradition," *Progressive Architecture* (June 1981): 75.

14. Pallasmaa, "Tradition and Modernity."

ing materials used and in the sense of proportion of the overall structures.

Regionalism in architecture, then, need not be constrained either by technological requirements or by adherence to stylistic ideologies. It need not be retrogressive. In principle, a regionalist approach can be taken with any building anywhere. At one extreme, of course, the simplest buildings are regionalist de facto, making use as they do of local materials and construction techniques. But at the other extreme, we have grown accustomed to the idea that the largest buildings look much the same wherever they are located. Architectural critic William Curtis states, "The skyscraper is [a] building type which, on superficial inspection, appears to be a rootless piece of international equipment like a Boeing 707. But it too can be 'regionalised,' not through the attachment of a little period dress (e.g., horseshoe arches) to a routine plan and structure, but through a critical re-examination of type in terms of climate, patterns of use, structure and *the abstraction of* devices from tradition."[10] (Italics added.)

We have been conditioned to believe that office towers should be the same on all sides and that that uniform façade more often than not takes the form of floor-to-ceiling glazing. They are so in London with an average of four hours' sunshine a day and an average temperature of 14°C, and Los Angeles, with nearly nine hours' sunshine and an average temperature of 24°C. In principle there is nothing to prevent architects from designing fenestration on such buildings using glazing panels, blinds, brises-soleils, and revetments in ways appropriate to the local climate and light. Such designs could be determined with reference to old buildings in the locale, but, more importantly, they could be derived from first principles, bearing in mind the technology and materials available. The problem with this approach is that, except, perhaps, in the hands of the most talented architects, the costs of such architecture would be greater than for conventional building. The outlook is perhaps less bleak for product design. While commercial development is often driven primarily by cost, there are some areas of product design in which the market demand for added-value goods permits greater expenditure on design and materials.

Perhaps the greatest hindrance to the wider practice of regionalist architecture has been a psychological one. Architects, who often have far greater creative autonomy than designers, are quite simply afraid of making fools of themselves. As the architectural writer Peter Buchanan has noted: "Scared of exercising their imagination (often trained not to), embarrassed lest their designs be dismissed as parochial or arbitrary, too many architects—

instead of attempting some synthesis between tradition and contemporary potential, and between man-made and its natural setting—continue to design buildings shaped solely by economics, regulations, catalogue components and construction."[11] This fear afflicts designers to an even greater extent.

Self-consciousness and self-doubt reinforce this fear. Pallasmaa wonders: "Is it possible to alter the course of our culture? Is the resuscitation of regional architecture in post-industrial and Post-Modern society feasible? Indeed, can authentic architecture exist at all in the metaphysical materialism that we live in? . . .

"In today's neurotic architectural climate, the intellectual construction seems to be often more important and more central than a sensory and emotional encounter with the architectural work. The fierce quasi-theorising and intellectualisation accelerates alienation and separation from social reality, instead of supporting the integration of architecture and culture, artefact and mankind."[12]

The design climate is unquestionably less neurotic and less intellectualized than the architecture climate. Designers, however, must deal with their clients' timidity as well as their own. The advice to both professions would seem to be to throw caution to the winds and have a go. The result might not be great design or great architecture, but it would at least have a certain authenticity.

Two examples at opposite extremes of American-built culture show that such an attitude can produce new work that is seen to belong. Across America, individual mom-and-pop enterprises have been supplanted by national franchises, with a consequent homogenization of highway architecture. In 1981 *Progressive Architecture* noted that both this usurpation and the ensuing backlash boom in nostalgia had eroded architects' confidence in regional experimentation. It offered encouragement to try again: "These roadside motels, diners, and gas stations made use of local vernacular building traditions and symbols in a way that lent an indigenous quality to even the most self-conscious efforts."[13]

Hope for those who believe that it is impossible to reclaim any true cultural identity in today's world came from a 1988 article in *Architectural Review*. Rather than shut out the endless flow of images from other cultures that comes from international contact and media, it advised, architects should remain open to all influences: "Regional character may be achieved—and usually is—from totally contradictory ingredients. Frank Lloyd Wright's American architecture synthesised themes from North American and Mexican Indian cultures, and European architectural history as well as traditional Japanese architecture."[14]

Nationalism in Music

Music has been called a universal language. Since the rise of the nation-state, however, many composers have sought not universalism but nationalism in their work. Nationalism initially was not only a positive reflection of various political developments, it was also a reaction against the monopoly of excellence seemingly held by Austrian and German musicians. During the late nineteenth century it was Romanticism in the persons of Richard Wagner, Gustav Mahler, and others that determined the nature of music across Europe. As the century turned, Romanticism gave way to the dry, academic music of the Second Viennese School of Arnold Schönberg, Alban Berg, and Anton Webern.

At various times, composers in other countries rebelled against both Germanic Romanticism and the atonal music that followed it. In search of something new and different, some turned to the folk music of their native lands, music that they felt was threatened by the continuing Germanic hegemony.

The genealogy of this musical dominance stretches from the Bachs to Haydn, Mozart, Beethoven, Schubert, and beyond. Of course, these composers' music also had its roots in local folk song. But the continuity of talent, patronage, and tuition in Austro-Germany gradually permitted this music to draw away from its humble origins. Understandably, this abstraction seemed all the greater to musicians in other countries who learned according to the German model.

Even outside Europe, German music was seen as the enemy. In the first paragraph of his famous book, *The New Music 1900–1960,* Aaron Copland set the context clearly: "Few music lovers realize to what an extent we are dominated in music by the Romantic tradition of the 19th century. A large proportion of the music heard nowadays was created in that century, and most of it came from German-speaking countries. Nothing really new was possible in music until a reaction had set in against that tradition. The entire history of modern music, therefore, may be said to be a history of the gradual pull-away from the Germanic musical tradition of the past century."[15]

The earliest assertions of musical nationalism came from Russia in the mid-nineteenth century, first from Glinka and then from the group of composers known as "The Five"—Balakirev, Borodin, Cui, Mussorgsky, and Rimsky-Korsakov. A strong nationalist strain continued into the Soviet era, often under powerful political control. In Czechoslovakia, first Smetana and then Dvořák and Janáček sought to break away from what was happening in neighboring Germany and Austria. Smetana saw himself, a little immodestly perhaps, as "the creator of the Czech style in the branches of dramatic and symphonic music—exclusively Czech."[16] He did not raid the library of folk music but concentrated on making strenuous claims for his own music as *the* Czech music in his comments and in the titles he gave to his pieces. In both countries, nationalism was intended to be anything but xenophobic. "The national substance of Russian or Czech music was a condition of its international worth, not an invalidation," according to the music scholar Carl Dahlhaus.[17]

Although it was Romanticism, in effect a German movement, that these composers sought to escape, it was paradoxically the Romantic spirit that facilitated the expression of national character. Its preoccupation with literary and pictorial themes allowed composers to portray their countries in music. In France, for example, Debussy reacted against the smothering presence of Wagner and created music in a personal idiom that was heavily influenced by the French Impressionist painting of the time. Debussy's dramatic break made it easier for other French composers to pursue their own alternatives to Germanic music. The output of Erik Satie, members of "Les Six,"such as Darius Milhaud and Francis Poulenc, and others was strongly individualistic. It was not Debussian and could never be said to constitute a single French style. But these composers did share a common will to defuse the ponderous music of the Germans and those in France, such as César Franck, whom they thought to be rather too much under the German spell.

An interest in national music also took hold in Britain and the countries of Scandinavia and central and eastern Europe. The vehicle for nationalism was often folk music. It is interesting to note that this music was often of a doubtful national pedigree itself, but the national classical music that was created from it has been none the less effective for that. The success enjoyed by nationalist music reveals that music is, in a sense, not the universal language sometimes supposed. But the composition of national music does not demand that other influences be excluded. As in architecture, it is better to be aware of all that is happening and to synthesize a national music from a combination of sources and examples both local and distant. It was in this manner that Stravinsky influenced Copland, for example. Copland writes of Stravinsky that "he borrowed freely from folk materials, and I have no doubt that this strongly influenced me to find a way to a distinctively American music."[18]

The attitude of composers seeking to give expression to their national character is similar in many ways to that of regionalist architects. Both groups must strive to create a synthesis of old and new, of indigenous material and modern technique, if they are to create works with a regional or national

15. Aaron Copland, *The New Music 1900–1960* (Macdonald, 1968).

16. František Bartoš, *Bedřich Smetana: Letters and Reminiscences* (Artia, 1955).

17. Carl Dahlhaus, "Nationalism and Music" in *Between Romanticism and Modernism* (University of California Press, 1980).

18. Aaron Copland and Vivian Perlis, *Copland* (Faber and Faber, 1984).

character. And as both groups show, it also does no harm—indeed it can be beneficial—to remain open to outside influences. This is welcome news for designers who, if engaged in commercial practice, can scarcely avoid exposure to international trends through their clients, colleagues, and the press.

Because music travels easily, it serves as a cultural ambassador. National music must be written not just for consumption by those nationals but also for listeners around the world. The best national music is not incompatible with performance and broadcasting worldwide. Likewise, it could prove to be the case that a product designed to reflect particular cultural attributes could be exported just as successfully as, and perhaps more successfully than, a "global" product. As the British composer Ralph Vaughan Williams realized: "It is because Palestrina and Verdi are essentially Italian and because Bach, Beethoven and Wagner are essentially German that their message transcends their frontiers."[19]

Three case studies will suffice to illustrate the issues, dilemmas, and contradictions facing those who would create or re-create a national style. The evolution of nationalist music in Hungary and Britain provides two very different examples of the renewal of tradition. Musicians in Hungary undertook a painstaking effort to catalogue and reinterpret a wealth of folk music as the country made the transition from a fragment of the former Austro-Hungarian empire to a full, independent nation-state. Britain's musical tradition, on the other hand, was unbroken politically but at risk from accelerating industrialization. The third, and very different, case is provided by the United States. After the Civil War the United States was a new country seeking to consolidate its identity, and unlike nations in Europe, it required the outright invention of a musical tradition.

Hungary's is the clearest case of the searching out of an endangered national tradition and the guaranteeing of its subsequent survival through creative reinterpretation. As the music historian B. Szabolcsi tells it, events got off to an uncertain start in the nineteenth century, when Ferenc (Franz) Liszt and others sought "the development of Hungarian music into 'universal art,' 'world idiom,' with the help of Western means of expression, within the range of European culture."[20] But Liszt, as the customary modification of his given name implies, rarely set foot in Hungary and was not even fluent in the language. Furthermore, "the Hungarian material at his disposal was not really genuine . . . he had no opportunity to become acquainted with real folk tradition . . . and therefore had to content himself with the music received through his friends: the often third-rate, current material of the 'verbunkos,' the 'czardas' and the popular song."[21]

At the end of the century, Béla Vikár toured the country recording folk songs with a phonograph. The composers Béla Bartók and Zoltán Kodály then swelled the collection, which ultimately became the grandly titled *Corpus Musicae Popularis Hungaricae*. Their research was thorough, genuine, and sincerely motivated. In his own composition, however, Bartók could not be accused of merely recycling traditional tunes. Where he did incorporate folk themes, he did so without compromising his contemporary formal technique. Bartók is still regarded by many as an exemplar of how to give meaning to tradition in the context of modern creative practice.

Bartók described three approaches he took in his work: he might either provide accompaniment to an unchanged or slightly varied folk tune; "not make use of real peasant tunes, but instead invent some sort of imitation of a peasant tune"; or, "distil the same atmosphere as peasant music."[22] Nebulous as these prescriptions are, their utilization in works of stature such as the *Concerto for Orchestra*, the *Divertimento for Strings*, and the string quartets shows that a variety of methods can succeed in expressing a national culture. Bartók's music, both that tending toward the modernistic and that tending toward the folkloric, has proved both innovative and durable. The composer himself believed that *all* his music benefited from his delving into local tradition. The musicologist J. Manga agrees: "Bartók maintained that the first results of research into peasant music ensured a firm basis for a rapid development of modern art music. The guiding influence of folk-music on Hungarian composers has been all the stronger in that they have always been in the vanguard of folk-music research."[23]

Once again, the veracity and cultural purity of the folk sources was not paramount. During the course of his research, Bartók, like others before him, had noted that the traditional *verbunkos* that had developed from Gypsy band music had themselves already been subject to Western formal influences and had been refined by pockets of foreign cultures present in Hungary. Indeed, the fact that they were not seen as immutable in the folk tradition may have encouraged Bartók and others to adapt them once again. Bartók wrote that "although the new style shows an organic relationship with the old style in its rhythms (and to some extent in its melodic patterns), its tunes are quite different in character because of their essentially different construction . . . undoubtedly the result of Western formal concepts."[24]

Today, the precise history of the folk sources and the treatment they were given are of secondary importance. Now the music of Bartók and Kodály itself is the tradition. More than anything else, it was the concurrence of these two composers of world

19. Ralph Vaughan Williams, *National Music* (Oxford University Press, 1934).

20. B. Szabolcsi, *A Concise History of Hungarian Music* (Corvina Press, 1955).

21. Ibid.

22. J. Manga, *Hungarian Folk Song and Folk Instruments* (Corvina Press, 1969).

23. Ibid.

24. Ibid.

stature that helped secure the new Hungarian musical identity. "Their example pointed the way to the generation following," explains Szabolcsi. "They discovered and placed Hungarian folk music in the centre of national culture and subsequently developed a monumental new art in the spirit of this folk music."[25]

British musical nationalism emerged as a creative force when the British empire was at its peak and gathered momentum as the empire declined. Its leading proponent was Ralph Vaughan Williams. Echoing some designers today who find nationality expressed in other arts but not in their own, Vaughan Williams saw signs of national identity in painting and poetry more readily than in music. Nevertheless, he did identify the music of Hubert Parry as seeming more English than most, and it was Parry who was instrumental in setting up the Folk Song Society in 1898.

Vaughan Williams retained a close association with this society and instigated his own research into Britain's disappearing folk music. However, he doubted the value of the efforts of those who sought to establish an English music based solely on folk song. He exhorted members of the Folk Song Society rather to put theory into practice. According to the musicologist Michael Kennedy: "Vaughan Williams did not believe that by using folk song composers could invent a national music ready made— 'we simply were fascinated by the tunes and wanted other people to be fascinated too. . . . We are now taking folk song for granted, whether we like it or not, as part of our natural surroundings.' These were the tenets of Vaughan Williams's musical faith. Paradoxically—for his whole career is one of paradox—he exemplified them yet he contradicted them. His nationalism was avowedly conscious; never was it self-conscious. There never was a less 'typical Englishman.' It has been suggested that by consciously assuming a nationalist mantle he restricted the development of his own musical personality. There is no evidence to support this view. Through a conscious nationalism he discovered a means of self-expression. Upon a foundation of folk song and other equally important influences—Purcell, the Tudor composers, and the hymn-tunes—he erected his own personal style which was his natural voice."[26]

By his writings and by example, Vaughan Williams laid the groundwork for the emergence of a strong English school. He and his contemporary, Gustav Holst, were perhaps all the more able to establish their musical nationalism in a land that had been relatively isolated from foreign influence. In simple terms, their music was often characterized by close-textured writing for strings. Other works made use of plaintive oboe themes. Casually structured rhapsodies and pastorales, either based on folk tunes or written so as to suggest that they were, contrasted strongly with the rigid formalism of German music. Works such as Holst's *Egdon Heath* and Vaughan Williams's *The Lark Ascending* were not weighty or particularly influential in the musical world at large, but they were and still are much liked and played in Britain.

These composers' achievements made way for a new generation of British composers who were able to push forward with the synthesis of traditional elements and modern compositional techniques. Like Vaughan Williams and Holst, Benjamin Britten took inspiration from Britain's literary tradition with settings of the work of British poets in his *Spring Symphony* and *War Requiem*, major compositions that were both British in mood and modern in construction.

Vaughan Williams had advocated a conscious—but never self-conscious—nationalism. He advised students that to write "synthetic folk music" was no less valid than to do what they did customarily at music school, which was to write synthetic music in the style of leading composers of the day. His advice was given nearly a century ago when Strauss, Elgar, and Debussy were the admired models. It is nonetheless pertinent in the light of current attempts by design schools such as Cranbrook Academy of Art in Michigan, Les Ateliers in Paris, and the Royal College of Art in London to encourage their students consciously to build on their countries' design vernacular. These efforts in design are scorned by some critics and ignored by much of the commercial sector, but the musical parallel suggests that such conscious nationalism can succeed.

The question of artificiality in national music was to prove of particular concern to American composers. It was not, however, a problem to Charles Ives, who is today recognized as the first champion of American music. Ives did not earn this title because he consciously wished to establish such a music; indeed, he did so by default. His work was largely unperformed during his lifetime. He got little feedback from audiences, critics, or fellow composers and was thus able to develop a strongly individual style. Ives's sympathies were not folkloric but were allied with the New England transcendentalist writers such as Emerson and Thoreau who were his contemporaries. In his book, *Music in a New Found Land*, Wilfrid Mellers tells how Ives drew liberally from other composers as well as from vernacular sources such as the town band of which his father was director. He did this in almost complete isolation. "So, working alone, without public or performance, Ives embraced within his embryonic art, America's musical past, present, and potential

25. Szabolcsi, *A Concise History.*

26. Michael Kennedy, *The Works of Ralph Vaughan Williams* (Oxford University Press, 1964).

future....The sprawling, amorphous texture of Ives's music is like the early American scene itself.... In accepting his environment, chaotic though it was, as a basis for the creation of order, Ives resembles another heroic figure, Frank Lloyd Wright, who insisted on the organic relationship between Man and nature precisely because, in a new world, man seemed to have asserted his whim, rather than his will, with promiscuous blatancy."[27] Ives produced a sort of musical collage that combined high and low cultural sources ranging from European Romantic music to music from streets, bars, and churches. It was multilayered, discordant, and brash, just like American city life.

Ives was very much an exception to the general trend in early American music-making. At first, composers had found the Romantic mood in Europe appropriate to a time when pioneers were opening up a new continent. The musicians of the American Romantic movement celebrated national events in works whose titles were based on the landscape and on Native American stories, but that were nevertheless middle European in style.

As in Europe, the prevalence of Romanticism duly precipitated a reaction. According to an authoritative history of American music, "Folklorism was hardly unknown to the European Romantics. . . . Ultimately America came to share this aspect of Romantic thought. The problem for composers was: what was American musical folklore? . . . all too simplistically they looked to the most 'primitive' kinds of music in the nation, the music of the American Indian and the Negro. That there might be other 'folkish' music in their past and under their very noses, that the vernacular tradition of popular music might provide a usable stock of invigorating source materials, seems not to have occurred to most of these composers."[28]

The selectivity in the identification of suitable sources was one of several ironies in the creation of an American musical tradition. The United States has always been a melting pot; American nationality is available to anyone who makes the journey (at least, during those periods when the country has welcomed immigrants). Thus, one of the prime movers in the search for an American music was the Bohemian Antonín Dvořák whose symphony *From the New World* adopted Negro spiritual themes and who promoted the idea that such tunes were appropriate source material for "American" compositions. And, somewhat later, the Frenchman Edgard Varèse wrote his *Amériques* and established the International Composers' Guild in New York to promote the creation of twentieth-century American music.

In such an atmosphere, it was unlikely that an American music based on simplistic folkloric criteria would last. The music that settlers brought with them—the austere Protestant liturgy and folk tunes from the British Isles in particular—turned out to be just as influential. Simple hymnlike tunes were well matched to the open spaces of the new continent and the innocence of its people. In time, this music was modified by Negro influences, with shifts in rhythm becoming gradually more pronounced as ragtime and jazz grew to maturity. Other composers sought to echo the collective attitude of the people rather than their origins. According to the musicologist I. Sablosky, Edward MacDowell, for example, wanted to hear "American music echo not folklore but 'the youthful optimistic vitality and undaunted tenacity of spirit that characterizes the American man.'"[29]

One composer is generally agreed to have united all these disparate threads in his music and in doing so to have laid the foundations for the United States to become a major force in twentieth-century classical music. Aaron Copland produced compositions that made use of jazz, blues, and folk music from his own Jewish tradition and from other traditions. He also endeavored to express more intrinsically the qualities of the American landscape and way of life. Yet the fact that Copland was able and inclined to do this was due in no small degree to his studies in Paris, where he gained a new perspective on his own culture and was exposed to composers such as Milhaud and Stravinsky, who were actively creating new music for their lands.

Copland's music runs the gamut of modes of national expression. *Appalachian Spring* and the opera *The Tender Land* borrowed and altered traditional melodies, including a well-known Shaker tune in the former piece, while his music for films such as that made of Thornton Wilder's play, *Our Town,* had the best of excuses for more blatant celebration of Americanness. Copland demonstrated his dexterity with a range of music that was sometimes national and at other times nationalistic, but he was nevertheless aware that a line had to be drawn somewhere. Referring to *A Lincoln Portrait*, he wrote: "I was skeptical about expressing patriotism in music—it is difficult to achieve without becoming maudlin or bombastic, or both."[30] Copland gradually lost interest in overt nationalist expression after the Second World War, but by then an American music was flourishing, and young composers were at last able to look to local masters rather than across the Atlantic for instruction.

Copland had never been shy about stating his nationalist aim. He wrote, for example: "I was intrigued with jazz rhythms, not for superficial effects, but for use in larger forms, with unconventional harmonies. My aim was to write a work that

27. Wilfrid Mellers, *Music in a New Found Land* (Barrie and Rockliff, 1964).

28. H. Wiley Hitchcock, ed., *Music in the United States: A Historical Introduction* (Prentice-Hall, 1969).

29. I. Sablosky, *American Music* (University of Chicago Press, 1969).

30. Copland and Perlis, *Copland.*

would be American within a serious musical idiom. Jazz offered American composers a native product."[31] "Copland absorbed the temper of big-city life at a level below conscious understanding. . . . Copland's music, as the creation of an urban America, had a real and profound affinity with some aspects of jazz: which affinity did not, however, involve imitation of the superficies." Along with jazz, Copland evinced a "slow harmonic movement," "lack of lyrical growth," and passages that "embrace all the physical and nervous energy of city life." *Quiet City* "is both Negroid in its blues notes and Jewish in its incantatory repetitions. . . . "[32] It was the sum of all these qualities, not the fact of any one of them, that made Copland's music unique. To his audiences, its uniqueness became its Americanness.

By the mid-twentieth century there was no shortage of influences. Ives had been "discovered"; George Gershwin had placed Negro music firmly in the mainstream and drawn together the worlds of opera and Broadway. Bartók, Stravinsky, and Schönberg had fled Europe, bringing new ideas. A diverse clan of younger American composers set to work. Sablosky was able to conclude, "Anxiety over the emergence of 'an American music' had waned as it became increasingly clear that there were to be several American musics."[33]

31. Ibid.

32. Mellers, *Music.*

33. Sablosky, *American Music.*

The Lessons for Design

Because artists more often than not take their cue from foregoing developments in their own field of art, it can happen that one person substantially creates or revives a regional or national style. This can be effected as it was by Bartók, by dint of meticulous research, or as it was by Smetana, by the adamant declaration of a fait accompli. Other artists will then develop that style even though they may have no avowed regionalist or nationalist agendas of their own.

The experience both of architects and of composers suggests that the success of regionalism has less to do with raw materials than with the panache of execution. In some cases the cultural ingredients are somewhat arbitrary, as the American examples of Frank Lloyd Wright and Aaron Copland show. In other cases they are entirely spurious. All this should prove reassuring to designers who worry where the sources for their regional design are to come from.

The musical precedent is most useful in dispelling another qualm that designers might feel with regard to regional expression. At the behest of foreign clients, the most able designers happily produce goods that are of a style that the client and its market will find acceptable. Only composers come close in approaching this chameleonlike behavior (evidenced in works such as Debussy's *Ibéria*, Milhaud's *Saudades do Brasil*, Copland's *El Salón Mexico* and *Danzón Cubano*… the list is endless), although when they impersonate another nation's style it is more often for their own amusement than for the specific satisfaction of a client. As Dahlhaus argues, this does not mean that a composer's genuine national style is devalued by his or her ability to adopt another national style when it suits. Neither does it mean that the impersonation is necessarily inferior: "To assert . . . that Glinka is 'authentic' when he writes pieces of Russian character, but 'inauthentic' when the stimulus is Spanish, would be absurd (and the musical nationalists always avoided making any such claim)."[34]

It would seem, then, that anything goes. Is national character really so malleable? To answer this question it is necessary to decide, of national character and individual character, which is the chicken and which is the egg. Dahlhaus asks: "Do individual characteristics proceed out of the national substance, or is the concept of what is national formed by generalization on the basis of individual characteristics? (In the latter case, the concept is necessarily formed at a secondary stage, but it is no less an 'aesthetic fact' for that.). . . . if a composer intended a piece of music to be national in character and the hearers believe it to be so, that is something which the historian must accept as an aesthetic fact, even if stylistic analysis—the attempt to 'verify' the aesthetic

premise by reference to musical features—fails to produce any evidence. . . . It is possible to regard nationality . . . as a quality which rests primarily in the meaning invested in a piece of music or a complex of musical characteristics by a sufficient number of the people who make and hear the music, and only secondarily, if at all, in its melodic and rhythmic substance. To express it summarily: so long as gypsy music in Hungary was regarded as authentically Hungarian, it was authentically Hungarian; the historical error has to be taken at its face value as an aesthetic truth."[35]

This same rationale may be translated with some modification to the field of design. In the process of creating a manufactured artifact, it is not only the individual designer and his or her national character that must be taken into account but also a number of collective intermediary characters, such as those of the client corporation and of the intended customer base. For the creation of a national style to endure, whether in music, architecture, or design, it must be appreciated as such by the consumer. This suggests that in commercial design the creation and acceptance of national products would be facilitated if they were explicitly marketed as national. However national design comes to be created, the examples of music and architecture show that the conscious act of creation can lead to enduring work of quality. It also shows that that act of creation can be more direct than many designers may currently believe possible.

34. Dahlhaus, "Nationalism and Music."

35. Ibid.

Countries

In the window of an electrical shop that lies in the shadow of the Gothic cathedral in the city of Ulm, a city sacred to the memory of Modernist product design, there sits amid the gleaming sculptural white and black appliances a 1930s-style radio with a prettily fretted wooden grille over its loudspeaker. Its package proclaims it as an *Echtholzradio* ("real wood radio") *mit Nostalgie-Look.* It is a salient reminder, here of all places, that the story of German design is not just the story of the Bauhaus and its progeny. *Kitsch,* after all, is a German word.

Notwithstanding this, the orthodoxy of design excellence in Germany has been established according to certain precepts of the Bauhaus and, more particularly, of the Hochschule für Gestaltung in Ulm that succeeded it. The Bauhaus existed from 1919 until it was shut down by Hitler in 1933; the Hochschule lasted no longer—from 1955 until, its funding curtailed by the local (Stuttgart) government, it closed in 1968. The Ulm school had—and continues to have—an influence out of all proportion to its modest number of teachers and pupils. Some of Germany's leading designers attended the school. Others who went there stayed in academia, and it is their proselytizing more than anything else that accounts for the durability of Ulm values both within Germany and abroad. Many of the younger generation of German designers absorbed the Ulm philosophy secondhand in this way. The result, according to Klaus-Jürgen Maack, managing director of the Erco lighting company, is that "all designers today, even if they don't know where Ulm is, are somehow in the tradition of Ulm." The question of whether the Ulm school has influenced German taste or whether it was German taste that made the Ulm school what it was is by now unanswerable.

The products of one company exemplify German style for the design-conscious consumer. That company is Braun. Braun's electrical products—hair-care and kitchen appliances and shavers—emerge from an in-house studio of just seven designers. The modest scale of this operation does not, however, prevent the company from stating its philosophy in the most portentous terms. The company's "Truthfulness Principle" lays down that "the first Commandment for product development . . . is to cater to the true needs of the people for whom

[the products] are intended. The products should be and look exactly as these people wish the objects with which they live to be and look." An admirable aim but one quite clearly not always met by the products themselves. They show a magisterial taste at work. Braun's range is among the most closely controlled of any consumer-goods manufacturer. The fact is that Braun's design has scaled the heights since its foundation in 1955, not by asking consumers what they wanted but by its own single-minded and unswerving commitment to a particular ideal—that of the Ulm school. The "Ergonomics Principle" continues by stressing the convenience of Braun products. Yet despite their elegance and proclaimed functionalism, it is, for example, almost impossible to insert batteries correctly into one of Braun's shavers on the first try. And what would be a bells-and-whistles "feature" of a product from the United States or Hong Kong—the voice-activated shutoff for an alarm-clock—is justified as a triumph of ergonomics at Braun. In general, the axioms that follow from these principles betray the inflexibility of an ideologue. This is at its most strident in "The Functionality Principle," which determines that Helvetica is the obligatory typeface for "conveying an advertising message completely and comprehensively."

That ideologue is Dieter Rams, the director of product design at Braun since 1962. He joined the company under the patronage of Hans Gugelot, the Ulm School professor who had been instrumental in establishing Braun's design philosophy. Gugelot set the tone for Braun's severe style in 1955. Rams has been a diligent custodian of that style, safeguarding it and refining it where possible in the years since. Rams is fond of saying that products should be "like a good English butler. They should be there when you need them and in the background when you don't." Rams's "butler," however, is a male model in an Armani suit; he finds it very hard to stay in the background. The designer favors black and white in place of color and pure geometric forms with meticulous but minimalist detailing or graphics.

According to a catalog of his life and work, "Dieter Rams acts like someone who has a very keen sense of hearing, but who is forced to live in a world of shrill dissonance." His office at the Braun headquarters just outside Frankfurt is spotless and precisely laid out. His house, a mile or two away up the hill in a village, is equally pristine. He drives an immaculate black Porsche 911, which is kept in a garage.

Though he is one of the world's best-known designers, Rams is quick to point out that his life is nothing like that of a Milanese such as Ettore Sottsass. He has no private studio, although he has regularly designed a few pieces for companies other

Hair dryers
Dieter Rams
Braun

In Dieter Rams's book, even color represents compromise.

BMW 3 Series car
BMW, 1991

850 table
Dieter Rams
Vitsoe, 1985
Photograph by Ian McKinnell

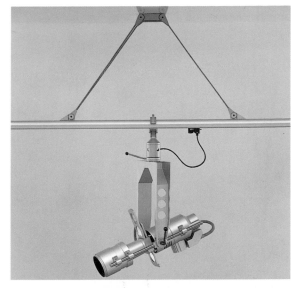

Lighting fixtures
Erco Leuchten

*Erco exercises sufficient
direction even over foreign
designers that their work, such
as the 1991 fixtures by Roy
Fleetwood (top) and the 1987
Eclipse by Mario Bellini
(bottom), conforms to the
company's high standards.*

606 bookshelves
Dieter Rams
Vitsoe, 1960
Photograph by Ian McKinnell

862 chair
Dieter Rams
Vitsoe, 1986

Meat cutter
Busse Design Ulm
Krups

Kitchen scales
Busse Design Ulm
Soehnle, 1988

Aroma Art coffee maker
Oco Design
Melitta

than Braun, most notably for Vitsoe, a Frankfurt furniture company run by a Dane. Rams's situation is not unusual in Germany where the commitment to *gute Form* is often strongest within corporations and where, as a consequence, there are comparatively few large design firms. This commitment is a product of the *Unternehmenskultur* (literally "corporate culture" or "enterprise culture" but conveying a sense of something much more durable in German than is implied in these terms' fashionable Wall Street and City usages) that is widespread in German industry. The best manufacturers do not only have the cultural confidence to employ and trust product designers, they also have the industrial wherewithal to ensure that the results of their endeavors will be solidly built and reliable in use. A typical Italian company, by contrast, does well in the former department but often lacks the technological base to ensure this degree of quality. Thus, a German automobile designed by Giorgietto Giugiaro will still be more reliable than a similar car by the same designer produced by an Italian manufacturer. German design firms, for their part, tend to be more strongly rooted in the real world than in other countries; more of their work goes into production, and less is done with recreational or polemical intent.

The Vitsoe work shows Rams's style at its purest. At Braun he is occasionally obliged to give way to marketing demands. The compromise clearly pains him, and he suggests that this was not always the case. A recent range of pastel-colored alarm clocks was a sign of the times. Surely they are not postmodern? "They look like the old alarm clocks which had a bell on top," Rams admits. "The idea was to translate something of the old into new materials, but I would never call these postmodern." Nevertheless, it is interesting that the pastel clocks do not appear alongside their black and white siblings in the company literature.

In principle, Rams remains true to the values he has always held, and he entertains the hope that the world will come around to his view in time. Meanwhile, there is kitsch all around. "It's terrible to go to a lot of these fairs. You can see it all over the world. Germany too? Of course. In general, though, people are becoming more and more aware of what design is and what it means. Ten years ago, they didn't know." Rams lectures and teaches and is chairman of the Rat für Formgebung, Germany's design council, but he also works in more mysterious ways to win converts to the cause of timeless Modernism. While Vitsoe is in sympathy with Rams's design ethic, it comes as a surprise to find him now taking on commissions for Alessi, a company that has done more than most to overthrow the Modernist idea of the product. But Rams finds solace in the Italian firm's

new mood: "They want to come back—I won't say to the Ulm style—but to basics."

Erco is another firm that embodies unsullied Modernist principles. Klaus-Jürgen Maack's pitch that Erco sells "light, not lighting fixtures" reflects the dominance of functionalist ideals. The company's lamps are designed, not like those of, say, the Italian firm Flos, as objects for contemplation independent of what they do, but as a means to an end. Erco works with designers of international repute, yet the process it uses to ensure that it gets what it wants is utterly German. "If a Bellini works for us," says Maack, "he has to work in a totally different way than he would for other clients. With other clients he's 99 percent Bellini. In our case the brief is already 80 percent Erco.

"We have a more puritanical approach to design than the Italians—we have more Protestants than the Italians—and so the acceptance of pure design is more advanced. I'm sure the Italians will be doing it too in ten years' time." Maack says this somewhat tongue-in-cheek—his exaggerated view is the butt of a long-running joke with Ettore Sottsass, whose own jest is to claim that Memphis is a Catholic revenge for the puritanical Bauhaus. Nevertheless, the conviction of the rightness of the functionalist view and of the prospect of its ultimate triumph is one often heard in Germany.

Braun and Erco continue a tradition of in-house design or design direction set in motion by AEG when it appointed Peter Behrens to design its buildings, products, and a corporate identity in the early years of the twentieth century. Behrens was also a pioneer of functionalist design and, with Hermann Muthesius, was instrumental in establishing the Deutsche Werkbund in 1907. Klaus Lehmann, a professor of product design at the Staatliche Akademie der bildende Künste in Stuttgart, credits Muthesius with introducing both the doctrine of unadorned form and the preachiness with which it has been spread through the education system. Influenced by Shaker and Puritan design, Muthesius taught that beauty of form without adornment is both useful and satisfying. This dictum was taken to heart by the Werkbund, the Bauhaus, and Ulm and its diaspora in the form of leading firms such as Busse Design in Ulm itself and Neumeister Design in Munich, whose principals are Ulm alumni.

The flip side of this credo is a degree of conformity that some find unnerving. This is especially evident in corporate graphics. Berlin typographer and designer Erik Spiekermann scorns the near ubiquity of the Helvetica typeface. At least half of Germany's top companies use it. Even those that compete with each other—BASF and Bayer, BMW and Daimler-Benz, Siemens and Nixdorf—largely share their cor-

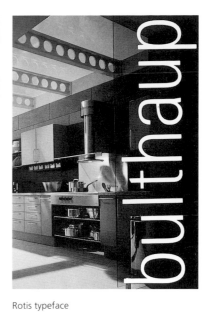

Children's bicycle seat
Busse Design Ulm
Römer, 1988

Company reports
BASF, 1991

Many of Germany's leading corporations choose Helvetica as their typeface.

Rotis typeface
Otl Aicher

Aicher's Rotis typeface has been adopted by kitchen manufacturer Bulthaup.

Inter-City Express high-speed train
Neumeister Design
Deutsche Bundesbahn

Initial design work by Neumeister Design was based on wind-tunnel tests but led to a radically different shape for Germany's answer to the French TGV.

Standard-office furniture line
Andreas Brandolini
Prototypes Designwerkstatt
Berlin, Berlin 1988
Photograph by Idris Kolodziej
Copyright Designwerkstatt
Berlin

Allegroh faucet
Phoenix Product Design
Hansgrohe, 1988

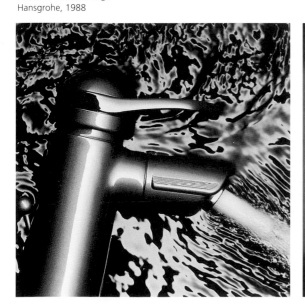

Top: Poster
Ott and Stein
Berlin Chamber Opera, 1988

Bottom: Poster
Ott and Stein
Berliner Festspiele, 1987

Graphic design in Berlin is more free-spirited than elsewhere in Germany, but is still generally governed by tight rules of typography and composition.

Perforated sheet-metal bow tie
Gabriel Kornreich, Büro für
Gestaltung
1989

porate lettering style. "It's all good stuff," says Spiekermann, "but it doesn't mean that the German public is design-conscious, and it doesn't mean that German clients are design-conscious."

There are signs of a loosening up. The best-known German design firm of recent years has been Frogdesign. To foreign eyes, much of the group's work still looks Germanically pure and simple, albeit with bolder curves and colors. To some Germans, however, even this small shift of emphasis is a revolution, enough to thrust Frogdesign into the front line of the avant-garde. Some call what Frogdesign does postmodern, but given that its products are founded on sound ergonomic principles and hold true to the Muthesian precepts of *gute Form,* this seems a trifle extreme.

In graphic design, one of the most important figures of the Ulm period was Otl Aicher, who developed the pictograms for the 1972 Olympic Games in Munich. No other series of images more effectively sums up the Modernist ideals of simplicity and universality. And yet in one of his last projects, even Aicher appears to have recanted, with the design of a new series of typefaces called Rotis that combines the sans-serif style of Modernist fonts such as Helvetica with properties of traditional serif lettering. The German kitchen manufacturer Bulthaup was among the first to adopt one of the Rotis faces for its company logotype. Countering the Modernist doctrine that proclaims the virtue of sans-serif legibility, Aicher commits what would once have been a heresy by averring that serif faces are not entirely without merit after all, although in an idiosyncratic book on typography that introduced the Rotis faces, he produced a functionalist justification: "This new typographic program does not espouse formal diversity, but . . . promotes a higher reading economy. . . . We need a more intelligible language without chaff or husk, free from vacuous aesthetic formalism. That must be matched by a new typography that does not—as is so often the case in our computerized world—dispense with aesthetic standards altogether."

These are small signs of accommodation to a world of changing design priorities. In general, Germany's federal structure works to maintain the status quo. There are many big cities but, until reunification at least, no single focus where an avant-garde could gain momentum. Frankfurt, Cologne, Düsseldorf, and the rest are important regional centers, but they are comfortable, provincial, and slightly dull. Dieter Rams feels that the federal structure that gives power to the *Länder* also weakens design education. There should be three good schools in the country, he believes, rather than ones in each region. The regions do vie with one another, however. Rivalry between Daimler Benz's dignified

Mercedes, made in the (largely Protestant) Swabian city of Stuttgart, and the flashier BMWs, made in the (largely Catholic) Bavarian capital of Munich (the blue and white of the BMW logotype are the colors of Bavaria), is especially strong.

The missing focus, of course, was—and is—Berlin. Renowned before the Second World War as the country's artistic center, Berlin has given rise to much of Germany's recent alternative design. Even before the reunification of the Federal Republic with the former communist Democratic Republic in 1990, Berlin could claim to be maintaining its cultural heritage despite—or perhaps because of—its isolation within East Germany. Before the Wall came down, there was something of the feeling of a ghetto. "Berlin was a refuge for extreme people and new ideas," says Theres Weishappel, a member of a young, multidisciplinary cooperative called Büro für Gestaltung.

It was in Berlin, during the 1980s, where some of these people began to question the unquestionable. Like many Berliners, Erik Spiekermann finds something sinister in the humorless moralism of design in what even West Berliners used to call "West Germany." In Berlin, he says, their rules count for less. "Because there's no commercial viability anyway, we might as well not listen to the gurus. Let's have a good time and ask questions rather than give answers." Much Berlin design is polemical and prototypical; little of it is manufactured.

Many designers believe that Berlin's isolation from the mainstream of German life, and especially from its commercial life, has allowed its special character to flourish. "On the weekends, you can't go to the country," says Angela Schönberger, director of the Internationales Design Zentrum in Berlin. "So everything concentrates around culture in its many aspects—high culture and subculture." In the absence of business investment, Berlin's culture became its industry. Bernard Stein and Nicolaus Ott, for example, have designed more than two hundred posters, mainly for local cultural events. "Now," says Stein, "much more business will come to Berlin. I don't know how that will influence the culture, but it will change the city."

Ott and Stein's work is vibrant, but hardly anarchic. Spiekermann, too, does not always appear to make full use of the freedom Berlin offers. His company, Metadesign, also produces posters, but Spiekermann himself is more interested in designing forms and signage for the post office and local transit authorities and designing typefaces. One recent job was to coax the ultraconservative *Wall Street Journal* through a gradual editorial redesign. "I'm not a Neville Brody," says Spiekermann. "I'm not that expressive sort of typographer. I like forms and

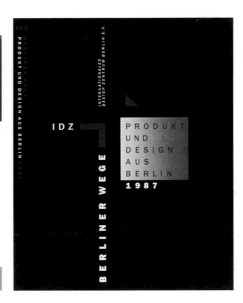

Far Left: Company literature
Metadesign
Fontshop
Photograph by Jons Michael
Voss

Middle: Poster
Metadesign
Herman Miller, 1989

Left: Poster
Metadesign
IDZ, 1987

German graphic design is produced often in one-man studios. Erik Spiekermann's company, Metadesign, is a rare example of a larger firm.

Coffee maker
Busse Design Ulm
Emige

Hat prototype
Kunstflug
Prototypes for Abet Laminati
S.p.A./Abet GmbH and
Designwerkstatt Berlin, Berlin
1991
Photograph by Idris Kolodziej

Train schedule terminal
Kunstflug
Düsseldorf Airport, 1989

Kunstflug subverts the norms of information graphics with its warped airport signage.

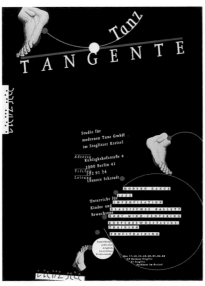

Far left: Party invitation
Theres Weishappel, Büro für
Gestaltung
1988

Left: Poster
Theres Weishappel, Büro für
Gestaltung
1987

Precedente II chair
Gabriel Kornreich
Prototypes Designwerkstatt
Berlin, 1988
Photograph by Idris Kolodziej
Copyright Designwerkstatt
Berlin

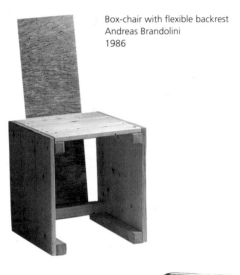

Box-chair with flexible backrest
Andreas Brandolini
1986

Threeswinger conference chair
with folded writing support
Stiletto Studios
Prototypes Designwerkstatt Berlin,
1988
Photograph by Idris Kolodziej
Copyright Designwerkstatt Berlin

*The New German Design
movement produced radical
furniture that made fun of
conventional Bauhaus wisdom.*

schedules and so on. I like to solve a problem. I am very Germanic."

Far more challenging is the work of the Berliners who have created what quickly became known as the New German Design. According to Schönberger, their experimental furniture and objects are characterized by an intellectual or ironic touch. They have formed groups with unusual names that celebrate their origin (Berliner Zimmer and Berlinetta) or carry a cross-border appeal (Cocktail and Stiletto) to distinguish themselves from traditional design firms.

New German Design does not aim to present a mindless opposition to the rule of functionalism, but it does hope to bring a new flexibility to bear. The impresario behind the movement is Christian Borngräber, who established the Designwerkstatt as a forum for the manufacture and presentation of its prototypes. "Say it this way," Borngräber remarks. "I'm not against Rams; I'm against the stiffness that says German design has to be like Rams." Not everybody liked this message: after the first exhibitions of the New German Design, Borngräber received hate mail from conventional industrial designers.

What was it that proved so offensive? The wilder examples of New German Design are often clumsy assemblages of scrap materials—hunks of wood, chipboard, rusty iron, sheets of polyethylene, corrugated cardboard. Elegance is less important than the expression of a verbal idea through the design. One of the neatest examples is the Consumer's Rest chair by Stiletto, which is simply a supermarket trolley stripped of its wheels and with its sides bent out to form an armchair. The idea compensates for the quality of the materials and finish—a complete reversal of the tenets of *gute Form*. Constructivism is a strong influence on New German Design, in opposition to the slick ergonomics and styling that so often disguise the construction of conventional products such as the chairs produced by Germany's powerful office-furniture industry.

Although Berlin is the natural home of the avant-garde, several other cities have found it in themselves to tolerate a token group of experimenters. Kunstflug (literally, "art-flight") in Düsseldorf and Ginbande (loosely, "nothing") in Frankfurt are examples. Neither is as anarchic as the more extreme members of the Berlin avant-garde. Ginbande, indeed, won widespread praise for its ingenious Tabula Rasa prototype, a long table and bench seats that fold like an accordion into a compact storage box.

Having formerly designed lamps that use fluorescent tubes and tree branches to achieve a quasi-religious effect, Kunstflug recently installed an interactive terminal to give train schedule informa-

tion at the Düsseldorf airport. The design openly mocks conventional German design, much of which surrounds it on the airport concourse. The terminal is a brightly colored skew-angled frame supporting a display monitor. An illuminated sign overhead indicates its presence to arriving passengers. It uses the same orthodox Modernist typeface as the rest of the airport signage, but the designers have cheekily warped the lettering.

These rebels are now gaining greater acceptance in the world they set out to challenge. Ginbande's Tabula Rasa was adopted by Vitra, the German manufacturer whose office furniture symbolizes all that the New German Design opposes, as one of its Vitra Editions. Andreas Brandolini, perhaps the movement's brightest star, is also now working with Vitra. The question these designers must ask themselves is whether their work can move into the mainstream without sacrificing its spirit or whether it will do so only to remain ghettoized in collections of prototypes, such as the Vitra Editions, that have little relevance to the company's commercial production. After all, as Borngräber states, "It's ridiculous if you are still calling yourself avant-garde after a decade."

This avant-garde may in any case find itself cut off by powerful currents that suggest a very different future. Reunification may alter the priorities. Perhaps because the two homes of the Bauhaus—Dessau and Weimar—lie inside what was East Germany, or perhaps simply because the Bauhaus was a creation of a united Germany, East Germans look upon that school with even more fondness than their countrymen in the West. "We have no Ulm. The Bauhaus was the last strong influence that we got from our history," says Andreas Trogisch of the graphic design company Grappa, before quickly adding: "When we talk about a Bauhaus aesthetic, we mean Herbert Bayer and Jan Tschichold, not the results of the Bauhaus in our new-build houses, those cartons. Those are not the Bauhaus, but people think they are."

There is a concern to retain the best aspects of East German communism and Bauhaus social commitment for design in the new economy. "We identify with projects only if the social and political connotations are acceptable to us. We do not see only the aesthetic product," says Trogisch. The same situation has existed in the past, according to Annette Musiolek, editor of *Form und Zweck,* the official design magazine of the East German Council for Industrial Design, now shut down. In the absence of a market and its demands, she says, designers have focused on functionalism. Given the tools for the job, the ability of designers educated under the communist system is to design for longevity. They have little understanding of markets or of why

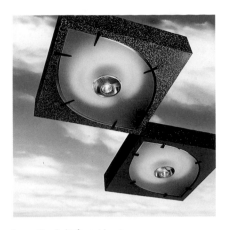

Eye ceiling light for grid system
Herbert Jakob Weinand
Prototypes Designwerkstatt
Berlin, 1988
Photograph by Idris Kolodziej
Copyright Designwerkstatt
Berlin

Prototype wing laminates
Element and Zick-Zack-Welle
Joachim B. Stanitzek
Prototypes for Abet Laminati
S.p.A./Abet GmbH and
Designwerkstatt Berlin, Berlin
1991
Photograph by Idris Kolodziej

Right: Prototype wing laminates
Patchworks
Michel Feith
Prototypes for Abet Laminati
S.p.A./Abet GmbH and
Designwerkstatt Berlin, Berlin
1991
Photograph by Idris Kolodziej

Below, right: Wiblingen light
system
Andreas Brandolini
Design Gallery Weinand, Berlin,
1987
Photograph by Idris Kolodziej

*Berlin has been a hothouse for
creative rebels who reject the
conformity elsewhere in
Germany.*

Below:
Little Sisters seating system
Andreas Brandolini, 1989
Photograph by Wilmar
Koenig/Fotografie für
Architekten

Bottom: Kassel living-room
carpet
Andreas Brandolini
1987

Tree-lights
Kunstflug

*Elsewhere in Germany, there is
a smattering of avant-garde
groups, seemingly one in each
major city. Kunstflug is based in
Düsseldorf.*

LT 1 and LT 2 table and
standard lamp
Joachim B. Stanitzek
Prototypes Designwerkstatt
Berlin, 1988
Photograph by Idris Kolodziej
Copyright Designwerkstatt
Berlin

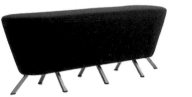

Above: Poster
Grappa
Künstler Agentur der DDR,
1988

Left: Restaurant lighting and
interior
Volkmar Nickel
Hotel Berlin

*Volkmar Nickel's startling
interiors for the Hotel Berlin in
what was East Berlin were
created in an attempt to
attract guests from the West.*

Food mixer
Ralf Seifert, Klaus
Beringschmidt, Matthias Zorn
VEB Polygraph, 1989
Photograph courtesy Amt für
Industrielle Formgestaltung

Posters
Grappa
1989

Product and graphic design in what was East Germany aimed to emulate that in the West. They often fell well short not because the designers lacked training but because of poor printing and manufacturing technology.

Alarm clock
Bernd Stegmann
VEB Uhrenwerke Ruhla, 1987
Photograph courtesy Amt für Industrielle Formgestaltung

design should be led by whims of fashion. The functionalist, problem-solving mentality is ingrained, even if the resources have rarely been present to implement any solution.

The vast majority of design in East Germany, such as it was, was done by and for the government. Most designers were employed in *Kombinate,* the state-run conglomerates. Like communist manufacturers elsewhere, the *Kombinate* sought to imitate Western consumer-goods design. They had to look no further afield for their ideal than to the products of Braun. In the new atmosphere there is no prerogative to stick to forms from the past. "Eastern European countries aren't so closely interconnected now," says Musiolek. "Each has its own history for the first time since the war—and its own problems."

There have been very few independent design groups in the Eastern sector. In the 1970s the authorities obliged all craft and design firms employing more than ten staff members to become so-called Socialist craft production associations, complete with regulations and economic plans. These restrictions have been lifted, but the independents remain small and ill equipped. Some may pool their resources, but even so, they will find it hard to undertake the complex product design or corporate identity work that will be demanded by the new businesses expected to grow up in the reunited Berlin now that it has been made Germany's capital city once more.

Lighting designer Volkmar Nickel, for example, spent fifteen years struggling to evolve his own style, stymied by the low-tech industry available to him. His lighting for a hotel restaurant in the Alexanderplatz is as controversial as anything by his colleagues in the West. Ironically, the design was commissioned with the specific aim of attracting Western tourists. Grappa's work, too, is produced in a somewhat artificial climate. "We have good training but bad circumstances and low technical standards," says Trogisch. "But because we use more simple technology, I think it makes our work more essential." As is the case in West Berlin, Grappa's clients are mainly in the cultural field. Unlike their colleagues in the West, however, these designers' prospects of attracting commercial work were diminished with the fall of the Wall, for they must now compete against more "professional" Western design groups and advertising agencies. This is not the only detrimental aspect to the opening up of the East. Volkmar Nickel runs his lighting factory with five colleagues. But already, one has deserted to the West and its high wages. West Germans view the drift with hostility as arrivals threaten to undercut local prices for services.

The Germans have given themselves five years to iron out these temporary difficulties and achieve

parity between East and West. In the longer term, the likelihood of a reappraisal of Ulm and Bauhaus values is strengthened by consumer demands for environmentally responsible design. Klaus Lehmann believes that Germany is well placed to lead in this area, with a naturalist sympathy that stretches from the Romantic era to the success of the Green movement during the 1980s. Annette Musiolek predicts that the residue of Socialist idealism combined with Green consciousness will lead to the development of products intended for longer life and available in fewer varieties. Faced with the new constraints of bringing East Germany into the consumer culture fold and with the need to create "greener" products—both matters of great concern to ordinary German people—it could well be that a new functionalism will gain ground in the coming years. The fathers of Ulm would be proud.

Poster
Grappa
1989

Holland is a tight little country. Its population of 14 million squeezed into just 41,000 square kilometers makes it one of the most densely populated developed nations. Much of its area lies below sea level and must be protected from flooding. As a result, there is here, perhaps more than in other nations, a sense of a whole country's having been designed.

This is something that the Dutch themselves point out, and it is something that influences new thought in design. Wim Crouwel, director of the Boymans-van Beuningen Museum in Rotterdam, and formerly with the Amsterdam firm Total Design, writes of his artificial surroundings in the catalog for the "Dutch Design Portraits" exhibition for the 1989 Nagoya international design conference: "It is this completely designed situation that—in return—is an interesting source for new design. By design, we make our country livable day by day."

It is perhaps because the Dutch have had to unite against the sea that they are more accepting of the idea of the overall plan, the grand design, in other aspects of their lives. Graphic designer Gert Dumbar explains: "A major part of Holland has always been shaped by human hands, by the official sector. We are a small country, so it is easy for the official sector to oversee the situation." While the countryside is designed to protect against flooding, the cities, too, are purposefully shaped both by their canals and by modern urban planning strategies implemented after the Second World War. Public design programs—signage, advertising for cultural events, stamps, and money—all have a contemporary design content far greater than in most other countries.

The generally high standard of design is also evident in Dutch products. According to Peter Krouwel of the industrial design firm Ninaber Peters Krouwel: "The supposed identity of Dutch design is not due to design faculties and academics. The influences of Dutch cultural history, the flat and geometric landscape, the climate and the people's stiff character in combination with the manufacturing in small series with low investment, are of greater importance." These conditions all contribute toward making Dutch institutions—led by the example of the government and its departments—some of the most understanding design patrons to be found anywhere.

In manufacturing there is a correlation between the scale of operation and of the market, and the materials and finishes used in many products. Philips is an anomaly. Like the fashion company Mexx and a number of other multinational corporations for which the Netherlands is well known, the firm merely happens to be based there, although it contributes mightily to the nation's exceptionally high volume of trade. In general, however, says Krouwel, many products still come into being locally, designed for a small market and for small manufacturing runs: "The small scale of industry enables the Dutch designer to create an intense relationship with top management. In this way, the designer gains a big influence on each decision. We strive for noble, venerable, durable, and beautifully made products. The design process is a struggle with functional aspects, traditional and aesthetic preferences, technology, marketing, and human factors. The moment this struggle is won and the commission is accomplished"—and this is the distinctiveness of Dutch design—"we try to go a little further, to give the product an extra kind of radiation."

In this respect, Dutch design has something in common with Danish design. Both countries have wealthy, design-literate populations who appreciate products designed and made locally that incorporate greater attention to materials and finishes than equivalent products from, say, Germany—which might be formally similar but, because they were produced on a far larger scale, would afford correspondingly less "extra radiation."

This quality is seen in Ninaber Peters Krouwel's own work—the Romeo and Juliet diabetes management system for Diva Medical Systems or an intelligent telephone for the Dutch post and telephone company, PTT—with their crisply cut, pure geometric arrangements in plan or elevation. It shows, too, in the bold or unusual accent colors of Ninaber Peters Krouwel's Babybob cradle for Dremefa; Holland Processing's information display unit for GVB, the Amsterdam public transport service; or laboratory instruments for Analyser/Industries by the Landmark design group. Though very much contemporary, these products, like much in Dutch life, still hold to the ideals of Modernism. This is not surprising given the appearance of the Dutch cityscape. Several native architects were key figures in laying the foundations for the International Style. New buildings show no loss of confidence. Not for the Dutch the pilasters and pediments of the postmodern. All is rectilinear white and gray integrity with occasional nods to De Stijl in splashes of primary color.

In a way Holland is a natural home of the International Style. What could better meet the conflicting demands of a native population with a Calvinist heritage and the quantities of Chinese, Indonesians, Greeks, Italians, and others who came to this liberal haven with the Dutch sea trade or to avoid persecution in their homelands? Modernism here is not a style but a way of life. A recent exhibi-

Information unit
Holland Processing
GVB Amsterdam, 1986

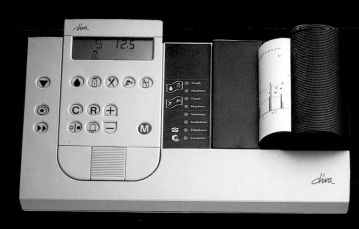

TeleOmega intelligent
telephone
Ninaber Peters Krouwel
PTT Telecom, 1986

Romeo and Juliet diabetes
management system
Ninaber Peters Krouwel
Diva Medical Systems, 1986

Telephone booth
Landmark
Royal PTT Nederland/PTT
Telecom, 1988

Babybob car seat
Ninaber Peters Krouwel
Dremefa, 1990

*Some people find a
connection between the flat
Dutch landscape and the
tendency in design often to
reduce compositions to linear
and planar elements.*

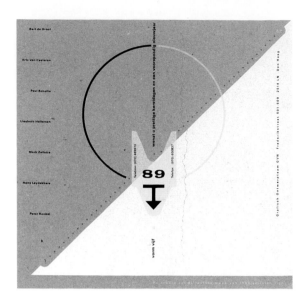

New Year's card
Vorm Vijf

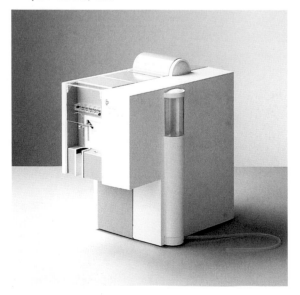

Chemical analyzer
Landmark
Analyser/Industries, 1990

tion in Rotterdam, "Nederland 2050," was merely interesting for its predictions for Dutch life sixty years hence: high-speed transportation, new habitation patterns, and farming from the sea. It was amazing for its unquestioning belief that those cities, houses, and products of the future would remain so firmly rooted in Modernist taste.

As in Switzerland, the compactness of the country encourages a strong awareness of what is happening in the next town and hence a strong competitive spirit that acts to maintain standards. The principal design schools have been the Gerrit Rietveld Academy of Art in Amsterdam and the Delft Technical University. The Rietveld Academy produced the central figures of Modernist Dutch graphic design, Wim Crouwel and Jan van Toorn. Both have concentrated on teaching the sound problem-solving skills of Modernist doctrine. Schools in Breda and in Philips's city of Eindhoven have recently challenged the established graphics and industrial design teaching with a more adventurous and lighthearted approach. The Delft school has the world's largest faculty for industrial design but was at its most influential in the 1970s, soon after its foundation, with teachers (such as Crouwel again) who were directly influenced by the Dutch avant-garde designers and artists of the interwar years—Gerrit Rietveld, Piet Zwart, and Piet Mondrian—as well as by the broader strain of European Modernism.

The art and design of Rietveld and Mondrian has become so well known internationally that it is hard to estimate its true importance to contemporary Dutch culture. While banal thefts from these artists, such as that used by L'Oreal in its "Studio" range of cosmetics packaging, can escape with impunity in the United States, in the Netherlands any such liberty would quickly be censured. Gert Dumbar found this out the hard way when in 1982 his studio produced a poster for a De Stijl exhibition in which the perspective of a photograph was used to pull the elements of a flat Mondrian canvas into three dimensions: "It caused a row in Holland because it was nothing to do with Mondrian."

The underlying influence of these men and of others less well known outside Holland, such as Paul Schuitema and Gerard Kiljan as well as Zwart, is still harder to assess. Gerard Hadders of the graphic design company Hard Werken in Rotterdam points out: "People talk of Piet Zwart as if he were a household name in the 1920s and 1930s, but of course he wasn't."

Zwart's contribution was sufficient to make the Dutch capital where he worked a center of typographic innovation. "Modern typography was developed in Russia, in Germany—and in the Hague," says Dumbar. As Dumbar hints, an intense rivalry

exists today among the designers in Holland's principal cities. This is seen most dramatically in graphic design. Many city authorities and institutions make good use of local designers, and the large bodies of work produced in their name in turn tend to predicate local "schools" as well as local loyalties. It is generally agreed that Amsterdam is most conservative, Rotterdam most adventurous, with the Hague somewhere in between. This hierarchy is interesting in itself since Amsterdam, with its Royal Concertgebouw Orchestra, the Rijksmuseum, and the Stedelijk Museum, is the cultural center, Rotterdam is the center of commerce, and the Hague is the seat of government. Unlike most countries, the design for government and commercial clients is more often innovative than that for cultural institutions. Government work may seem tame by Rotterdam standards, but it remains remarkable according to almost any international yardstick.

This local variety is achieved within a basically Modernist framework. Not only have the Dutch shunned the glib prettiness of postmodern graphics, they have also expunged most traces of anything premodern from their environment. In the 1960s Total Design was dominant, its signage at Amsterdam's Schiphol airport and other commissions setting a severe tone. This was a time when, as Total Design's creative director Ben Bos puts it, "Holland was the 'new Switzerland.'"

Quite a loosening-up has taken place since then. In recent years, Wim Crouwel became the man every young Turk loved to hate. Gradually, more intuitive work came to the fore, from Anthon Beeke, formerly a Total designer, from Studio Dumbar, and from Hard Werken. "Modernism of the 1960s was very strict in nature, whereas Modernism now is very liberal and varied," says Hadders. Crouwel, van Toorn, and their peers grew up with letterpress and have been unwilling or unable to adapt to the freedoms offered by offset lithography, he suggests. What Hard Werken did with type was seen as grotesque by the old guard. "They were appalled on one hand and envious on the other." By using strange colors and rediscovered, often rather clumsy, typefaces, Hard Werken signified its break with the immediate past. Studio Dumbar's signage for the Rijksmuseum also combines Modernist common sense and a new irreverence with internationally recognizable pictograms overlaid onto pertinent fragments of old masters. Even Total Design has broadened its formula, with some recent work using the Dutch-made Aesthedes computer in an effort to escape from old dogmas. What is remarkable about the results, however, is not how computer-generated they look but how like other Dutch and Total Design work they are.

Table
Pastoe

Holland's trading history makes it home to international corporations such as Philips and Mexx. Companies such as furniture manufacturer Pastoe also look overseas, using designers such as Shiro Kuramata and Shigeru Uchida.

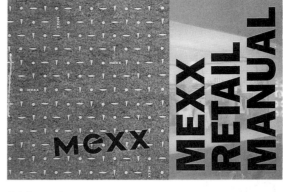

Retail manual
Mexx

Helena chairs
Bořek Šípek
Driade, 1988

Lamp
Pastoe

L260 cupboard
Pastoe, 1983

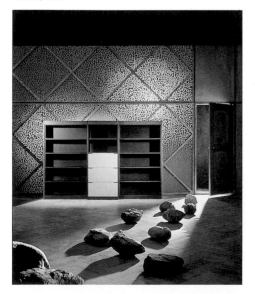

Report 1987

The National Investment Bank of the Netherlands

87

The National Investment Bank of the Netherlands

4 Carnegieplein
P.O. Box 380
2501 BH The Hague
The Netherlands

Telephone (070) 425 425

Kieler Woche

22.-30. Juni 1991

Kiel week sailing event
poster
Ben Bos, Total Design
Kieler Woche, 1990

Poster
Jan Paul de Vries,
Samenwerkende Ontwerpers
Volksbuurtsmuseum

Annual report
Wim Verboven, Total Design
Nationale Investeringsbank,
1987

Exhibition poster
Studio Dumbar
Zanders Papier, 1990

*Strong leadership by
designers such as Wim
Crouwel latterly of Total
Design and Gert Dumbar has
established a distinctive voice
for Dutch graphics.*

Book jacket
Hard Werken
Uitgeverij Bert Bakker, 1990

Signage
Studio Dumbar
Rijksmuseum Amsterdam, 1985

Studio Dumbar took a characteristically sardonic view of its client's "product" when devising signage for the Rijksmuseum.

Corporate identity and literature
Marianne Vos, Samenwerkende Ontwerpers
Drukkerij Mart Spruijt, 1989

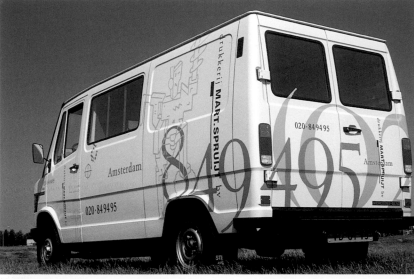

Corporate identity
Studio Dumbar
PTT, 1989

Cover and inside spread from
annual report
Frans Lieshout, Total Design
Suiker Unie, 1988

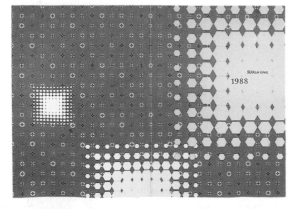

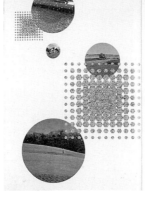

Dumbar's most visible work has been a new corporate identity for PTT, which was privatized in 1989. Here the seriousness lies in the strictness of the basic logotype and the irreverence in the wide variety of ways it may be used. The logotype is a partially "deconstructed" arrangement on a grid of squares. The platonic shapes and primary colors clearly echo the art of De Stijl. Elements of this central design—boxes, rules, and circles—may be removed, resized, and collaged back together to create further designs, sometimes by Dumbar, other times by the up-and-coming studios that PTT's design department makes it its business to seek out. This sophisticated approach allows everything from mailboxes to PTT buildings and coffee cups to bear the PTT signature without actually spelling it out in letters. Dumbar could only have brought such a complex identity into being for a company that was both acutely aware of its design heritage and also, because of the small geographic spread of its operation, able as he says to "oversee the situation."

PTT is an exemplary client. Like many companies, it established a tradition of corporate patronage, first by buying art and later by setting up an in-house design department responsible for commissioning the best designers of the day. But unlike, say, London Transport, which took a similar approach, it has not faltered, and its influence on other Dutch businesses has been great. "The Dutch belief in design is because of companies like PTT, and companies look like PTT because of the Dutch belief in design. It's impossible to separate the two," says Henri Ritzen of Studio Dumbar. But why, in Holland, does support for design go beyond the lucky chance of occasional patronage and become a continuing policy? "It has to do with the visual tradition of our culture," says Dumbar. "We have contributed major painters to the history of art—Rembrandt, Vermeer, Van Gogh, Mondrian. Art is part of the cultural structure; we steal our ideas from the laboratory of fine art."

In turn, the degree of understanding of design PTT expects from its public is astonishing by other countries' standards. At the Post Museum in the Hague one room is given over to an exhibition of stamps, past, present, and future. The designs run from 1920s woodcut expressionism and Piet Zwart photographic pieces through mainstream Modernism to the present. A slide presentation explains PTT's graphics program, even down to why it uses Univers 65 type.

But the strongest evidence of the pervasiveness of design in Dutch life is its money, much of it designed by Ootje Oxenaar, who also runs PTT's design department. In the Netherlands, by all accounts, people wait with bated breath for each new guilder denomination to appear. One recent note has a colorful diagrammatic windmill as its centerpiece, following a policy of replacing figureheads with more abstract objects. All the notes are more refined in color and composition than most other currencies. And whereas the dollar bill is signed only by treasury officials, the guilder bears the signature of its designer. It shows the value the Dutch place not only on their money but also on their design.

Public sector patronage is an important factor in the excellence of Dutch design. Postage stamps such as these are among the features of daily life that benefit. The post office design program is overseen by RDE Oxenaar, who has also designed some of the country's banknotes.

Right: Currency
RDE Oxenaar and others

Below: Postage stamps
PTT, 1989

Top: Anthon Beeke

Middle: Lex Reitsma

Bottom: Mart Warmerdam

Denmark

"The pleasing geometry of most Danish designs comes from the demand of function," says Steffen Gulmann of the Eleven Danes Design partnership. "A beautiful tool is beautiful because you can feel that it has the optimal function."

"Danish designers try to make their products good tools," agrees Jens Bernsen, director of the Danish Design Centre, "tools with which the user identifies. The aim is to make them so good that the user simply forgets about them and goes on with the task."

"Tools" is a word that crops up frequently in discussions about the Danishness of Danish design. There is even a Danish design magazine called *Tools*. The principle of simple functionality, which lies behind the talk of tools, applies across the board in Danish design, from graphics to products, furniture, and architecture. It is one of the ingredients contributing to perhaps the strongest national design identity in Europe.

The unity of this look is helped by the fact that Denmark has a small land area and a modest population of just over five million. Its population is more ethnically homogeneous than those of many other European countries and enjoys a high standard of education. For these and doubtless other reasons, too, the Danes appear to be at ease with themselves about their identity. This is indicated in design not only by unity across a range of products but also by a marked continuity down the years. It is often hard to tell whether a chair or a coffeepot dates from the 1950s or the 1990s, and Danes would in any case hesitate to prefer the latter over the former simply on the basis of its newness. "Denmark is one of the very few countries where famous design classics are also popular with the ordinary Dane," says Bernsen. "Many of the Danish designs which you find in museums all over the world you also find in hundreds of thousands of Danish homes."

Denmark changed comparatively late but comparatively rapidly from being a nation of farmers to being an industrial country. In the process of this transformation, the craft culture of the former weathered the passage into the new field of design better than in many countries. Today, says Jørgen Palshøj of Bang and Olufsen, "the protection of the knowledge we have of crafts is important to us. It reflects the fact that we have a lot of small industries." The craft tradition, combined with the small scale of many manufacturers, explains why many of them favor wood, natural textiles, and leather and why these materials as well as newer

ones, such as aluminum and plastic, are treated with an uncommon degree of honesty and a feel for their tactile and structural properties.

It is taken for granted that man-made objects should be simple, natural, and plain. "The Danish 'Jante law' [a customary piece of good advice] prohibits excess and showing off, so therefore grand lavish products are a no-no," explains industrial designer Anders Smith. This axiom applies both to the objects themselves and also to the process by which they come into being. Danish people have little interest in waiting to see what the next fashion will bring. They continue to hold in high regard products that may have become museum classics but that nevertheless continue to serve their function. In some cases, sales of such products are still rising.

But as Smith explains, there is an important corollary to this fondness for longevity. "Limited production volumes and the focus on what is really needed to solve a problem have bred a way of designing products that last a long time and are relevant even after the technology is obsolete." Put another way, many products are simply not up-to-date. This is a problem because it restricts Danish competitiveness and the problem will grow in importance with the approach of the European single market. An exception to this general rule applies in the case of a number of small companies that have grown by successfully establishing a dominant position in a niche technology. Brüel and Kjær, a maker of acoustical measurement equipment, is one example, digital drawing scanner manufacturer Contex another. How to assimilate the demands of modern technology on a wider scale without sacrificing the craft heritage is a central question in the current design debate in Denmark.

Danish design has been a largely private affair, concerned with providing practical solutions to everyday problems. It has never ostentatiously sought the international limelight. It came to wider notice only because it threw up a handful of world-class designers at the same time. Some, like Arne Jacobsen and Jørn Utzon, were architects, others were craftsmen who made their name in furniture design. According to Steffen Gulmann: "Danish design as it is known today had its origin in furniture created by designers such as Hans Wegner, Arne Jacobsen, and Poul Kjærholm. In all the work you will find the combination of function and a very refined beauty which presents itself in a natural way."

As early as the eighteenth century, Danish furniture was highly regarded in Europe. In the absence of much in the way of raw materials, crafts-men worked mainly with wood, a tradition that continues today with established manufacturers such as Artzan and Schiang and newcomers such as Orla

Windmill
Danwin

Denmark's strong environmental record does much to determine materials and forms in Danish design.

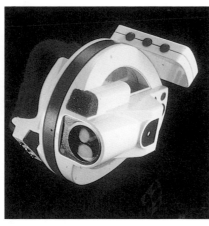

Far left: CB radio
Anders Smith
Danitas Radio, 1990

Middle: Video camera prototype
Anders Smith, 1988

Left: Directional system for
blind swimmers
Anders Smith, 1989

*As elsewhere in Scandinavia,
ergonomic considerations are
often uppermost in Danish
designers' minds.*

Ice scraper
Erik Magnussen, Eleven Danes
Design
Q8 Petroleum

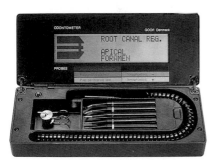

Dental odontometer
Lennart Goof, Eleven Danes
Design

Left and right: Tableware
Erik Magnussen, Eleven Danes
Design
Stelton

*Where the form of a product is
not conditioned by human
contact, it is free to assume more
austere shapes seen to good
effect in Erik Magnussen's work
for Stelton.*

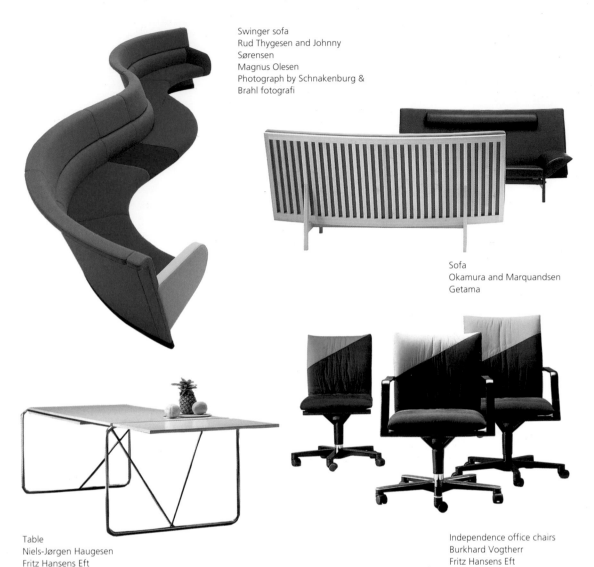

Swinger sofa
Rud Thygesen and Johnny
Sørensen
Magnus Olesen
Photograph by Schnakenburg &
Brahl fotografi

Sofa
Okamura and Marquandsen
Getama

Table
Niels-Jørgen Haugesen
Fritz Hansens Eft

Independence office chairs
Burkhard Vogtherr
Fritz Hansens Eft

Beovision television
David Lewis
Bang and Olufsen

Beocom 2000 telephone
Lone and Gideon Lindinger-
Löwy
Bang and Olufsen

Albæk, a company that has diversified into furniture production from shipfitting. Jørgen Gammelgaard, a professor of furniture design at the Royal Academy of Fine Arts, the country's principal design school, for example, follows in the footsteps of Arne Jacobsen with his furniture for Schiang. His Skagen stacking chair is a typically simple construction of metal frame and maple wood seat and backrest with a functional and material directness but also great refinement in its balance of line and plane.

In the 1960s, well before the Danish Design Centre came on the scene to promote companies' use of design, the success of Danish furniture designers inspired industrial companies to pursue a higher standard of design for their products. Louis Poulsen, Grundfos, and Danfoss were among those to take this path, but the best-known name internationally was the home-entertainment equipment company, Bang and Olufsen.

In 1988 a prominent Danish industrialist was quoted in the magazine of the Danish Design Council, offering the opinion that Denmark had produced just four companies that really understood international marketing. The four were Lego, Royal Copenhagen, Carlsberg, and Bang and Olufsen. The magazine went on to suggest that these were all design-based companies but then left it at that. In fact, these companies neatly summarize four very different approaches to design. Royal Copenhagen survives by the reproduction and marketing of tradition in its fine china. Lego's success was of the "eureka" variety—it took a spark of design genius to realize the new possibilities of plastics technology that would duly revolutionize the world of children's construction toys. Carlsberg's beer is not designed, but the way it is presented through packaging and advertising is carefully judged. Only the television and audio manufacturer Bang and Olufsen uses design in the conventional way of an Olivetti or an IBM: to maintain a market position as it introduces new products over a period of time.

Yet Bang and Olufsen is no mirror of the design policy of these corporations. It has no in-house design department. These days it does not even employ a design manager. Jørgen Palshøj, who used to have the title, explains that the formal existence of the position had little meaning: "A very strong corporate culture influences the design."

Some Danes agree with Bang and Olufsen itself that the company's work is not typically Danish, although it is one of the first examples of Danish design quality that springs to a foreign mind. Confined to a country of limited resources, Bang and Olufsen's design leadership is a means of survival. "We accepted years ago that we are not big enough to run a major production line like the Japanese," says

Skagen chairs
Jørgen Gammelgaard
Schiang

Beolink 1000 audio system
David Lewis
Bang and Olufsen

David Lewis was born in Britain but has been instrumental in establishing Bang and Olufsen's distinctive designs, which are often seen abroad as typically Danish.

Palshøj. "We found that being smaller you will always be late on the learning curve. In electronic parts, you can halve the price each time you double the volume, but with the mechanical parts it is different. The mechanics are less dependent on production volume, and this may be one of the reasons why we are eager to keep a strong mechanical component in our products. The mechanics are also closely related to craft. When we select materials and decide a product's finish, we pay a lot of attention to craftsmanship of the sort that we find mainly in the furniture industry." The implication of Palshøj's remarks is that the electronics receive less attention and may suffer some of the technological obsolescence that Smith mentions as a commonplace shortcoming among Danish products. Certainly some hi-fi buffs would claim that, for all its good looks, Bang and Olufsen's equipment does not represent the state of the audio art.

The attention to formal detail is well illustrated by the remote-control unit designed for the Beolink 1000 system by David Lewis, an Englishman long resident in Denmark, who, with Jakob Jensen, has largely set the modern style for Bang and Olufsen's products. It is made of cast aluminum, not the crummy plastic molding used by some manufacturers, and is pleasing to hold. "At least once a year we get young engineers coming and suggesting we mold it in plastic," says Palshøj. "They say it would be much cheaper and the tool would last longer. But if you put it in your hand, you get the answer. We use it as an example of design consciousness." The weighty metal case serves an ergonomic function, drawing heat from the hand so the unit does not become sweaty and unpleasant to hold. "That's the kind of design understanding that has been built up inside the company for many years," remarks Palshøj.

If such practical thoughtfulness were the end of the story, Danish design would quite probably not look anything like it does. There is a less easily articulated, but no less vital, quality that distinguishes Danish products from those of other countries, even from those of neighboring Germany and the other Scandinavian countries with which Denmark is often grouped (and where ergonomics and practical matters are also frequently foremost considerations).

This quality adds a cerebral dimension to the essentially practical concern of making products fit for their purpose. Per Mollerup, the editor of *Tools* and director of Designlab, a visual communications firm, describes it as "a certain quest for quiet qualities. In the graphics done by my own company this is seen as a quest for simplicity." Designlab is one of Denmark's major corporate identity firms, numbering Bang and Olufsen and Danish State Railways among

Sciang
home

Det Danske Teater 🎭

Logotypes by Designlab

Top: Schiang furniture company
Middle: Home realtor chain
Bottom: Det Danske Teater

Graphic design displays the same clarity seen in furniture and product design.

"Den lille lune" book for home insulation
Rockwool

its clients, although it is much smaller than its British or American counterparts. The quiet simplicity appears, for example, in Mollerup's logotype for Schiang, in which a simple green isometric outline of a chair substitutes for the letter *h*. "In formal terms, Danish design tends to be simple and elegant," adds Bernsen. "Yet it is a demanding simplicity that is not achieved at the cost of compromising the interests of purpose, manufacturing, construction, use, or relationship to the environment imposed upon an industrial product. When a simple solution is sought in such a complex situation, the result often achieves a natural beauty. Some of our most sophisticated modern industrial designs are a subtle and skillful play with proportions. In rare cases they achieve an ultimate refinement."

There is a distrust of complex and solid forms where the construction is hidden. Planar and laminar architectures are preferred, whether in plywood chairs or in wafer-thin hi-fi equipment or in central heating radiators made by Hudevad. Stretching a point, the ideal might be the monoliths in the film *2001*—pure shape with a contemplative presence. Part of the logic behind this extraordinary preference may be that small companies, unable to invest in expensive tooling, find simple shapes unavoidable and resolve to make the most of limited circumstances. According to John Stoddard of London's IDEO, which recently set up an office in Jutland to serve a growing roster of Danish clients, "In craft-related products they like organic forms, but elsewhere it is geometric-based—elegant, formal, geometric. The archetypal Danish form has proportions of one by five by twenty, say. Germany wants reliability, toughness, engineering. Denmark has to have elegance and this slightly more human feeling." IDEO's design for the Dancall 5000 cordless telephone is comparatively complex because of its technical requirements, but it still has some of this sharpness to it. "There's very little softening on it to say 'handle me,'" notes Stoddard. "That's deliberate to some extent, but also to some extent forced on us by the technology."

It is the impact of technology above all that is likely to condition the future of Danish design. The style that the world sees today was nurtured by a loose confederation of smallish companies producing low-technology goods such as furniture, lighting, and tabletop products. In recent years many of these companies have become part of larger enterprises that export a high proportion of their wares. They must upgrade the technological content of their goods in order to compete abroad. The obvious case in point is office furniture, a field that has become highly technocratic in the United States and Germany, but in which Denmark, historically a leader in furniture design, now lags in comparison.

Denmark is better positioned in other areas. As the only Scandinavian member—so far—of the European Community, Denmark serves as a useful bridge between the two regions. It is also ready to serve as a gateway to the Baltic countries if and when the occasion arises. Denmark's principal offering to the countries of the European Community is its progressive record in environmental and social policy. Some Danes worry that closer links with Europe will lead to a dilution of the country's position on these matters. If, on the other hand, Europe follows Denmark's example, the future of Danish design looks rosy. "The Danish design tradition fits very well with the growing awareness of the environment and substitution of the throwaway culture for longer-lasting products," says Steffen Gulmann. "The joy of developing a relationship with the tools that surround you in daily life will be a dominant trend."

Cordless telephone
IDEO
Dancall Radio, 1990

It was the Emperor Napoleon who called the British a nation of shopkeepers. Nearly two hundred years later, little appears to have changed. It is surprising to learn that Britain has fewer shops per unit of population than any country in the European Community as well as a comparatively low level of personal spending in those shops.

The difference is that Britain's shops are more noticed. During the 1980s, under the administration of Margaret Thatcher (whose father was a shopkeeper), retail design seems to have become a replacement activity for the design of the products that shops sell. The upshot, according to Rodney Fitch of Fitch RichardsonSmith, one of the super-firms that grew to dominate the British design scene during the decade, is that "this country gives a false view of the role that designers play in the retail process."

The decline of British manufacturing has brought with it an upsurge in the service industries. Design has paralleled this development to the extent that it is now hard to find examples of high-quality products designed by Britons for British clients, while the design of everything else, from corporate identities to television graphics and advertising, has boomed and is often more sophisticated than elsewhere in the world.

If one person were to be credited with generating an awareness of modern design in Britain it would be Terence Conran. Britain had largely shunned European Modernism between the wars. Isolated proponents of the new style did exist, of course, many of them immigrants from elsewhere in Europe and some staying only a short time before moving on to greener pastures in the United States—Serge Chermayeff, Marcel Breuer, the furniture makers Gordon Russell and Jack Pritchard of Isokon, and the graphic designer F.H.K. Henrion are among the better-known names. They had an effect on British design that was out of proportion to their numbers but insufficient to transform Britain at large into a Modernist nation. The difference is immediately apparent today if one compares Britain with the Netherlands, the country "on the Continent" with which it otherwise has most in common. Conran appeared on the scene in the 1960s with a cozier form of modern design based in part on postwar trends from Scandinavia. Initially a designer and manufacturer of textiles and furniture, he became a household name only when he became a shopkeeper. Through the Conran Design Group, however, he had a still broader impact on the British environment, both directly and indirectly.

The Conran Design Group itself set the style for many High Street stores, including those, such as Habitat and Mothercare, owned by Conran himself. It also nurtured a number of other designers, such as Rodney Fitch (Midland Bank, Asda), Stewart McColl (Halifax and Leeds building societies), and David Davies, who was responsible for many of the Next clothing stores. At its best, the retail design profession has sought to retain some of the sign-painting tradition that is still much in evidence on the façades of sole-proprietor local shops and public houses. But because the retail business is dominated by a comparatively few nationwide chains that wished to establish a uniform presence, the designers they appointed began to employ an inferior form of corporate identity in their work. The High Street homogeneity is compounded by the fact that so many of the firms share similar roots. "Everything could be more sensitively done. No one would argue against that," concedes Fitch. Subtlety was not the priority during the Thatcher years, however. Where once a new retail identity and shop design were intended specifically to bring more people into the shop, now it seemed that the order of the day was change for the sake of change. Consumers grew wealthier; retailing boomed and with it retail design. Both businesses were poorly protected against the effects of the recession that began abruptly at the end of the 1980s.

Related service sectors experienced an equally vicious cycle of rapid growth and painful slump. First advertising rode the wave, led by Saatchi and Saatchi and followed by Martin Sorrell's WPP. The design sector soon fell into step. It became more important for organizations of all sorts—stores, big companies, small companies, even government agencies and political parties—to be seen to have this thing called design than for the design actually to communicate any substantial new message to the public. As business boomed, several design agencies went public. One of Britain's many design magazines publishes a stock index of publicly listed design firms. According to a recent *Financial Times* report, seven of the world's ten largest design networks are based in Britain. Of these, three are publicly quoted, but by the end of 1990 all three were at their lowest ebb, valued at only 20 percent of what they were worth the year before. The flagship design firm of the era, Michael Peters Group, filed for bankruptcy in 1990.

Some view the misfortunes of the service sector with ill-hidden glee. They regard its difficulties as vindication of their belief that Britain should be manufacturing more goods, rather than advertising, marketing, and selling goods that are often made abroad. Others see these vacillations as the "teething problems" of building a prototypical service-oriented economy as British manufacturing continues its long-term decline.

Retail design
Rasshied Din Associates
Next

Logotype and retail interior
Fitch RichardsonSmith
Esprit du Vin wine store

Bank chain styling
Fitch RichardsonSmith
Midland Bank

Mail order catalog
Newell and Sorrell
Body Shop

Logotype and retail interior
Fitch RichardsonSmith
Dillon's bookstores

Once a "nation of shop-keepers," it is almost possible now to see Britain as a nation of retail designers.

Apparel
Vivienne Westwood

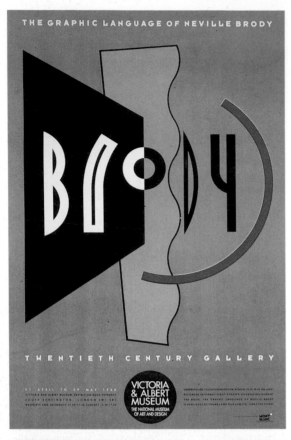

Top: Poster
Neville Brody
Victoria and Albert Museum,
1988

Bottom: Realtor signage
Neville Brody
Pilcher Hershman

Neville Brody's influential graphics serve as an antidote to the fake tradition on offer elsewhere.

For their part, there never was much talk of the quality of design from these big groups. It fell to a small band of designers working as individuals or in small studios to give voice to any criticism. Most effective among them was the graphic designer Neville Brody, who railed against the worthless and transient values of the "design industry" in a front-page article in the *Guardian*. "Design in England has become a commodity," observed Brody. "Suddenly, you couldn't sell something unless it had an element of 'design' in it, even if it was badly designed."

Industrial designer Geoff Hollington finds something of the same banality among product designers. "There's something generic about the work of London design consultancies," he says, with the implication that the London firms are the only ones most people stop to consider. In fact, there are a few mavericks who distance themselves from events in the capital. James Dyson, near Bath, and Paul Atkinson, in Leicester, retain some of the spirit of invention that characterized British creativity of the Victorian age.

But it is graphic design that has occupied center stage. In a political climate that has encouraged an awareness of big business, stimulated share ownership, and set about privatizing a raft of nationalized industries, it is not surprising that the greater part of this attention has been focused on the field of corporate identity. Although American firms have long predominated in this sphere, their British rivals have caught up with them in recent years by leading a trend toward "friendlier" design.

A fluent brushstroked figure of the virtue Prudence, representing the Prudential insurance company, is one of the best examples of the type. The new symbol for the private telephone company British Telecom, unveiled at the beginning of 1991, uses a similar technique in a bid to compete more effectively for business overseas. Both logotypes were executed by the firm Wolff Olins, whose director, Wally Olins, suggests that the nature of the design is itself a direct result of conditions imposed by the nascent service-dominated economy: "It happened here simply because some identity consultancies took a particular view of the situation at a particular time. It will happen elsewhere because underlying this is the issue of social responsibility and the acceptability of the company. A company can no longer isolate itself from society; it will have to become more socially responsible and to do that it will have to become more open and hence more friendly."

Olins's observation about the openness of corporations will also come to apply to the public sector. Following the example set by the privatized utilities, several government departments adopted fashion-

able, frequently crass, identities during the 1980s. They will have to do more and better to convince the public that they intend to change the poor attitude to providing service that still lurks behind the new façade. Wolff Olins itself is at work on the daunting task of providing an identity for London's demoralized and inefficient police force.

The few designers who are charting their own course, unswayed by the fashions of the moment or by the lure of big money, are doing so largely in obscurity. Brody is the conspicuous exception to the rule. He came to prominence with his editorial design work for *The Face,* a magazine of the 1980s' youth culture. Brody's design language has several readily identifiable components culled from Dada and Constructivism, though his images have a freshness all their own. Along with record-sleeve designers Peter Saville and Malcolm Garrett, and Terry Jones of *i-D* magazine (a rival to *The Face*), Brody used bold images or ideas, often cheap in execution, in reaction against the slick overproduction prevalent in these fields and against the impersonal quality of mainstream graphic design in general. These designers appropriated elements from earlier periods in design in the manner of certain fine artists of the time. "We brought to graphic design a sense of fashion," says Saville. "We wanted to draw a parallel between the discipline we were in and what we were into—fashion, music, shopping."

Brody's route from the punk music culture to magazines of varying degrees of trendiness was only the beginning of a thread by which his ideas spread. Brody's work in these areas is now seen by many as having had a profound influence on design in advertising and in the retail area, even though Brody himself has done no work in these fields. Brody's easily identified style was widely imitated, something that he abhors but also understands: "I don't support what has been happening on the High Streets. All my work has been geared against that. In Britain, partly because of the size and the speed at which information travels, a small setup can have a great impact. Say someone opens a shop, does a certain sort of design, and the shops works . . . a large chain will be aware of that shop and will then want to be part of that trend. In America, for example, it would take much longer for something to reach through."

Is there any crossover between this scene and the popular stereotype of British design abroad—all tweeds and Jaguar automobiles, Burberry raincoats and Barbour jackets? Surprisingly, it appears that there is. In a 1983 issue of *Design,* a magazine published by the government-funded Design Council, Peter York, the *soi-disant* style anthropologist and author of the *Sloane Rangers' Handbook,* hit the nail on the head when he described some early symp-

Left: Corporate identity
Wolff Olins
Kuwait Petroleum International,
1986

Below: Record cover
Peter Saville
Orchestral Manoeuvres in the
Dark, 1981

*An element of visual or literate
wit characterizes much British
design such as this record cover
by Peter Saville and company
identity by Wolff Olins that
plays on the word* Kuwait.

*With the Prudential identity,
Wolff Olins coined a fluent
Matisse-y style to make large
companies seem more
accessible. Michael Peters
followed suit in work for
Powergen and the Conservative
Party.*

Corporate identity
Wolff Olins
Prudential Corporation, 1986

POWERGEN

Corporate Identity
Michael Peters Group
Powergen, 1989

Corporate identity
Michael Peters Group
Conservative Party, 1987

Logotype
Alan Fletcher, Pentagram
Victoria and Albert Museum

Television graphics
Robinson Lambie-Nairn
Anglia Television, 1987

ANGLIA

Top: Shopfront , Paul Smith

Above: Shopfront, Laura Ashley

Shopfront, Colefax and Fowler

toms of the emergence of an "Anglo" style. He noted that the musician Bryan Ferry of Roxy Music had opened the doors of his historic country house to readers of the glossy *Interiors* magazine. It was a near-ultimate fusion of punk and pageant.

The British tend to regard anything that might be labeled "culture" with suspicion. They are far happier with the notion of "heritage," and a thriving industry has grown up to sell "British heritage" to whomever wants to buy. Fashion designer Ralph Lauren and interior decorator Mario Buatta purvey their interpretation of British tradition at one remove in New York. But the British are equally assiduous at doing it themselves. Laura Ashley and Paul Smith sell their fashions and home decor worldwide. Design-conscious Britons despair of it all. "A lot of the stuff seen abroad, particularly in the U.S., is a grotesque caricature of what actually exists," says Olins. "It's part of a distorted, plastic, Disneyish, research-based national identity which has got very little to do with the real thing. It's shorthand which distorts any kind of subtlety."

Irrespective of the sincerity with which it is exploited for commercial ends, there is some truth in the stereotype of the British country life-style that stems from a society that has always stressed its class distinctions. "It may be that the British upper classes are more into inheritance and tradition," says Grey Gowrie, a former Minister for the Arts, now chairman of Sotheby's, and himself an earl. "They're trying to make a statement by showing that something has been in the family a long time and that it's not a reproduction. But it's also a design thing: People pay very expensive decorators to get that look."

The British aspiration to an aristocratic life-style expresses itself very differently from that in France. Where the French upper classes have always placed great importance on the decorative arts, a tradition that accommodates a thriving design avant-garde today, the British have been more conservative in their preferences. The high proportion of home owners in Britain today is a factor: A permanent abode permits furniture that is solid; mortgage repayments demand that it be cheap. As a proportion of their income, the British spend less on furniture than other Europeans.

The British prefer to take their avant-garde in the form of images for consumption in two dimensions rather than three. One recent advertisement on British television showed a man in "designer" clothes and "designer" stubble going to a junkyard, welding up a leather seat from an old car, and taking it back to his spacious loft to be admired by his soulmate, clad in black silk lingerie. The sign-off line was "Less is more." The commercial was for beer, but that's not what matters. The ad revealed how the public

The furniture of Jasper Morrison exemplifies a quiet practicality that some see as typically British.

Top: Chair
Jasper Morrison
SCP, 1986

Bottom: Birch ply chair
Jasper Morrison
Cappellini, 1989

Thinking man's chair
Jasper Morrison
Cappellini, 1988

Flipper table
Matthew Hilton
SCP, 1987

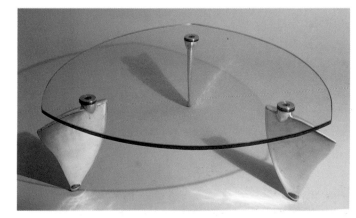

Sofa
Jasper Morrison
SCP, 1987

Top: Land-Rover Discovery
RSCG Conran Design
Austin-Rover, 1989

Above: Rover chair
Rod Arad
One-Off, 1981

A sturdy comfort remains one of the most important aspects of British automotive design, seen recently in the Land-Rover Discovery, and admired tongue-in-cheek by Ron Arad with his Rover Chair.

humors and neuters an avant-garde that is trying to break into the cozy world of interior and furniture design. These designers, whether they intend to or not, form an opposition to the English sensibleness of Conran and the design-led retail empires.

The designer of the chair in question, Ron Arad, is not British at all, but Israeli. Remembering the legendary English love for the car, the chair, called Rover, is his one "English" piece. As with the previous generation, several of the more experimental designers practicing in Britain have come from overseas—Danny Lane, who creates furniture in glass, from the United States; product designer and architect Daniel Weil from Argentina; and furniture designer André Dubreuil from France. Often drawn to Britain by its pop and punk culture, such designers have stayed because what Britain withholds in rapturous enthusiasm it does at least grant in tolerance. Even their radical design must find its outlets, as Lane dryly points out, not in galleries but in shops.

More British is Jasper Morrison. The basement apartment where he works is seedy and yet genteel in a peculiarly English way. A gas fire glows feebly in the clammy atmosphere. The plaster is peeling, but *Madama Butterfly* is on Radio Three. Tea is served. Morrison is concerned with using materials in an appropriate manner, an approach that hardly applies to Lane's glass furniture or Arad's sheet-steel armchairs. "An honest treatment of materials negates ornament as a requirement for modern living," he says. His work is a very English mix of Puritanism and sensibility, seen clearly in an ingenuous chair designed in 1989. It is made of birch plywood, thick pieces for the legs and back and a sheet of three-ply for the seat. The materials cost just seven dollars. The plywood is cut by laser. Its lines are straight and its angles crisp, except for one subtle undulation in the back legs that gives the chair its life. "It's a plus starting with a cheap material," notes Morrison. "It's upgraded by the way it's used. Generally, I try to achieve something quite humble in its materials and not screamingly loud in its shape, but I don't go out of my way to make my furniture look British."

Martin Ryan's designs have some of the same qualities. His St. Stephen's Chair has a matte-black, tapered steel-tube frame and legs, which give it an elegant lightness. "That chair would probably sell better with thicker legs," he concedes. Some of his other work is more blatantly historicist, for example the Queen Bess table and chair with their re-creation of the folds of Elizabethan costume. In all his design, Ryan is concerned that the pieces be well made. "A lot of the stuff around—André Dubreuil's furniture to some

Gourmet food processor
Kenneth Grange, Pentagram
Kenwood, 1987

The faring to provide a firm base for this food processor reflects British pragmatism. A similar German product might not have such a detail.

Telephone
Jonathan Miles, 1988

British students show a greater willingness than British companies to question the conventional wisdom of form.

extent—is crude in the way it's put together. It presents a bad image for English furniture," he complains. Where Dubreuil and Arad rely on radical ideas, Ryan and Morrison employ sound workmanship—a key word—in a quiet way to create quintessentially British design.

The same quiet spirit informs the best product design. Kenneth Grange is the industrial design partner within the Pentagram firm and is Britain's senior figure in the discipline. Like many British product designers he now finds that the majority of his clients are overseas, often in Japan. "I was on a TV program there," he recalls, "and they asked me why I thought Japanese manufacturers are employing me. I found that it was about reliability, that compared to Italian designers the British fit more closely to the Japanese behavior in terms of delivering what they say they are going to deliver and in having a more immediate interest in and responsibility for the manufacture of goods. The downside may be that we are not as vivacious and theatrical and adventurous. We are also very interested in the function of products. We bring a lot of concern about the performance of a product, and that leads to invention as well."

Grange finds a high level of skill in the sculptural aspects of British product design, the fruit of a cultural tradition common to German and Scandinavian form giving. By European standards, there is also more willingness to accommodate the wishes of clients. British designers, he concludes, are moralistic, but not so moralistic as the Germans, and pragmatic, though not so pragmatic as the Americans. His own work for Kenwood, a British kitchen-appliance manufacturer, exemplifies these qualities with a sort of lived-in Braun look. "I'm flattered by the association with Braun because they've been a terrific dose of salts through the entire design community, but at the same time I think that things need a little warmth." Grange's Gourmet food processor for Kenwood achieves its warmth by a flaring of the product casing at the base. "That idea to flare it out comes instinctively to me," remarks Grange. "Which comes first—the idea for it to be more stable in truth or to look more stable—or whether it's the need to have a bit more warmth and humanity in the thing, I'm not sure, but Dieter Rams wouldn't do it like that unless there was some absolutely manifest reason for doing it."

British designers are perhaps less surefooted when it comes to product styling. "You may find an aspect of wit, of humor, which you would not typically expect to find in an Italian product. You may also find ingenious markings on switches and catches and things," says Grange. But Geoff Hollington sees those same markings in a rather different light: "The fundamental form of a lot of stuff is quite hard and

Savoy cutlery
David Mellor Design, 1989

Queen Bess chair
Martin Ryan
Portfolio Furniture, 1988

St. George sofa
Martin Ryan
Conran shop, 1989

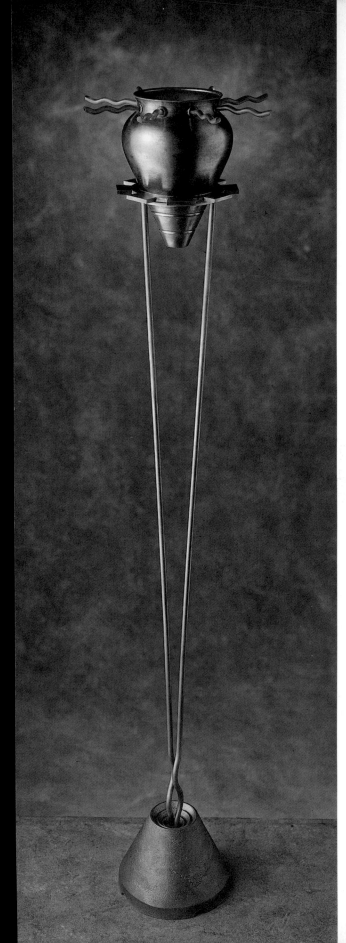

technocratic, but then you see evidence of a last-minute panic to soften it up by putting on pink and gray bits and bobs. The only accommodation that's made is with color."

Examples of outstanding British product design are few and far between. Radios for Ross Electronics by Graham Thomson of Product First and Paul Priestman's stoves for Belling are among recent successes. This is not because Britain produces too few or untalented designers but because there are few manufacturers, and fewer still who are committed to good design. Indeed the schools, most notably the Royal College of Art, produce designers of a caliber far in excess of that demanded, or apparently understood, by most British companies.

Often the best opportunities come from abroad. Geoff Hollington works with the American Herman Miller company, where, after years of struggle and compromise working with British furniture manufacturers, he has the resources and the client has the confidence to allow concepts to be fully developed. Seymour Powell, one of London's most successful product design firms, finds that two-thirds of its business comes from outside Britain. It designs kitchen equipment for the French company Tefal and motorcycles for Japan's Yamaha as well as the domestic manufacturer Norton. The proportion of Seymour Powell's business from overseas would be still greater were it not for a large contract to design a train for British Rail that will be the successor to Grange's 125 High Speed Train of 1976. Destined to run on what may by then be a privatized rail network, Seymour Powell's design aims to recapture some of the awe and romance of Britain's late steam age. "If we trace its bloodline back," says Richard Seymour, "it's through 'Mallard' [a record-breaking steam locomotive] out of the Pacific Class. It's got the power and the glory."

Some designers, like recent Royal College of Art graduate Anthony Dunne, have gone abroad altogether, in his case to work for Sony. Others have stayed in London but also work almost entirely for Japanese clients. The Japanese have identified and supported a school of design that has little to do with either conventional design for mass production or the traditionalism of the heritage industry but that combines a baroque handling of materials with craftsmanship and witty historical reference. The architect Nigel Coates has made his name in Tokyo with his entropic but sophisticated theme restaurants. Others have followed in his footsteps, among them Pirate Design Associates, which has found manufacturers for sensual, craft-oriented products such as audio equipment and lighting that it never would have found in England. It is ironic but hardly surprising that it is the Japanese, always searching

for new consumer sensations, who are the new patrons of British design of all types.

Britain was the cradle of the Industrial Revolution and the site of the design community's first reaction against it, in the guise of William Morris. Some commentators today hold Morris and the Arts and Crafts movement responsible not only for the enduring rusticism but even for the parlous state of the British manufacturing industry. It seems appropriate now that Britain should be the first country to wrestle with its postindustrial persona.

Tourism and tradition, heritage and royalty are all part of the mix. So are the financiers and investors of the City of London. So are the media businesses of the 1980s, temporarily indisposed as they are, recovering from their decade of success. Clearly, not all countries can fulfill this destiny. But neither is it necessary, today, for each trading nation to maintain a mix of manufacturing and service industries, merely for an overall balance to be maintained among those nations. The trend is causing deep concern. Should the country attempt to revive its manufacturing industry? Or should it take the new, untried road? Britain may find some solace in the fact that it has designers to cope with both eventualities.

Left: Uplight
Pirate Design
Daiko, 1990

Despite public conservatism, Britain is home to many radical designers often working for clients overseas.

Noah chair and stools
Nigel Coates
SCP, 1988

Radio
Daniel Weil and Gerard
Taylor, 1981

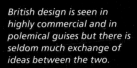

*British design is seen in
highly commercial and in
polemical guises but there is
seldom much exchange of
ideas between the two.*

Radio
Product First
Ross Consumer Electronics

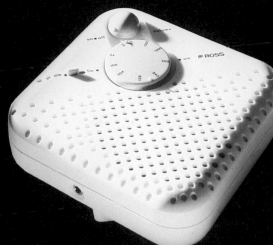

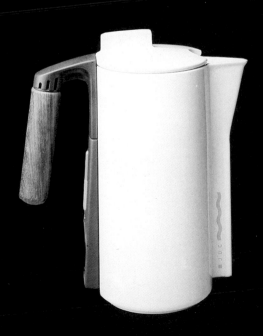

Stove
Priestman Associates
Belling, 1990

*The jug kettle is a peculiarly
British product for which there
is a market large enough to
interest multinational
manufacturers. The Philips
design has less of a British
character than a project by
Geoff Hollington, however.*

Left: Jug kettle
Hollington Associates, 1986

Above: Jug kettle
FM Design
Philips UK, 1990

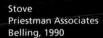

France

When students at the Paris design school Les Ateliers assembled for a project to devise objects that would display a specifically French character, they revealed more than they intended about the difficulty of consciously attempting to design in a national idiom.

Some participants were French, others were foreign students, but both groups were equally happy to seize the chance to lampoon the first cliché of Frenchness that came to mind. Food and sex were popular starting points for some of the more tongue-in-cheek projects.

On a subtler plane, Jeffrey Casper, an American exchange student, created a pencil sharpener with blade and handle formed of a single, intricately shaped sheet of steel that simultaneously managed to celebrate its materiality, technological ingenuity, and sensuous form. Frédéric Thevenon came up with a red velvet Walkman with diamanté controls, which he described as "decorative and impractical—typically French." Michel Fougère designed a hearing aid as a piece of jewelry, reasoning that if glasses can be modified to become fashion accessories for the shortsighted, then the deaf should be afforded the same right.

Serious or flippant, these proposals had something in common: None was to be admired from afar. All were things to touch and feel. Only bodily contact made them complete. To this extent they were as French as fine food, fashion, jewelry, and toiletries. "France has always been known for luxury design," comments Liz Davis, director of the international studio at Les Ateliers. "[The French] are very good at haute couture, perfume, and everything connected with luxury markets."

The reason for this lies in French social history of the eighteenth and nineteenth centuries. While in other parts of Europe economies were becoming more industrial and the people more emancipated, France remained a strongly agricultural economy in the grip of a powerful aristocracy. At court, style held sway over substance. When it came, the French Revolution did not bring a rejection of the trappings of privilege but an aspiration for them from the middle classes. Initially the preserve of the aristocracy, *les arts décoratifs* were admired first by the bourgeoisie and later by the peasant class. Even now, nearly half the world's luxury goods are French-made.

France's priority remains the decorative arts today. Many people still regard *all* design as no more than that—a decorative art. Davis explains: "The English and the Germans have got used to buying a

newly designed product because it's cheaper; it works better; it's easier to clean; it's more efficient ergonomically. In France at the moment, I'm not sure that the idea of a complete product rather than a styled product interests the public. But after Italy's great design boom, and with everybody now talking about Spain, there is in France a wish also to have a design identity." Even if the contemporary furniture of Philippe Starck has captured the imagination of the international design community in its attempt to fulfill this wish, the fact remains that the majority of the French public are happier with reproduction Louis XVI. The Minister of Culture, Jack Lang, despairs of the conservatism of the French. "They were shocked by the Impressionists," he reminds.

While the phrase "decorative arts" has a French ring to it, "design" is a dirty word in France, one of many on the growing list of banned words that represent official attempts to purge the French language of Anglo-Americanisms. Despite reproofs, however, "*le design*," remains in current usage. "*Création,*" the approved word, crops up mainly when tied around with bureaucratic red tape, in the titles of bodies such as the Centre de Création Industrielle at the Centre Georges Pompidou in Paris.

The difficulty with nomenclature is an indication of French efforts to preserve or re-create a national identity in many things. This semantic curiosity means that design has been thought of differently in France from other industrialized countries. The word *design* has much the same pejorative connotation for the French as *designer* used as an adjective does in English. "The connotation design has is not a good one because it enforces a separation between the well designed and the not designed," observes industrial designer Jean-Pierre Vitrac. "We need a new design between high style and hypermarket nondesign."

Under the presidency of François Mitterrand, there has been an increased effort to ensure that design by whatever name is understood more clearly and used more effectively. Most of the media coverage has fallen on a few conspicuous acts of patronage in the public sector. For industrial design it is an uphill struggle to gain widespread acceptance. The comparatively few large corporations with a consistently strong design image—auto manufacturer Citroën, kitchen equipment maker Moulinex, household appliance company Terraillon—have in-house design departments or ties with independent designers. But for smaller firms, the *petites et moyennes entreprises* that make up the bulk of industry, the story is very different. They traditionally do their own design through an internal *bureau d'études* (which often has responsibility for all research and development activity), without the

Below: Juicy Salif juicer
Philippe Starck
Alessi

Arome-Extra
coffee maker
Jean-Louis Barrault
Moulinex, 1989

Et La Guillotine Rata Les Pieds
Louis XVI chair
Christian Duc
VIA, 1989

Nord-Sud chair
Studio Naço
General Council of Belfort,
1989
Photograph by M. Pignata-
Monti

Above: Plastic sunglasses
Vitrac Design
Alpha-Cubic

*Jean-Pierre Vitrac is rare among
French designers in being at
home with plastics as well as
more luxurious materials.*

Top: Knives
Vitrac Design
Sedasco

Above: Gloves and
driving glasses
Vitrac Design
NSX Gear/Honda

Dr. Glob chair
Philippe Starck
Kartell, 1988

Walter Wayle II clock
Philippe Starck
Alessi

Food processor
MBD Design
Ronic

*This design aims to put distance
between itself and European
competitors with a combination
of technical innovation and
unusual styling.*

Chocolate packaging
MBD Design
Valrhona, 1987

Eurotybox economizer
thermostat
MBD Design
Delta Dore, 1990

services of a professional designer.

The inclination among smaller companies to make do in this way means that there are comparatively few strong design firms and little outstanding product design. But Claude Braunstein, managing director of Plan Créatif, finds some cause for optimism: "If I compare French with German or British production, I think French technical products are not as good as the Anglo-Saxon. But Anglo-Saxon design also has a conformity. You can see the same Ulm-school rules and lack of imagination. There are some qualities to French design that permit fresher ideas which are innovative and look different." Plan Créatif itself is an independent successor to the Paris office of the British PA Design, and its work has a consequently European feel, most notable in its design of faucets for Porcher.

Another leading firm, MBD Design, has conceived a product of more distinctively French character in its work for kitchen-equipment manufacturer, Ronic. Ronic's competitors are companies like Braun and Philips. "We wished to create differentiation in a market largely standardized in its codes and forms," explains MBD's Yves Domergue. "The idea was to break the rules by a certain organization of the forms. We tried to distance ourselves from the culture of functionalist design and rediscover our style." In France it is not done to create visual innovation without technological innovation to justify it. "This is a very French idea," notes Domergue. "Hence we used a horizontal-lying motor to give a new form and reappropriate our national style." With the services of industrial designer Jean-Louis Barrault and its in-house design resource, Moulinex, Ronic's main domestic rival, has long created successful products in a generic European style. Now it, too, is reported to be working on designs with more distinctive character for the local market.

A few of the most characteristically French products draw together engineering innovation and decorative tradition: Many French cars have quirky features and a feeling of *grand confort* that are distinctly absent from, say, their German competitors. Citroën especially has made a name not only with technically advanced suspension and sleek exterior styling but also with eccentric instrument design and layout and soft seating that contrast markedly with the strict ergonomic logic of a BMW or Mercedes.

Conscious attempts to unite the engineering and decorative strands of French design have not always been so successful, however. Working for a china manufacturer in Limoges, for instance, Elixir, one of the new generation of Paris design studios, tried to introduce a new technique from Germany for thermostatic injection molding of the porcelain. This would have opened up new decorative possibilities, enabling the designers to introduce relief patterns on the surface of the china for the first time. The client remained unconvinced.

In general, the split between the decorative arts and engineering-based design runs deep. France's design schools perpetuate the differences, with the Ecole des Beaux Arts and the Ecole Camondo representing the artistic tendency and other schools, such as that at Compiègne, near Paris, producing strong technical designers. The Ecole Nationale Supérieure de Création Industrielle, generally known as Les Ateliers, is the first French school devoted entirely to industrial design. Set up under the joint auspices of the ministries of industry and culture, Les Ateliers hopes to cover all bases.

While product design languishes in the absence of a reconciliation between the decorative arts and engineering, the two disciplines thrive in mutual isolation. French engineering design is second to none, especially in railroad and aviation technology. Periodically, the world is reminded of this with a demonstration of engineering prowess. Gustave Eiffel did it with his tower a hundred years ago. The Concorde supersonic airliner and the TGV (*Train à Grande Vitesse,* or "high-speed train") had the same effect more recently, impressing foreigners and bolstering national pride. Engineers in France are highly regarded, and great prestige attaches to the fruits of their labors, as seen, for example, in the huge nuclear program and in government plans for every home to have a Minitel interactive data terminal.

Giving expression to the engineer's work is important in these high-profile projects. Several Paris design firms have played their part. Plan Créatif's Vecteur division has designed rolling stock for the Paris Métro and other subway systems around the world. MBD Design is working on a high-speed rail link in Florida. But the symbol of this success remains the TGV, the latest version of which, the Atlantique, has been styled by Roger Tallon and ADSA Design Programme to suggest the pace and romance of the technological revolution. The train is a far cry from the wind-tunnel rationalism of its German competitor, the ICE Train. Even a static product such as Alcatel's Minitel terminal by Enfi Design has some of the same urgency about it. The recent move by Luigi Colani, the designer of fantastical streamlined planes, ships, and other objects, to Toulouse, the center of France's aerospace industry, is another indication of the importance of styling in the expression of technological leadership.

Behind France's grander triumphs of design and technology, says designer Pierre-Yves Panis, there has

Left: Telephones
Jean-Louis Barrault
Mecelec, 1985–1989

Right: Train à Grande Vitesse
Atlantique
Roger Tallon, ADSA Design
Programme
SNCF, 1989
Photographs by Lafontant

*Jean-Louis Barrault and Roger
Tallon are two senior figures
who have given French design
an endearing quirkiness.*

Right: Da-Tong Chine furniture
Ronald Cecil Sportes
Photograph courtesy Victoria
and Albert Museum

Below: Shelving
Eric Raffy
Christian Farjon, 1988

Bottom: Bao chest
Jean Nouvel
VIA, 1987
Photograph courtesy Victoria
and Albert Museum

*Led by the government-funded
VIA agency, France has re-
emerged as a creator of original
furniture.*

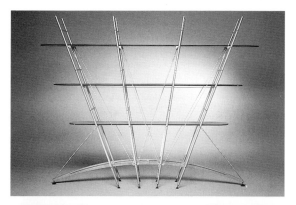

Corporate identity and exterior
design
Lonsdale Design
Accor, 1984

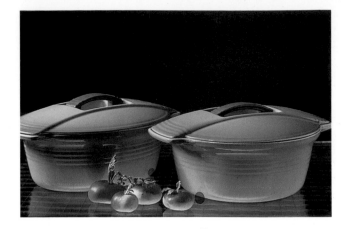

Futura ovenware
Jean-Louis Barrault
Le Creuset, 1988

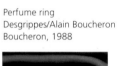

Perfume ring
Desgrippes/Alain Boucheron
Boucheron, 1988

Mustard container
Desgrippes
Amora, 1985

Corporate identity
Desgrippes
Credit Agricole, 1988

Corporate identity
Carré Noir
Le Bon Marché

Faucet
Plan Créatif
Porcher

Corporate identity
Plan Créatif
Guardian Royal Exchange, 1989

Graphics
Plan Créatif
Gare Montparnasse

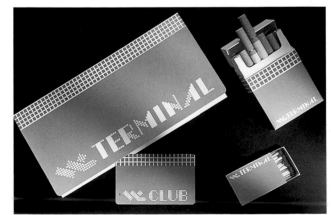

been "what we call the *raison d'état*." Plan Créatif's Claude Braunstein confirms the view: "If you look at the fields where we are strong—trains, atomic research, telematics—they are always fields that have been pushed by political will and government investment."

The most powerful symbols of French nationhood are architectural. These monuments have also been pushed by political willpower although they transcend particular ideologies. They stretch from the palace at Versailles, built in the seventeenth century for the Sun King, Louis XIV, to the Arc de Triomphe, commissioned by Napoleon, to the "people's palaces"—the Centre Pompidou, the Louvre pyramid, the Bastille Opera House and others—of contemporary democracy. Though the buildings are intended to celebrate the French nation, the largesse today extends worldwide. The 1970s' Centre Pompidou was designed by the Anglo-Italian duo of Richard Rogers and Renzo Piano; the Louvre pyramid by the Chinese-American I. M. Pei. Among the *grands projets* of the Mitterrand presidency, Jean Nouvel's Institut du Monde Arabe is the best work by a local architect. Some find it hard to regard these architectural and technological dinosaurs with due pride, however. "Why do we focus on big projects?" asks Jean-Pierre Vitrac bitterly. "Because we have nothing to show behind them. French people *dream* about technology. The Germans and Japanese invest more with less fuss."

The conspicuous patronage also extends to graphic design. Grapus, a cooperative that emerged from the *événements* of 1968 and was once identified by its angry, expressionist style, won a state commission to design signs for La Villette park in Paris—one of the Mitterrand *grands projets*. The program simply takes three pure shapes (a triangle, a circle, and a square) and three primary colors (red, green, and blue), and uses them in different combinations to signify different activities in different regions of the Villette complex. "The problem was that it is a place with lots of features, all very different," says Grapus member Pierre Bernard. "So we thought that the only solution was to organize something very clean, very Swiss and functional." Grapus recently stepped deeper into establishment territory, having won a competition to design signage for the Louvre. Taking the controversial glass pyramid entrance to the museum as its starting point, the Grapus team came up with a logotype and a scheme for implementing it on museum literature. The main symbol was a triangular prism lit from within, clearly echoing the Pei design. Suitably museumlike typography for the words *Musée du Louvre* complemented the clean geometric

— Préparez votre visite avec nous

Above: Corporate identity
Grapus
Musée du Louvre, 1989
Photograph by Andre Lejarre

Left: Corporate identity
Grapus
La Villette, 1987

The revolutionary graphic design cooperative Grapus began life during the 1968 riots. It has recently attracted establishment clients and has influenced other design groups such as Zanzibar't.

Exhibit visit ticket
Zanzibar't
La Villette, 1988

Ville de Lille

ILE DE LA RÉUNION

Top: Logotype
Kheops
Conseil de la Ville de Lille, 1984

Above: Logotype
Kheops
Ile de la Réunion Regional
Council, 1988

*No French city or département
is complete without its logotype
often executed in a racy style.*

Above and left: Flying object
desks
Thierry Blet/Catherine LeTeo, Elixir
Narbur, 1990

Below: Cutlery
Catherine LeTeo, Elixir
Alessi, 1987
Photograph by Christian Julien

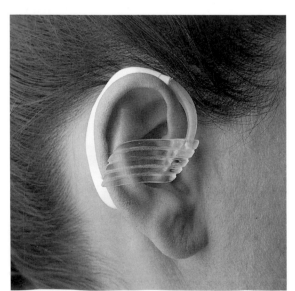

Hearing aid prototype
Michel Fougère, 1988
Photograph by M. Pignata-
Monti

*This project was one of many to
emerge from an examination of
French character at the design
school Les Ateliers.*

Above: Lolamundo table and chair
Philippe Starck
Driade, 1988

Philippe Starck has become the international media voice and image of French design.

Below: Romantica chair
Philippe Starck
Driade

centerpiece. The museum authorities liked the implementation on letterheads, posters, and the rest, but not the logotype itself. They felt it was too reminiscent of the multimillion-franc pyramid, a sore point with many Parisians.

Although France is a strongly centralized country, and it can sometimes seem that Paris is the only city that matters, there is an equally strong belief that design can convey pride in the provinces. Powerful mayors in regional centers such as Nîmes and Bordeaux have followed the Parisian example and commissioned civic buildings from prominent architects. Individual départements, towns, and suburbs have commissioned graphic identities. The Kheops design firm has designed logotypes for the towns of Boulogne and Lille and the Pas-de-Calais département in the north, for example. Another group, Zanzibar't, has won support from Paris suburbs Saint-Denis, Le Blanc-Mesnil, Val-de-Marne, and Nanterre, as well as from places further afield, such as Montluçon in the Auvergne.

Kheops's style is flexible and commercial. Many of its corporate identities comprise a sketchy motif and brash type. The symbol for the Ile de la Réunion, a French département in the Indian Ocean, is a colorful example: a scribbled sunset behind a volcanic island with the name in a less-than-classic typeface below. Zanzibar't has a very different credo. Some of its designers came from Grapus, and like Grapus, Zanzibar't combines Swiss clarity and a preference for a single, powerful graphic idea with an abrasive, painterly expressionism. And like Grapus, Zanzibar't has strong political and aesthetic ties to the raw-edged poster-making tradition of Eastern Europe, especially Poland, the homeland of Ewa Maruszewska, a Zanzibar't principal. What is interesting is that both groups' work was seen as appropriate by their respective client authorities, irrespective of stylistic leaning.

Neither has the state limited its patronage to those grandiose architectural and technological creations which, apart from meeting their ostensible function, have a beneficial side effect as symbols of French culture around the world. One hope of Valorisation de l'Innovation dans l'Ameublement (VIA), an organization established to promote new designers in furniture and the decorative arts, was that its example would inspire a broader section of industry to give more consideration to design.

VIA established the "Cartes Blanches" scheme, which each year enables a number of up-and-coming designers to work free of financial or client constraints and pays for production of prototypes of their designs. In addition, Jack Lang saw to it that Philippe Starck, Jean-Michel Wilmotte, and others gained eye-catching public commissions. In 1983, for

example, Starck created a suite of rooms in the Elysée Palace for President Mitterrand that set him on the road to international design stardom. Pierre Paulin had been given a similar commission a decade earlier, but Starck had the advantage of impeccable timing, coming along as the personification of French design in riposte to the Italian Memphis movement. Lang explains: "I proposed these young French designers in order to explain to the French people that they have to encourage modern designers. My purpose was to introduce a new art to the public consciousness." There is some consensus that the effect of the policy has been beneficial. Thierry Blet of Elixir comments: "We only started speaking about design in France ten years ago, since the government started speaking about it. Now design is like advertising, really necessary for the development of company strategies." Yves Domergue of MBD Design agrees: "We need the Starck phenomenon in order to recover our French identity in industrial design; it's happening now."

Of Starck's Frenchness there can be no doubt. It is something he plays up to the hilt with foreign journalists. He wears a beret, drinks only champagne, and has an accent just this side of Inspector Clouseau's in the Pink Panther movies. Among his peers he speaks a genteel old-world French at odds with his slobbish appearance. He is, says fellow interior designer Andrée Putman, "a *personnage*." Behind the ham-acting, there are less affected French traits. According to VIA director Jean-Claude Maugirard, his style combines a sense of humor with evidence of the fact that "he grew up bathed in technology." Starck often tells the story of how he lay as a baby under the drawing board of his father, an aeronautical engineer. In his own work Starck *fils* is not entirely without an engineering sensibility, but he has added the preoccupations with materials and form that are a distinguishing mark of the decorative artist. Starck's contemporary, Jean-Pierre Vitrac, agrees about the humor but thinks he is a technological rogue: "Starck is quite French in the way that he is not quite serious. He has a French ironic sense. But he has imagination only for jokes, never inventing anything new." In his Lolamundo table-chair for the Italian producer Driade, for example, Starck changed the material for the legs to polished aluminum while retaining a form traditionally associated with wooden furniture, rather than using the new material to discover a new form. "If he were genuinely creative," claims Vitrac, "he ought to use what contemporary industry can offer."

Perhaps Starck's real skill is to have made such efficient use of the media. He was one of five designers commissioned for the Elysée project. The others—Jean Martelle, Pascal Mourgue, Ronald

Afrika table
Garouste and Bonetti
Neotu

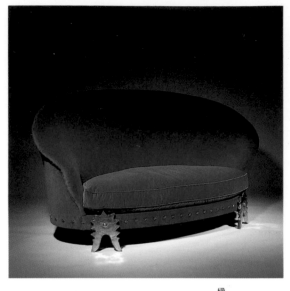

Carpet
Garouste and Bonetti
Editions Philippe Laïk

Blue sofa
Garouste and Bonetti
Neotu

Right: Fizz bar on wheels
Marie-Christine Dorner
Artelano, 1990

Below: Office of the French
Minister of Health
Marie-Christine Dorner, 1990
Photograph by Gaston Bergeret

Bottom: Presidential stand for
the military parades of July 14,
1990 and 1991
Marie-Christine Dorner
Photograph by Christoph
Kicherer

Headphones and packaging
Jean-Michel Cornu and
Véronique Malcourant
BST

Computer terminal
Nemo

*The spare technocratic style of
this design is in sharp contrast
with the opulence evident in
much French furniture and
furnishings.*

Ikmisou sofa, above,
Ikmisou table, right
Pascal Mourgue
Vecta, 1988
Photographs by Andy Post

Bianca M radio
Studio Naço
1989
Photograph by M. Pignata-
Monti

Sewing machine
Corinne Chiapello/Renate Eilert/
Loic Perois
Neste Forma Finlandia
competition, 1990

Desk lamp
Philippe Starck
Flos, 1988

Bar stool
Philippe Starck
Royalton Hotel

Jarra silver ewer
Jean-Michel Cornu and
Véronique Malcourant
Christofle

*There is a close family
resemblance in many
contemporary objects by French
designers. Similar forms recur
throughout the history of
French design and
decorative arts.*

Chair
Nemo
University of Brest

Sportes, and Jean-Michel Wilmotte—remained known mainly at home as the personable Philippe was hailed first in Milan and then around the world. Along with others such as Martin Szekely, Jean-Louis Godivier, and Marie-Christine Dorner, these designers share a certain spirit. This is unsurprising: Some learned from others; some worked for others; several attended the same design school, the Camondo. As a result there is more in common within this body of work than there is between it and contemporary design from Italy or Spain.

There are, of course, exceptions to this prevailing style. Superficially, nothing could be more different from the clean lines of a Starck classic than the furniture of Elizabeth Garouste and Mattia Bonetti, for example. Their work has been variously called Gothic, tribal, primitive, and ethnic. They use rough-hewn chunks of wood, straw, wrought iron, and papier mâché. Despite the ironic commentary these materials make on the rich leather, wood, and metal favored by their rivals, the tactile qualities are as important as those of more conventional finishes. Garouste and Bonetti have recently designed a lavish showroom for the *succès fou* of Paris fashion, Christian Lacroix. In many ways, their impossible, opulent work is in tune with the couture of their client, just as Starck at his best has an economy of line that gives his work something in common with the classics of Chanel, Dior, or Pierre Cardin, for whom he worked briefly as an art director at the beginning of his career.

A more convincing exception to the general trend comes from Alain Domingo and François Scali, two designers who make up the firm Nemo. "We are not interested in elegance," proclaims Scali. "We are not concerned about using leather and wood. We do not belong to the tradition of decoration or interior design. We are more concerned with industry." When Starck says, as he does in one of his many quotes, that *he* is not interested in elegance, you know it is not true. When Nemo says it, you believe it. Nemo's astringent alternative is at its clearest in a chair for the University of Brest. It is asymmetrical, with one leg jutting out to the side to enable it to be stacked. The frame is square steel tube, crudely welded at the joints and bent at the corners. The seat is made of tough but slightly

flexible fiber glass slats that are not bonded to the steel frame but simply jammed into holes pressed into it. They say, "The only poetry we have is the poetry of new technology. This chair would have no raison d'être if it were not constructed of glass fibre."

The odd exception duly noted, there is a remarkable family resemblance not only among recent French furniture but also among many decorative objects. Compare, for example, Starck's famous cast-aluminum ashtray, the horn-shaped lamp for Flos, and interior fittings for the Royalton Hotel in New York; the Bianca M radio by Marcelo Joulia-Lagares and Alain Renk's Studio Naço; the Specimen range of office accessories by Jean-Michel Cornu and Véronique Malcourant; and a sewing machine by Les Ateliers students Corinne Chiapello, Renate Eilert, and Loic Perois, which placed third in the Neste plastics company's prestigious "Forma Finlandia" design competition in 1990. It is remarkable how alike they all look. It is even more remarkable how closely they all resemble a bullet-shaped six hundred-year-old helmet from a French suit of armor kept in the museum of the Hôtel de Cluny in Paris. Could there be an atavism at work here in addition to the likeness among the present generation?

It was possible to see the new French furniture in a different light when it appeared, not, as so often, in the company of design from many countries at the international furniture fairs, but at the "L'Art de Vivre" exhibition of two hundred years of French decorative arts held at the Cooper-Hewitt Museum in New York during 1989, the bicentennial year of the French Revolution. This was furniture that had been designed in full consciousness of its contemporary international context to look different, even revolutionary—and, above all, not Italian. What was startling at the Cooper-Hewitt exhibition was not how different and revolutionary the work looked, but how clearly it belonged in the French genealogy.

Graphic designer Pati Núñez used to work out of an apartment in the Casa Milá, one of Antoni Gaudí's most noted buildings. The rooms were painted poisonous shades of purple and green. They were not rectilinear like yours or mine. There wasn't a sharp corner or right angle anywhere, and moody lighting made the swirling organic plaster moldings cast spooky, distorted shadows.

Not surprisingly, Núñez found the famous architect a constant presence. But then so do many of the designers who are leading the design renaissance in Spain in general and in Barcelona in particular. "Living in a Gaudí building was marvelous," says Núñez. "People liked it, but they said it influenced my work, that it was oppressive."

So Núñez moved. Her cosmopolitan work, which is influenced by Britain's Neville Brody, proves there is life in Barcelona without Gaudí. It also reflects another preoccupation in the city: the wish to underline its membership in the European and international communities. The large and ambitious design firm Quod also ensures that much of its work has a determinedly international appearance, with polished typographic logotypes for a variety of commercial clients. When it came to creating a symbol for the 1992 Barcelona Olympic Games, however, Quod's graphics specialist, Josep Trias, turned his back on such precision and opted for three bold brushstrokes in blue, yellow, and red depicting a hurdler in mid leap.

Here, the Catalan artist Joan Miró is the influence. Where it is appropriate to celebrate Spanishness or Catalanness, his painterly brightness has become something of a local trademark. Ironically, it was the American corporate identity firm Landor Associates that started the ball rolling. Its symbol for La Caixa bank in Barcelona used a red, yellow, and blue design culled from a Miró painting. Miró himself was retained to produce a tapestry incorporating the logo for the bank's headquarters. During the 1980s a host of companies have given themselves very similar identities, to the point where the *ramblas* are now dotted with splashy red, yellow, and blue graphics.

There is some justification both for the colors used and for the pseudoartistry. Red and yellow are the colors of the Spanish flag, and, more importantly, of the Catalan flag. The blue is taken either as a symbol of the Mediterranean, which is vital to Barcelona's prosperity, or perhaps as an echo of the shade used in the region for external household woodwork (it apparently repels flies). But there is another reading. The flag the Spanish Republicans

used during the civil war from 1936 to 1940 was a red, yellow, and blue tricolor. Half a century later, the flag is still banned, but there is nothing to prevent the use of its colors in other ways in what remains a region with strong Republican sympathies.

In other countries the adaptation of a painter's art to commercial ends might be found objectionable. In Spain, however, little fuss is made over the distinction between art for the galleries and art for the street. Miró's murals have long adorned Barcelona's plazas. The symbol Miró helped to produce just before his death in 1983 for the promotion of Spanish tourism was just the last in a line of such symbols he created as occasion demanded.

The natural coexistence of art and architecture that is such a local tradition was reinforced recently by a program to install public art in a number of Barcelona's plazas. Spanish and American artists such as Antoni Tàpies, Roy Lichtenstein, and Richard Serra collaborated with local architects such as Oscar Tusquets Blanca and the Martorell Bohigas Mackay partnership.

Barcelona's architecture, meanwhile, is gaining a huge boost from the Olympics. Jorge Carbonell, who is directing the building of the Olympic Village, says that the buildings for 1992 will be the best since the Tokyo Games in 1964. The city of Seville, capital of the Andalucían region, can be expected to make sure that its Expo in the same year will rival the Games' architectural splendor. Many of Spain's regions are striving to establish their own identities. In the Basque country, the Spanish region that generates the greatest wealth per capita, design is the most businesslike. In less industrialized regions like Andalucía and Galicia, on the other hand, it is the traditional crafts that flourish. The area around Valencia, another region vigorously seeking greater autonomy, has always been associated with furniture making, and many manufacturers are still based there.

But it is Barcelona, which has produced more than its share of the country's great artists and architects, that is the hub of Spain's design activity. The recent influences have been the city's great modern artists—Miró, Picasso, and Dalí—and the architects who preceded them, principally Antoni Gaudí. Long before this time, in the early eighth century, Spain and the southern part of France had fallen to invasion by the Moors from Africa. The Islamic influence is still seen in Spain's architecture, and Spanish designers have continued to find inspiration there.

Gaudí made a journey to Africa that provided the inspiration for some of his peculiar building shapes. Following in his footsteps, the graphic designer Javier Mariscal also seeks out the Moorish influence, which he has introduced in some of his

Tourism symbol
Joan Miró
Department of Tourism
Promotion, 1983

Cobi Olympic mascot
Javier Mariscal
COOB'92, 1988

Cartoonist and designer Javier Mariscal brought a refreshing irreverence to the Olympic mascot.

Right: 1992 Olympic Games logotype
Josep Trias, Quod
COOB'92, 1988

The art of Miró and the Catalan primary colors have inspired many logotype designs.

Bank logotype
Landor Associates
La Caixa, 1982

Barcelona'92

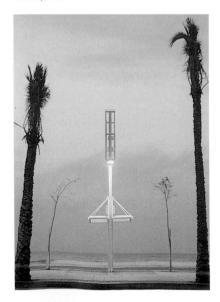

Capra chair
Esteve Agulló/Mariano Pi, Quod
Andreu Nort, 1987

Cambrils street lamp
Esteve Agulló/Mariano Pi, Quod
Lumex, 1989

graphic, ceramic, and carpet designs. "There is a close cultural link between the Spanish people and Africa," he says. "For me to go to Africa is a little like going to my grandfather's house—or like American people coming to Europe."

Sybilla, the young star of Spanish fashion design, draws on a variety of Spanish elements, mixing and remixing them to yield entirely original results. Her colors are the rich, earthy tones common to much Spanish clothing and are another Moorish inheritance. Her predilection for embroidered materials relates to Islamic traditions in the decoration of surfaces of all types. But like some designers in other disciplines, Sybilla has found that local industry cannot meet her demands—her clothes are made in Italy.

Spain's varied cultural history is not the only reason for the current strength of its design. Since the death of the dictator Franco in 1975, Spain has been reaping the rewards of its newly democratic society. Its rate of economic growth is higher than the European Community average. It is suddenly part of the international economic and cultural community, a fact that is reflected not only in the obvious economic prosperity of a city like Barcelona, with its Silicon Valleyish suburbs, but also in the freeing of long-pent-up creative urges.

At the end of the 1960s, still under the dictatorship, Barcelona was the only place in Spain offering anything close to the liberal attitudes and cosmopolitan life available so readily in Europe's other large cities. Mariscal fled to Barcelona from Valencia. Other Spaniards, such as Santiago Miranda, born in Seville, decamped altogether, to Milan. With his British partner, Perry King, Miranda has only recently begun to design for Spanish clients.

Spain's liberation has not only unshackled creative minds; it also, to a lesser extent, has determined how they work. The rapid acceptance of Spain into the international community has been met halfway by the Spaniards themselves, indicating their wish to belong. Spanish design looks to influences from abroad as a way to signify the country's new legitimacy in the eyes of the world. If Spanish furniture sometimes looks as though it came from Milan, and if Spanish products and graphics are sometimes rooted in the purism of the International Style, this is why.

It is in the design of furniture that the new freedom of expression has shown itself most proudly. A strong group of design "editors" and manufacturers provides essential backing for the local talent as well as for designers from abroad. Philippe Starck came to one, Disform, when he couldn't find a suitable

French company to arrange production of his designs.

As the declared capital of the Spanish cultural scene, Barcelona can hardly avoid comparison with Milan. Barcelona is to Madrid as Milan is to Rome: the former, at least in the view of their respective denizens, create wealth, the latter squander it. They have the same geographical latitude, the same proximity to the Mediterranean, a similar climate, the same predominant religion, and similar social attitudes. Norberto Chaves, formerly of the Barcelona corporate communications firm Chaves and Pibernat, remarks: "As in many things, Spain is immediately related to Italy, and Barcelona has historical links with the north of Italy. There is a shared degree of Latinity." (Some Italians disagree with this assertion, a clear indication that it is the Spanish who aspire to the condition of the Italians and not the other way around.)

In 1986 the Spaniards came in force to the Milan Furniture Fair. The excitement they occasioned even at this excitable event has proven to be a mixed blessing. It turned the spotlight on Spain all right, but this soon brought about a feeling locally that the attention was too much of a good thing. Many designers are now asking for a period out of the limelight, to polish their act in order to be able to compete equally on the European stage when the time is right.

There has been a more-or-less conscious wish on the part of Spanish designers to create work that is internationally acceptable. Really Spanish-looking work might have proved acceptable, but the quicker and surer route was to produce designs that built on the established codes of the Milan looks, from traditional to Memphis to Starck. This is why, when they show the work abroad, as Chaves points out, "they don't say 'Spanish design,' they say 'international design from Barcelona.' The best thing that Spanish design has done in the last few years has been to be international."

Some Barcelona designers see themselves in the Italian mold because they share a similar broad-based training in architecture rather than a narrower specialty in one design discipline. Like their Milanese counterparts, they consider themselves equally capable of designing a chair or a building. Oscar Tusquets Blanca is such a designer. Before he began to gain sufficient architectural commissions, he made his name designing furniture and household objects, principally for Italian companies such as Alessi and Zanotta. Tusquets's split loyalties are expressed in his Gaulino chair, an immaculately crafted wooden article that pays homage to both Gaudí and the Italian designer Carlo Mollino. The chair sets a deliberately awkward skeletal frame in opposition to comfortable

Left: Varius side-chair
Oscar Tusquets
Casas, 1986

Right: Varius office chair
Oscar Tusquets
Casas

The spindly nature of some
Spanish furniture is in marked
contrast with the Italian designs
with which they are sometimes
compared.

Manolete chair
Alberto Lievore
Perobell

La Vuelta table
King-Miranda
Akaba, 1986

Duplex stool
Javier Mariscal
BD Ediciones, 1983

The Moorish heritage is important in Spanish design, although it is rarely as obvious as in these carpets by Mariscal.

Above: Alfombra carpet
Javier Mariscal
Muebles Muy Formales, 1983

Left: Carpet
Javier Mariscal
CCI, Centre Pompidou, 1986
Photograph by J.D. Peauchet

Opposite: Gaulino chair, high version
Oscar Tusquets
C. Jane, 1989

The architect Antoni Gaudí is an inescapable source of imagery in Barcelona today.

polished wood and leather finishes. Despite—or perhaps because of—the influences spelled out in its name, the Gaulino chair, according to Tusquets, has nothing to do with the European styles of the moment.

In commissioning, manufacturing, and marketing, there are similarities but also important differences between Spain and Italy and elsewhere. Tusquets's Varius chair, designed for Casas, neatly embodies both the capabilities and the limitations that are characteristic of Spain. Casas is a division of Cassina of Italy and one of Barcelona's more technically sophisticated manufacturers, though still not up to the level of technological advancement of the Milanese. Tusquets intended the Varius to be an ergonomic office chair, but knew he lacked the resources to make the heavily engineered piece of machinery that is typical of Italian, German, or American producers. Instead he designed the Varius with a spidery appearance that passes deliberate comment on the Spanish situation, attempting to avoid the "overly sophisticated techniques" that might come from Milan. Other Spanish designers have reacted similarly to their circumstances. "As designers," says Tusquets, "we have to introduce reality, and design in the knowledge that some things here are well done and some are not." As a result, the five-wheel base of the office chair and the legs of the armchair look too meager to support any weight. Nevertheless, the design was acclaimed at a time when other office chairs were much of a muchness.

Tusquets's luxuriously upholstered Vayven armchair for Casas is very different. "I used my experience with the office chair but this is not an office chair. It is a very comfortable chair for normal house use, to watch television in, to read in." It comes complete with a built-in table, ideal, says Tusquets, for the TV remote control and a glass of whisky. This is a smart and surreal Spanish take on the American Barcalounger. The chair's concession to the avant-garde is that it is asymmetrical. The headrest is lopsided and the leather swells on the right arm to form an integral handrest, counterbalancing the little drinks table built into the left. Salvador Dalí was a personal friend of Tusquets, and the designer is happy to acknowledge the artist's influence in his work.

Although Tusquets and many other Spanish designers are, like their Italian colleagues, architects by training, there are notable exceptions to the general rule. Santiago Miranda trained in industrial design at a Seville school, with a strong emphasis on tradition and craftsmanship. Javier Mariscal began work as an underground cartoonist in the 1970s' Franco dictatorship and then turned to furniture

Port Autònom de Barcelona

The graphic design of Pati Núñez ranges from cool internationalism suited to Barcelona's port authority to spirited designs for local events and stores.

Top: Poster
Pati Núñez
Mercat de les Flors theater and
Ajuntament de Barcelona, 1988

Middle: Corporate symbol
Pati Núñez
Port Autonom de Barcelona,
1985

Bottom: Shopping bags
Pati Núñez
Vinçon, 1990

design at the beginning of the 1980s, joining the Memphis group in Milan. Like Tusquets's Varius chairs, the work of both these designers frequently has an attenuated appearance that comes of stretching limited resources. But it also is more graphic. Mariscal's three-legged stool designed for the Duplex bar in Valencia in 1980 perhaps owes a debt to Miró with its bright colors and fluid lines. But pop art, comics, and underground magazines remain his influences as much as any fine-art source, and his design, like much in Spain, is witty, ironic, and irreverent but entirely without the manifesto of irreverence of an Italian Memphis movement. If much of Mariscal's furniture looks like a drawing come to life, it should be no surprise, for this is exactly how he works. The approach is the same whether he is creating a graphic or three-dimensional design. Mariscal draws what he wants to see and then gives the drawing to his collaborator, Pepe Cortés, who determines whether the piece is structurally possible, makes alterations, and selects materials accordingly.

King and Miranda's Vuelta furniture for the San Sebastian company Akaba also relies on line rather than solid form. The designers bypassed the difficulty of manufacturing metal legs for the tables and desks by using bicycle wheel-forks bought from a local factory. An elegant—and easily made—bent chrome steel rod completed the leg design. Together the two elements have the air of a Duchamp "find" but also a pleasing baroque curve.

Considerably more conservative furniture comes from Alberto Liévore and Jorge Pensi, who manage a quieter marriage of international appeal and local sensibility. Here the materials are traditional ones of leather, wood, and metal used in more expected ways. There is an organic luxury to some of their pieces that contrasts with the uncomfortable look of much of the international avant-garde, whether of Spanish or other origin.

Spain seems to lack the crafts tradition capable of producing small runs of extremely high quality that exists in Italy, although it is better equipped in this field than other European countries. Woodworkers, metalworkers, seamstresses, and the rest did and do exist, but their services are not well coordinated and marketed. Mariscal—somewhat improbably—attributes the poor Spanish business sense to the enforced departure of the Sephardic Jews at the time of Columbus. The closed market that existed under Franco may provide a more convincing modern explanation. Some things can adequately be made. Reproduction Gaudí furniture—hulking carved wood chairs and tables for example—could not, in fact, be produced outside Spain because its craft labor is still cheaper than that elsewhere. Now an effort is being made in Barcelona to

bring glass, ceramic, and textile craft work up-to-date for current needs and technology with the establishment of a new crafts institute.

But it was industrial design that suffered the most under Franco. As a consequence, Spain is only now beginning to make up ground in the manufacture of consumer goods and is doing so too slowly for its own consumers. Spain's gross domestic product has been the fastest-growing in the European Community for several years. Consumers have the money and the taste for well-designed products, says Mai Felip Hösselbarth, director of design at the Barcelona Design Center: "The sensibility is there. The consumer in Spain is becoming very selective. He knows what he wants. He knows what is available in other countries. He is pressuring us now." Meanwhile, of course, imports are surging.

Logotype
Josep Trias, Quod
Institut Català de la Salut, 1989

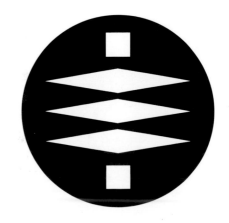

Josep Lluscá is a senior member of a comparatively small community of industrial designers. His work is necessarily more serious and functional than that of Tusquets, Mariscal, and the rest, but the influence of local art and architecture is still present.

Far left: Vaticana lamp
Josep Lluscá
Metalarte, 1988

Middle: Andrea chairs
Josep Lluscá
Andreu World, 1986

Left: Splendid pressure-cooker
Josep Lluscá
Fagor, 1986

Below: Calenda tape dispenser
Jorge Pensi/Carme Casares
Sabat Seleccion, 1989

Right: Olympia lamp
Jorge Pensi
Be-Lux, 1988

Text-Pert computer manual
Josep Trias, Quod
Ciència i Tecnologia Aplicada,
1988

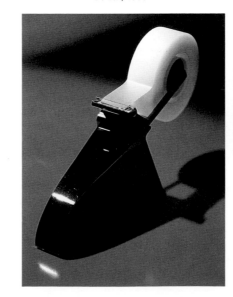

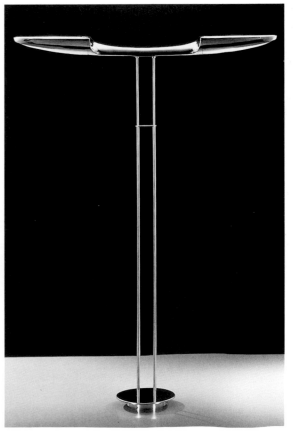

Many designers have little knowledge of Memphis, Tennessee, and still less of Memphis on the Nile. But of Memphis Milano they know all. This was the movement that made design headline material during the 1980s and, rather more usefully, caused designers the world over to reconsider how much fun it was legitimate to bring to their work.

Memphis could only have flourished in Italy and that to all intents and purposes means in Milan. Yet its members were scrupulously multinational. In addition to the movement's founder, Ettore Sottsass, there were, to be sure, a number of Italians, but also a Frenchwoman, a Briton, an American, a Spaniard, and others at various times.

In the 1960s it had been Florence that briefly played host to the radical design movements Superstudio and Archizoom. Gradually, more practically oriented groups were established, groups that were interested in using industrial materials and processes in their projects. The central figures of these groups—first Studio Alchymia and then Memphis— were practicing industrial designers, and it was natural that the spotlight should turn to Milan, the industrial center where they worked. Milan became a magnet for young designers keen to learn the secrets of Italian design and adopt its ways. Several successful studios are now run by immigrants who have found the Italian environment amenable, among them the Japanese Isao Hosoe and the Anglo-Spanish duo of Perry King and Santiago Miranda. The quality of Italian design has less to do with the star designers and their avant-garde projects, however, than with the commercial environment that, directly or indirectly, sponsors them. Alberto Alessi, who himself has drawn many foreign designers and architects to create products for his famous metal-ware company, explains: "We are right to think of Memphis as Italian, just as the Bauhaus was German. Italian design will continue to exist regardless of Italian designers because of the attitude of Italian industries."

The bulk of Italy's furniture industry is located in and around Milan, making the city a natural center for furniture designers. This, in turn, draws other designers. Olivetti, an important patron of design, is located nearer Turin than Milan, but its designers are usually Milanese. Only the Italian automobile industry is sufficiently powerful to secure local design services, notable among them the studio of Giorgietto Giugiaro, responsible for the design of many recent Fiats as well as of the original Volkswagen Golf. But in general, as former Memphis member Michele De Lucchi concludes, "Italian design is Milanese design. In Italy maybe five percent of the population knows about design, and all of them are in Milan."

Italian industry, and hence Italian design, centers on Milan, polarizing the country and bestowing upon it one of the sharpest north-south divides anywhere. There is some design activity in southern cities such as Naples, Bari, and Palermo, but it is more craft-oriented and Mediterranean in feel than that in the wealthy north.

Without substantial competition, Milan can seem self-obsessed. Its design magazines and the international furniture and other trade fairs held there only add to the effect. This vanity renders even the talented Roman designer Paolo Pallucco an irredeemable outsider in Milanese eyes, a rebel who could never be accepted into the Milan establishment as Milan's own rebels quickly are.

If, as Alessi suggests, it is the industry rather than the designers that makes Italian design what it is, then that industrial ethos deserves investigation. "We trust ourselves," is one of the first comments to emerge from many manufacturers who are patrons of good design. It comes from Sergio Gandini, president of the lighting company Flos, Enrico Cazzaniga of the furniture company Airon, and many others. It comes, too, from Renzo Zorzi, formerly director of cultural relations at Olivetti, who adds this corollary: "What you need is to know what you're doing, to have the right people doing it, plus a little daring, because the public does not like change." These people share a distrust for any but the most informal exercise in market research, relying instead on their own instincts backed up by no more than perhaps a straw poll of their dealers' opinions. One reason for this self-confidence is that many companies continue to be family-owned, something that distinguishes Italian industry from that in most developed countries, with the exception of Spain. Even Olivetti was family-owned until quite recently. Such intimate control may no longer be tenable for the largest companies, but it shows every sign of persisting in the small- and medium-sized companies that form the bulk of Italy's industrial strength.

Nonetheless, Italian designers are different from those elsewhere. Mario Bellini, a senior figure in the profession, attributes this to the fact that they are educated in schools of architecture. In an essay on "Italian style" Bellini wrote: "Today, however, at the very height of its good fortune, it might paradoxically be asserted that there is no such thing as an 'Italian style': the Italian style is the absence of any definite style . . . it has no unitary code or familiar elements that could be easily described or transmitted by teaching. And it is no coincidence that this new 'Italian school' has positively thrived on the lack of

Opposite: Telephone
Ettore Sottsass
Enorme Italiana

Portanuova shelf unit
Ettore Sottsass
Zanotta, 1988

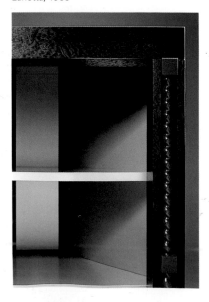

Lightlight chair prototype
Alberto Meda
Alias, 1987
Photograph by Aldo Ballo

For all the furor created by its movements and manifestos, Italian design is shaped just as much by technological innovation epitomized by Alberto Meda's use of ultra-lightweight carbon fiber.

Softlight chair
Alberto Meda
Alias, 1988
Photograph by Aldo Ballo

specific schools of industrial, furniture or interior design. Its culture of reference in fact has been and continues to be that of our architectural schools: still largely humanistic and multidisciplinary rather than oriented toward specialized professions." Architect Francesco Soro adds that this coupling between design and architecture has been a fact of Italian life since the sixteenth century, a lineage that suggests that contemporary bursts of what Soro dismissively calls "styling," because of its separation from functional demands, will be short-lived. It is possible that the various polemical movements in design also stem from a long-held idealism. According to Marco Cavallotti, general secretary of the Milan Triennale design exhibitions, the idea that the world can be changed through architecture (and design) persists in Italy more strongly than anywhere else.

Bellini argues that only architecture schooling can instill a sense of the roots and context that products need as much as buildings. He believes it is misguided to teach industrial design as an autonomous discipline, as it is taught in many other countries and as it is beginning to be taught in some schools in Italy: "It happens that the best-known Italian designers are architects. We do have schools preparing designers for urban design and furniture design; we do now have a few small schools of industrial design, but none of the famous designers came out of those schools. It is not by chance. I strongly believe that a school of architecture gives you a better understanding and a better background about what the living and habitative culture is."

Italy's architecture schools cannot claim all the credit for the healthy state of the Italian industrial and furniture design professions. Many of their alumni might well have become architects rather than designers had circumstances been different at the time of their graduation. "We had particular social and economic conditions after the last world war," explains Bellini. "A very open minded and energetic new industry needed industrial designers and so pushed architects to get involved with industrial design and furniture design. Also, there were not too many opportunities for architects to do architecture."

Convincing as it is, this argument does not completely explain the Italian preeminence in design. Some leading figures are designers first and architects second. This applies, understandably, to designers who have not been educated in Italy but who have adopted Italy as their home—Hosoe came as a mechanical engineer, King and Miranda as industrial designers—but also to some of the most influential Italians of the postwar period. Carlo Mollino was such a designer, and the furniture that came out of his Turin studio in the decade after the war contrast-

ed with the more architectural Milanese style. Marcello Nizzoli studied fine arts before moving, via the company's advertising department, to product design for Olivetti.

Recent Italian design has turned away from the seductive curves of Nizzoli's Olivetti typewriters and Mollino's organic furniture to assume a generally more angular appearance. Is this a reflection of the prevailing architectonic way of thinking? The architect-designers do not necessarily design in an architectural way, although the products of Sottsass, Bellini, and others frequently display a strong, ordered design in elevation and in plan. Perry King observes that this might be attributable in part to an architectural background, but he believes that it also serves a polemical purpose, enabling a designer to indicate a personal philosophy by means of a proposal, whether or not it goes into production; in Italy, published drawings of an unrealized design can be as significant as the real thing.

Countering Bellini's proposition that Italy's is a style-without-a-style, Alberto Alessi believes that there *is* an element of constancy to be found in the best Italian products. That element isn't tangible but is what he calls a "component of transgression," a willingness, even an obligation, to break rules. Alessi identifies three types of rule to be broken: the technological rule that says "it can't be done," confounded by Alberto Meda's ultralightweight carbon-fiber chair; the marketing rule that prefers to maintain the status quo by selling more of the same and shying away from the new, scorned by Olivetti's Renzo Zorzi and others; and the aesthetic rule that denies any break with what Alessi calls the "ruling figurative tradition" and that was spectacularly demolished by Alchymia and Memphis.

There is a feeling in Milan now that the polemical movements are a thing of the past. Italy's wealth has grown enormously since the 1970s, and there is ample commercial demand to distract designers from these exercises. There is also much building, and many, such as Michele De Lucchi and Mario Bellini, who made their names as designers are taking up the theme of their training and spending more time as architects. "I consider this a transition period in Italian design," says De Lucchi. "I don't find elsewhere the same element of crisis I find in Italy at the moment, as designers move into architecture and interiors away from objects."

Memphis was declared finished once it became clear that the monster of commercialism and the tyranny of taste that it had set out to challenge with its populist forms had consumed it, once Memphis became "collectible." Alchymia's last gasp was Ollo Design, which made use of brightly colored materials, plane surfaces, and patterns that echoed those

Miram 200 telephone
George Sowden/Simon Morgan
Olivetti, 1989

Italy is fertile territory for talented designers, such as the British pair of Sowden and Morgan, who came from around the world to work mainly in Milan.

OFX 420 fax
George Sowden/Simon Morgan
Olivetti, 1991

Mario Bellini's training as an architect has given his furniture and product design its strong profile.

Top: Praxis 35 typewriter
Mario Bellini
Olivetti, 1982

Middle: ET 55P typewriter
Mario Bellini/A. Chiarato
Olivetti, 1987

Bottom: ET 2500 typewriter
Mario Bellini
Olivetti, 1988

Far right: Onda Quadra shelves
Mario Bellini
Acerbis International, 1988

Top: Serenissimo table
Vignelli Associates
Acerbis International, 1988

Above: Tecnico table
Michele De Lucchi
Cappellini, 1988

Novecento furniture
Antonio Citterio
Moroso, 1988

Jewelry and wristwatch
Alessandro Mendini
Türler, 1988

*After Memphis and Alchymia,
Mendini remains one of very
few designers to make use of
decorative surface techniques.*

Le Lamentazioni chairs
Paolo Pallucco, 1988
Photograph by A. Callari

*Milan's concentration of
furniture designers makes a
Roman like the iconoclastic
Paolo Pallucco almost as
much of an outsider as
Philippe Starck.*

of the Italian Renaissance. One of its prime movers, Alessandro Mendini, reports that the decorative ideas explored by Alchymia and Memphis continue to be pursued by painters and fine artists, a reversal of the usual trend by which movements in art generally inform activity in the field of design. Mendini himself is one the few designers to explore pattern and ornament in a manner that, he says, effectively renders working on an item of furniture the equivalent of designing the façade of a building.

Early indications of the general shift in priorities came toward the end of the 1980s, as designers began to opt for a less decadent approach, looking back to the work of the Italian Rationalists in the 1930s. Furniture began to seem more true to the materials of its construction. Meanwhile, Solid, an international group of designers under De Lucchi, brought new attention and unusual grace to a range of everyday objects. "We developed the idea that it is possible to make progress in design through small, 'insignificant' objects," says De Lucchi. "If design is to participate in the evolution of the world's images, it is important to be able to evolve and manipulate creative work quickly and flexibly. What could be better for the purpose than small objects?" When in 1990 the Milan Furniture Fair, traditionally the media platform for radical movements, committed the heresy of moving from the fall to the spring, it merely seemed to be the final nail in the coffin of the Milan of the manifestos.

Away from the media posturing and the hastily assembled fair prototypes, there has always been a concern for craftsmanship and finesse with materials. Pierluigi Molinari, director of the Italian Designers' Association (ADI) in Milan, adds to the Italian ingredients of style and craftsmanship a third ingredient: technology. Contrary to popular belief abroad, Molinari rates technology as the most important of these three factors. Marco Piva, another ADI official, illustrates the argument with reference to Britain's Jaguar car company. The firm has the style and craftsmanship but lacks an open attitude to technology. "Jaguar is just reproducing something. It is the exact opposite of what is happening in Italy."

It is hard to fathom why Italy's manufacturers today—sons and daughters of yesterday's artisans and craftsmen—are able to maintain the small- and medium-scale production of the past and yet are apparently willing to combine it with the latest technology when their counterparts in other countries are failing to do the same. In the United States or Britain or Germany, the wish to remain small often means wallowing in the nostalgia of craft processes that have been left behind by mainstream industry. In Italy, even a designer with such a profound interest in history as Alessandro Mendini believes that

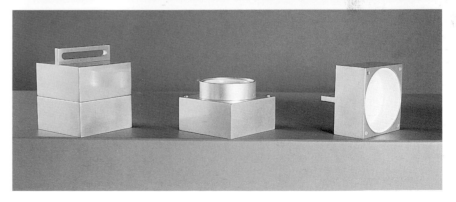

Top: Cups
Furriccio Laviani, Solid
1988

Middle: Napkin rings
Furriccio Laviani, Solid
1988

Bottom: Butter dish
A. Micheli, Solid
1988

Figura chair
Mario Bellini
Vitra, 1987

The sensual humanism that Bellini has brought to his office furniture and hand-held objects such as calculators for Olivetti is in contrast to his more architectonic approach seen, for example, in his typewriter designs.

Guya chair
Centro Studi Castelli
Castelli, 1987

Riccado bed
Mario Marenco and Franco Onali
Matteo Grassi, 1988

Some Italian furniture manufacturers have reconciled traditional craftsmanship with modern demands without becoming embroiled in highly publicized design trends.

Faucet
Mario Bellini
Ideal Standard

Right: Wizard gas hob stove
Roberto Pezzetta
Zanussi

Far right: Wizard refrigerator
Roberto Pezzetta
Zanussi

*Italy's designers are often
trained in schools of
architecture. As a consequence,
many products have the
qualities of small buildings.*

Trompe l'oeil cabinet
Piero Fornasetti
Photograph courtesy Design
Museum, London

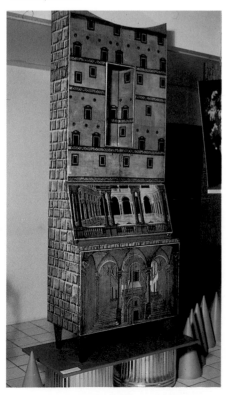

Left: Palio shelf unit
Massimo Morozzi
Giorgetti Matrix, 1988

Right: Electronic lathe head
positioner
Giorgio Decursu
D'Andrea, 1989

Above: Tea/coffee set
Alessandro Mendini
Alessi

Alessi's unstinting patronage of Italian designers has done much to define a national style that is widely admired.

Right: Il Conico coffee set
Aldo Rossi
Alessi

Far right: Tea/coffee set
Paolo Portoghesi
Alessi

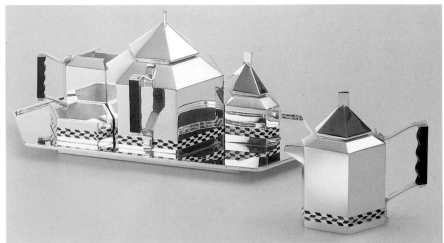

manufacturers must adopt the latest methods or risk the consequences.

There are other constants in Italian production: a wish to expend less energy, to use materials properly, and to deploy intelligence in place of resources. "This you can find all through our history," says Piva. "Because we didn't have raw materials or a big market all over the world, we always had to take care of what we were using. Each time we had to add more intelligence to the process." These are useful yardsticks against which to measure Italian avant-garde furniture, for example, against its European rivals.

These requirements appear to drive the craft and technological mentalities to work together, whereas in other countries they are driven into mutual opposition. Piva credits this to Italy's markets, which were, and to some extent remain, strongly fragmented into historically and culturally important regions: "The dimension of the market is very important. There was the time and the opportunity to produce something quite different in, for example, Milan from that produced in Venice only 200 kilometers away. This is quite different from the structure that you have in Germany or in England, because from the Industrial Revolution they were single countries." (Although the German nation coalesced in 1871, a decade after the unification of Italy, the former was already more closely knit, unified by a common language and an abundance of energy and raw materials, says Piva.)

Alberto Alessi believes that with its constructive coexistence of craftsmanship and high-technology production, "the Italian design industry is the spiritual heir to the tradition of the Arts and Crafts movement." Ruskin, Morris, the Wiener Werkstätte, the Deutsche Werkbund, and even the Bauhaus were critical of the production of their time. "They could never be defined as exactly serving industry," notes Alessi. A similar antagonism informs Italian design.

Alessi is well positioned to comment. His company's products very clearly carry the signatures of their designers. Yet they are made in a metalworking factory with three hundred employees near Lake Maggiore that can draw upon some very high volume production and is capable of investing hundreds of millions of lire in molds and tooling. All metalworking is done in this factory; only the final polishing is done elsewhere, in a network of far smaller factories better suited to this manual task.

Alberto Alessi has been assiduous in his patronage of designers from many countries. This, in turn, has made the name Alessi well known around the world. He says, "Alessi designs are both national and Italian. They express their national identity, but their product becomes Italian." Recently, four designers were invited to design knobs for the lids of a range of cooking pans designed by Mendini. The program required the designers to invoke something of their respective nations' characters. It may be a facetious illustration of national identities, but it is perhaps possible to deduce a superpower propensity for formality and a more playful, informal spirit from Europe and Japan: the Soviet and American knobs, by Yuri Soloviev and Michael Graves, respectively, are symmetrical and restrained; those by Philippe Starck and Arata Isozaki are eccentric, both literally and metaphorically.

The coexistence of craft and technology is a lynchpin of modern Italian design thinking. It is universally seen as a recipe for success, not a disadvantage in the European free market. Optimism expressed by Alessi, Airon, Flos, and others about their prospects contrasts sharply with the fretfulness of some companies in other European Community countries. The acceptance of technology by Italy's industry and designers is a necessary, if not a sufficient, condition for this comparative advantage to endure. While a commitment to style and craftsmanship continues to support the country's still largely unrivaled position as Europe's design showcase, Marco Piva adds the hope that after 1992 Italy could become Europe's technology workshop as well.

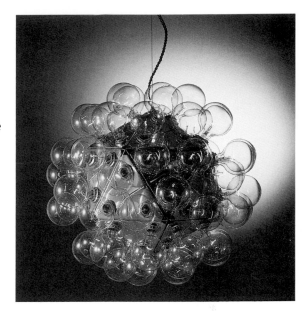

Cluster lamp
Achille Castiglioni
Flos, 1988

Twist collection
Paolo Nava
Airon Metalarredo, 1988

Swatch watches

Switzerland

The world knows Switzerland for its cheese and chocolate, for its cuckoo clocks and their successors, the Swatch watches. Designers know Switzerland for the International Typographic Style and the clean, doctrinaire elegance of its graphic design. Swiss Modernism was largely the creation of two design schools, one in the financial center of Zurich, the other in Basel, close to the French and German borders. Through their work and their teaching at these schools, Armin Hofmann, Emil Ruder, Josef Müller-Brockmann, and their followers ruled the roost from the 1940s until the 1960s. Then, in 1968, Wolfgang Weingart of Basel usurped the established order with what is still known as the New Wave. It seems that little of Swiss design has reached the wider world since then.

Given the strength of its reputation, it would be easy to imagine the Swiss style as a homogeneous entity in this tiny land. But Switzerland's designers would have you believe it is not so. They need little encouragement to tell you how what they are doing differs from what is being done in the next valley fifty miles away. "Lucerne and Zurich and Basel are completely different," says Hofmann, who still teaches occasionally at the Basel school. "The whole idea of Swiss graphic design is okay from far away, but when you look closer, you see the differences."

The differences are best articulated in the country's six main design schools. The aesthetics divide roughly along the borders of the historical cantons. In the capital, Bern, and in the big cities of Basel and Zurich—all German-speaking—the purism of the Swiss style is linked to Protestant Calvinism. In French Lausanne and Italian Lugano, on the other hand, the schools' styles are closer to those of the countries whose languages they speak.

Finally, there is Lucerne. Located in the middle of the country just north of the Alps, the Lucerne school is a hybrid of German language and Catholic religion. It's as near as Switzerland gets to a melting pot. And it is from here that some of the most interesting design is now coming. While the Frenchman John Calvin made his home in Geneva, Switzerland's own hero of the religious reformation of the sixteenth century was Huldrych Zwingli. According to Benno Zehnder of the Lucerne school, "Zurich is a Zwinglian Protestant town with a very strong work ethic and a belief in authority; Lucerne is the center of Swiss Catholicism." It has a colorful carnival and more ornate churches. "You feel the difference in the two colleges. It's almost anarchistic here. Lucerne has a philosophy, but not a visual ideology. Students don't have to work within a design language."

There is a general consensus in all the schools that the crusading zeal of Swiss Modernism is a thing of the past, although its values continue to haunt design teaching. Its legacy is a high level of graphic competence. There is little produced that is really bad, but neither, according to locals, are there many peaks of excellence. Design graduates tend to disappear into advertising, which graphically, even here, is rarely much to write home about. Billboards and print ads are tidier than those in France or Italy, for example, but they lack the punch of Herbert Matter's Swissair posters of old. Other fields, such as book and magazine design, or animation, are comparatively overlooked. Outside the advertising agencies, there are few group studios. Most designers work individually. In the past this was an advantage, with the artist/designer giving poster design its strength. Somehow, this is no longer the case. Something is missing. Within the comfortable code of Swiss conduct, there is a need to rebel.

Both the means and the will to change exist. Several years ago the Swiss government gave the go-ahead for the schools to give postgraduate degrees. The main schools welcomed the move and set up programs as soon as they could. Student uptake was slow, however, because it is easy for graphic designers to find well-paid employment in Switzerland (although not necessarily without compromising their integrity as designers). Few found a sufficient incentive to return to school. Nevertheless, with the first of those who did return now completing their studies, commercial Swiss graphic design could begin to regain some of the vigor it has lost in recent decades.

The difficulty, some teachers say, is for individual designers to shed their complacency. It is hard to become indignant about anything in Switzerland. The federated administration means there are no national politics on which to take sides. The world's youth rioted in 1968; the Swiss didn't have their demonstrations until 1980. In this neutral island in the middle of Europe, it is easy to forget that the chemical companies that create the wealth are raining acid on the Black Forest in neighboring Germany or that the components of Switzerland's watches are equally suited for use in missile guidance systems for other nations' defense contractors. It takes some effort to consider that things are not always for the best in this best of all possible worlds.

All this provides source material for new design. Even Zurich, the most conservative school, is struggling to evolve a new language distinct from the worn-out purism of the past. Ideology has given way to pluralism, according to school manager Benjamin Hensel and visual communications head Urs Fanger who says, "It's too nice. We don't like it. You have to fight against this purism and regimentation of life."

Poster
Paul Brühwiler
Filmpodium, Zurich, 1987

In the past, the type—often in Helvetica—on a poster was merely an inert adjunct to a central image. But Fanger believes an opposition of type and image can serve to highlight society's conflicts and contradictions. In this interplay between words and pictures, images are "supersigns," with meanings that may be ambiguous and accidental as well as direct and intentional: "You have the possibility to think in pictures and the possibility to think literally. The question is: What is the extent of each and how do they relate?" The juxtaposition of type and image that results from this thinking is sometimes interesting, sometimes less so. But it is always done in a polished manner. The typography is neat, the photographs apposite. It is hard to believe there is any anger here. Wolfgang Weingart is among the designers at other schools who doubt the value of Zurich's radical chic.

Weingart's own revolution of 1968, the misnamed and ageing New Wave, now falls well within the bounds of Swiss good taste. The layering of type that began as Weingart's personal effort to break away from the good taste of the time has evolved into a teaching tool at Basel, extending the function of typography from written to visual communication.

It sometimes seems as if the Basel design language has become every graphic designer's stock-in-trade. Weingart demonstrates the fact by picking a piece of scrap paper from the trash and doodling the trademark motifs that have come to mean New Wave in its most banal sense—the zigzag steps, the wide-spaced letters, the underlining, the partial frame around a design. As he draws, he explains: "I counted them once when I was judging a competition in Los Angeles—I found around twenty." Now the American interpretation of what they called the Swiss punk style is coming home to roost in Switzerland. Weingart is resigned to the rip-offs, to a method becoming a style, to the *words* of his design language becoming confused with language itself. "'New Wave' can hide a lot of mistakes," he remarks. "With my typography, I can hide nothing."

Weingart teaches three classes at Basel. His international typography class, made up largely of foreign students, is allowed to experiment widely in a manner that the students will find appropriate when they return home. His other two classes are made up of Swiss students only. "In these classes," Weingart told *Emigré* magazine, "we do classical, strict, clean, intelligent, structured typography because I know these people will stay in Switzerland and they'll need this here."

While Basel concentrates on the rigors of typography, Lucerne has an expressionist bent that stems from its strength in illustration. Lucerne has always attracted good draftsmen, and today the marrying of

illustration and design is one of the school's pedagogical aims. It is reinforced by the occasional presence of influential illustrators such as Paul Brühwiler. Though born in Lucerne, Brühwiler works mainly in Zurich. He lived in Los Angeles in the 1960s, working with Saul Bass and the Eameses before setting up his own studio. Back in Switzerland, he now designs posters for movies and political causes, having quit the corporate identity business. These are low-budget jobs; the writing is often done by hand for economic as much as artistic reasons. Much use is made of black-and-white images in order to cut enlargement and reduction costs. "It's like street art," says Brühwiler. The roughness is in keeping with the subjects, although the spirit of the work places Brühwiler closer to Eastern European poster art than to the Swiss tradition. Another angle much in evidence in the Lucerne student work is a witty literacy—playing with words and images to create a verbal rather than a visual punchline—perhaps a by-product of faculty member Benno Zehnder's years in Britain. This is not in the Swiss tradition either.

Hans-Rudolf Lutz represents a similarly liberated spirit in typography at Lucerne. The designer of a logotype, graphics, and videos for the rock band UnknownmiX and publisher of his own books, Lutz identifies with the student movement of the 1980s and pursues an aesthetic of resistance influenced by underground books and third-world graphics. Though ostensibly poles apart from the intellectual work of Weingart at Basel, Lutz's typography is still polished in appearance and eminently Swiss to the foreign eye.

The Lucerne school is trying to channel these new qualities into work that addresses issues of local importance. "We don't have enough designers who question the quality of life," says Brühwiler. Lucerne students have, for example, designed a poster campaign to make townspeople aware of air pollution caused by cars. An emphasis on the availability of lead-free gasoline and public transport made the project relevant and not merely rhetorical. Addressing a real issue like this, the students find the project rewarding and gain the added benefit that only a genuinely felt cause can generate the best creative work.

The fact that no one school has established an ideology to replace Swiss Modernism has opened the field. A second tier is making its presence felt. In the French-speaking part of Switzerland, the school of applied arts in La Chaux-de-Fonds, Le Corbusier's hometown, startled the establishment recently when undergraduate Magali Babey won a national schools' competition for the design of a poster for the conservation of Swiss forests. Her winning submission was simply a small splash of green blood on a white

Poster commemorating the
bicentennial of the French
revolution
Paul Brühwiler
Artis, 1989

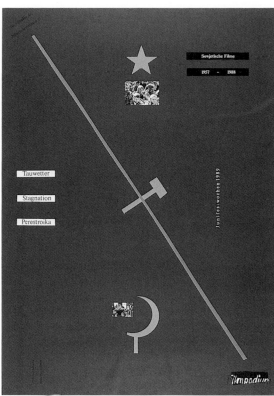

Poster
Paul Brühwiler
Filmpodium, Zurich

Logotype
Hans-Rudolf Lutz
UnknownmiX

*Even when it could afford to let
go, as in this work for a punkish
band, Swiss design usually
remains well-mannered.*

Poster
Fabienne Schrommer, 1990

DER WALD BLUTET, PFLEGEN WIR IHN!

Poster
Magali Babey, 1988

background with a simple caption reversed out from a black bar centered at the top of the poster. Accused of creating an innately Swiss design, Babey remarks tartly, "That's not a pejorative term."

The La Chaux school's sudden grab for the spotlight is all the more surprising because Babey is in only the first graduating year of a modest new graphics program. For now, perhaps, the ultra-Swiss look of her poster will help the school claim its place among the graphic establishment. Eventually, though, says professor Gilbert Luthi, the aim is to create a distinctive temperament by looking to France as much as anywhere else. Professors will visit from Lausanne and Geneva. "I love my German-Swiss colleagues," says Luthi, "but we also have a right to exist, don't we?" It is relevant that in a wider sense the Jura region in which La Chaux-de-Fonds lies has been no stranger to the separatist call.

The claims of each school to a discrete cultural lineage stretching back through the centuries are perhaps a little tenuous. After all, students at a given school may come from elsewhere in Switzerland. Many of the graduate students come from abroad. When they graduate, they are almost bound to end up working in Basel or Zurich if they stay in the country at all. The best teachers spend a good portion of their time flitting along expressways between the cities and their schools.

Aside from the legitimacy of their competing claims, the schools are in a state of flux, in stark contrast with the assuredness and evangelism of a generation ago. What we have grown accustomed to thinking of as Swiss design has come almost entirely from the German-speaking north of the country. With the more Catholic (and catholic with a small c) areas now in the ascendant, this may begin to change.

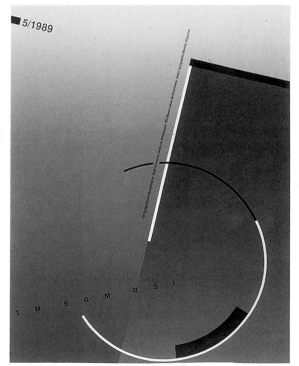

Poster
Anne Antonini, Ecole d'Art
Appliqué, La Chaux-de-Fonds
Société Suisse pour la Protection
de l'Environnement, 1990

Poster
Philip Melia, Kantonale Schule
für Gestaltung, Lucerne, 1988

AIDS prevention poster
Christophe Dubois
Aide suisse contre le
SIDA/L'Office fédéral de la santé
publique, 1989

Magazine cover project
Sylviane Giro, Ecole d'Art
Appliqué, La Chaux-de-Fonds,
1989

Hungary

Baby shampoo bottle
Alexandra Nagy
Gedeon Richter

An expressway now runs between capitalist Vienna and once-communist Budapest, twin capitals of the old Austro-Hungarian empire. Shortly before they snipped away the barbed wire that formed the border here, you could, on weekends, see rich Viennese and Munichers setting out in their big BMWs and Mercedes for a trendy couple of days behind the iron curtain. They would amuse themselves on the way to their cheap, chic breaks by terrorizing the locals in their Soviet-made Ladas, the underpowered cars that Hungarians drive for want of any auto industry of their own.

The Hungarians would be returning from their own, less easily afforded trips to Vienna. In 1988 Hungarians flooded Vienna to do their Christmas shopping, thanks to relaxation of border controls that year. One hundred thousand Hungarians spent $40 million in ten hours. It was estimated then that Hungarians had an additional $5 billion in hard currencies stashed away under their mattresses for future occasions.

The symbiosis is better than none at all, but it is not exactly what either country would wish. The Hungarians' Western aspirations have long been plain for all to see. An illuminated Levi's billboard flashes its message across the Danube to Buda from Pest. And on Béla Bartók Street, you can pick up one of Lee Iacocca's big-business manifestos in a secondhand bookshop.

Though Hungary was never the most productive country in what was the Eastern bloc, design here has more cause for hope than in some other places. There is an inventive spirit in Hungary, though the connection has seldom profitably been made between ingenuity and commerce. László Bíró, of the ball-point pen, and Ernő Rubik, of the eponymous cube, remain exceptional figures but are indicative of a largely untapped potential for innovation. Hungary boasts a comparatively high gross domestic product per head and an incipient Western-style consumer culture. There is a readier understanding here of markets and choice.

The Austro-Hungarian heritage exerts a strong stylistic influence. József Scherer, a teacher at the Hungarian Academy for Crafts and Design, notes that certain local industries exhibit a generic style that is equally welcome in Germany and Austria as well as in Hungary. The well-known local porcelain company, Herend, is one example. There are good reasons for the existence of some commonality with design from German-speaking regions. Hungary's power was greatest during the days of the Austro-

Hungarian empire. Its industrialization during this period was largely backed by German investment.

The security of empire nurtured an independent spirit in design. Zsolnay, another chinaware manufacturer, had a more Hungarian style, developing local variations on the Jugendstil of the turn of the century. In architecture, Odön Lechner, Budapest's equivalent of Barcelona's Antoni Gaudí, blended western Art Nouveau with Turkish and Arabic elements that reflect Hungary's historical eastern influxes. A local character was sustained through the period between the two world wars. Today, Zsolnay and other companies are trying to pick up those threads once again.

"A hundred years ago, Hungarian object culture was richer," says József Hegedűs, director of the Hungarian Council of Industrial Design. "One could sense the oriental influence and the Asian culture. The colors were so much richer. The impoverishment started with the breakup of the Austro-Hungarian empire and is closely connected with the impoverishment of the economy." The Council has mounted a study to find out what is hampering the enrichment of the material surroundings. "Why cannot colors break into the Hungarian vision?" asks Hegedűs. "No one wants to buy a car in a color other than white, for instance." Others are less sure a Hungarian style ever existed. The country is in the very center of Europe; it was subject to periodic devastation; and it is a place where traditions have had the pride stripped from them by successive waves of invasion—and an unlucky propensity for Hungarians to pick the losing side in any conflict.

Early influences come from the spareness of the Lutherans and Calvinists as well as the more ornate style of the Catholics who banded together to beat back the boundaries of the Ottoman Empire during the Reformation. Ornament fell into disfavor at this time. A more recent reason for Hungary's turning its back on more exotic influences may lie with the German-backed industrialization. That dominance, together with Hungary's central location, made the country ideal territory for the internationalism of the Bauhaus. Some Bauhaus luminaries, notably László Moholy-Nagy, were Hungarian themselves. The characteristic combination of functionalism and pure form is still apparent. This is evident in the annual competition run by the Hungarian Design Center. Director Mihály Pohárnok admits that no real benefit accrues to the winners without a free market, but for what it's worth, the awards do go to a design *team*— designers, engineers, and manufacturing technicians. One of the early casualties of the new non-communist administration was the Design Center, which was recently shut down by its paymaster, the Hungarian Chamber of Economy, for lack of funding.

Telephones
Varga and Venéczi Design
Service

*Hungary's poster-making
tradition, like that in other
Eastern European countries, has
risen well to the challenge of
recent moves to democracy.*

Right: Poster
István Orosz, 1989

Below: Poster
István Orosz
Hungarian Democratic Forum,
1990

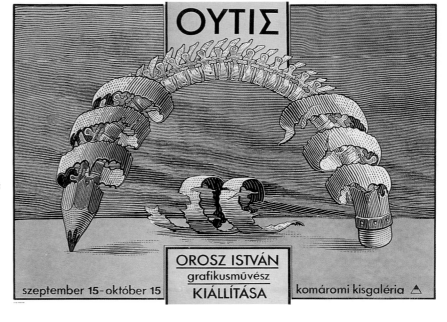

ΟΥΤΙΣ

OROSZ ISTVÁN
grafikusművész
KIÁLLÍTÁSA

szeptember 15 - október 15   komáromi kisgaléria △

ТОВАРИЩИ
конец!

Magyar Demokrata Fórum

Toiletries packaging
Alexandra Nagy/András
Kamarás
Gedeon Richter, 1989

*Some fields, such as toiletries
and cosmetics, support a high
degree of competition and
provide good opportunities for
designers.*

Above and below: Furnaces
György Lissák
KGYV

The pure Bauhaus abstraction of Lissák's design is a reminder of the enduring appeal in central Europe of elegant functionalism.

Right: Vehicle prototype
Varga and Venéczi

Designers are realistic about their chances of recapturing a Magyar mood. The future could see a more distinctively Hungarian style in furniture and ceramic articles, which are made individually or in small batches, as well as in fashion. The apparel industry remains close to tradition. Ilona Lendvay, for example, acquired a sound knowledge of popular and national costume at school before going to work for the Hungarian Fashion Institute. Here she continued her exploration of Hungarian themes that would be good export prospects, gradually seeking to blend Western and traditional styles. In the increasingly liberal atmosphere of the 1980s, Lendvay struck out in a new direction: "This time I was not interested in the pure rustic character but rather the forgotten national character in costume. I attempted as much as possible to express this character, but not adhering to any particular region. I achieved my goal in part with the assistance of the music of Zoltan Kodály." Lendvay's collection was shown in Paris in 1989.

József Scherer is trying to stimulate discussion on how to express a strong cultural consciousness in products, but many students and teachers are still thinking too traditionally, he says. They are unable to break with the idea of a closed market. The director of the Academy for Crafts and Design, András Mengyán, adds that his students are unlikely to find well-paid jobs in industry after graduating. And if, instead, they go freelance, producing small runs of decorative designs, they may fail through lack of instruction not in design but in techniques for the marketing of their wares.

It is a different story in graphic design. Senior figures such as György Kemény and Sándor Pinczehelyi continue to exemplify the painterly tradition that is characteristic of Hungarian poster making. Even run-of-the-mill billboards such as those portraying Lenin on the anniversary of the Bolshevik revolution are given more formal consideration than their subject matter really demands. The most recent posters, celebrating the transition to democracy and free elections, show a propagandist touch that is lighter than in the Soviet Union and in character with the national ironic sense of humor. In commercial graphics there is less liberty. The corporate identities for Palota, a leatherworks company, and Ibusz, the state travel agency, by József Scherer and György Fekete, are international in the way they play on typographic forms.

In fact, the big state companies have often been the best clients. They have had the proper channels for commissioning designers. Small companies, complacent with their captive market like small companies anywhere, tend not to be able to see what is wrong with what they have. The upshot of this is that the short-term prospects for designers may be poor as their former clients undergo realignment in the new economy. This is not to say that government clients always encourage the best work. Iván Dankánics recalls that when he was asked to design an exhibit stand, his remuneration was by the square meter—"so it pays to use a bad idea many times, instead of one big, powerful idea once." Dankánics has been able to do better work for cultural clients in Austria, where he can gain access to better materials and printing equipment.

Life has been no less limiting for product designers. György Lissák is a rarity in enjoying the best of freelance design work and in-house security. Most of his work is in heavy-duty apparatus for a metallurgical company. Furnace design is everywhere unique to its context, says Lissák. So although the company bought licenses from a British firm, the design was not appropriate. Lissák was free to redesign unsatisfactory details on the original products and, more important, to impose his own aesthetic. He notes that "Hungarian designers are always complaining: '*I* designed something and *they* spoiled it.' That's not the case with these furnaces."

Some low-cost consumer-product fields can support absurdly fierce competition between rival manufacturers. A quite disproportionate amount of design effort is spent on cosmetics, for example. Alexandra Nagy is a leading creator of Hungarian packaging design. Her main client, the Gedeon Richter pharmaceuticals company, has idolized her work by naming two of its shampoo products Alex and Sandra. Resources are limited but Nagy gets round this by using bright colors and ingenious forms. A range of children's bath products, for example, has brightly colored rings that nest around the bottles and clip together, becoming a toy. Although materials are often less than ideal, the German-made tooling is of high quality, and so the form of a container can occasionally be quite intricate, something Nagy exploited in her tongue-in-cheek bottle for export to the Soviet Union, whose top resembled the onion-dome of St. Basil's Cathedral in Moscow. Nagy has designed for Gedeon Richter since 1972, always packaging new products. She recently redesigned an old package for the first time. The event is a significant indication not only of Hungary's growing consumerism but also of one industry's willingness to use design to meet changing demands.

Telephone booth
Tibor Varga, István Tarcsik, Imre
Néder, Antal Hornyák
1984
Photograph by Molnár Géza

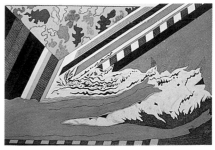

Interior panel for hotel
Polgá Csaba

Cosmetics packaging
Alexandra Nagy/Márta Koós
Gedeon Richter
Photograph by Janos Kovesdi

*An onion-dome cap refers to
local architecture or perhaps
pokes fun at former masters in
Moscow.*

Below: Corporate symbol
József Scherer and György
Fekete
Ibusz Hungarian Travel
Company, 1981

Bottom: Corporate symbol
József Scherer and György
Fekete
Palota Leather Goods, 1984

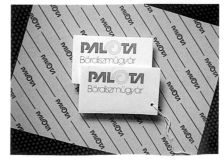

Yugoslavia

"It's not very useful to talk about Yugoslavian design," states Janez Suhadolc, "because the country is so divided into different cultures." More than any other European country, Yugoslavia is courting spontaneous disintegration as its myriad constituent communities seek to reassert their voices in the administrative vacuum that has existed since the death of President Tito in 1980.

Among Yugoslavia's republics, Slovenia has been the most forthright in expressing itself. Just before Christmas 1990, its two million people voted overwhelmingly to become an independent state. Yugoslavia as a whole has always been a somewhat artificial creation. The country only coalesced after the First World War and was held together under Tito's comparatively liberal brand of communism. Yugoslavs are paying for that liberalism now. Their country bypassed Eastern Europe's revolution in 1989 to remain one of the few that is still notionally communist. It has its full measure of the economic problems that this political condition so often implies.

The breakup is occurring along historical fault lines. The richest republics, Slovenia and Croatia in the north and Bosnia in central Yugoslavia, fell within the boundaries of the Austro-Hungarian Empire. They are comparatively wealthy as well as liberal in outlook and are pushing for independence from Serbia and the south, which was once under Ottoman rule. Slovenes resent Serbian dominance and would rather ally themselves once again with richer countries to the north. The mayor of Ljubljana would like to be able to call his city the Salzburg of Yugoslavia (or Slovenia). It is uncertain whether the Yugoslavian centrifuge will stop at a Swiss-style federation or go whirring on to full-blown secession.

Suhadolc is an architect and designer and a teacher at the design school in the Slovenian capital of Ljubljana, one of two national schools. The other is in the national and Serbian capital Belgrade. Most industrial designers have not been to these schools; instead, like their peers in neighboring Italy, they have backgrounds in architecture. Graphic design has been enlivened by Yugoslavs returning from schools abroad in places as politically and stylistically distinct as Poland and Italy.

Product design since the Second World War has been generally dull, though perhaps less dire than in some other places in Eastern Europe. "Design in Yugoslavia was certainly heavily under control of the ideology of so-called self-managing socialism," says Suhadolc. "But compared to that in the Eastern bloc,

Janez Suhadolc's furniture echoes the Slovenian Baroque style of the architect Jože Plečnik.

Anton chair
Janez Suhadolc
1988

Josef chair
Janez Suhadolc
1990

Typewriter
Selma Arnautovic
Unis Dizajn, 1990

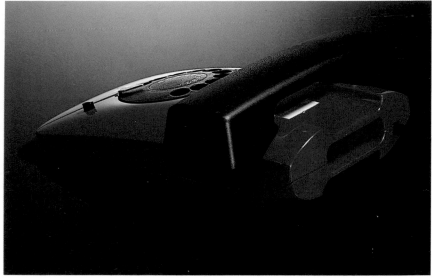

Telephone
Davorin Savnik
Iskra

Furniture, such as "American Colonial," is one of Yugoslavia's principal exports but the country also has a thriving avant-garde.

Pyropos chair
Boštjan Debelak
1990

Hieronimus chair
Boštjan Debelak
1990

Sixtus chair
Janez Suhadolc
1988

Corporate symbol
Borivoje Ljubicic
Mediterranean City
Games, Split, 1979

Wine labels
Mateje Rodici
Progresexport

Lok armchair
Branko Ursic
Stol, 1988

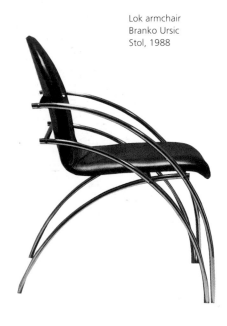

Vhutemas armchair
Oleg Hržić
Artresor, 1985

*Hržić's furniture makes eclectic
references to design trends in
both Eastern and Western blocs
reflecting the dual training and
outlook of many Yugoslav
designers.*

it was quite remote from the hard-core communist norms."

The most praised consumer product to come from Yugoslavia in recent years has been a telephone designed by Davorin Savnik for the communications company Iskra in the late 1970s. The design was promptly copied by many manufacturers, though no benefits accrued to Savnik, Iskra, or Yugoslav design. The product can be read as an object lesson in the country's political history and geography. It is ostensibly a functionalist design, suggestive of Germanic design values. Yet its gentle convex form is curved in a more elaborate manner than is really necessary. In combination with its bright color, the shape hints at the proximity of Italy. Both influences would have been present in Slovenia and the other northern provinces of Yugoslavia from the time when they fell within the boundaries of the Austro-Hungarian empire. Sadly, the telephone is a far-from-typical piece of design. Few products of any excellence can survive both the lack of consumer spending power and legislation that until recently restricted companies' use of external design consultants.

Much of the interest in Yugoslav design centers on the furniture industry. Yugoslavia exports traditional furniture, much of it cheap "colonial style" pieces for the American market. These are manufactured in huge plants, mainly in Serbia, rather than in anything like the small but versatile workshops that encourage experiment by avant-garde designers in Italy. Each factory employs thousands of people, including its own in-house designers, but their contribution is simply to fit reproduction styles from all periods and countries into their manufacturing regimen.

Designers seeking to develop new forms in furniture get a poor response from these companies. The craftsmen exist to produce new work economically, but there are laws—overdue for change, say designers—that offer no incentive for small series production. Meanwhile, a number of designers are prolific in their creation of prototypes that show the new potential. Freed from much likelihood for production of their own work, independent designers have opted to explore the rich rather than the austere side of the Austro-Hungarian heritage. In the past, the architect Jože Plečnik, a pupil of the Viennese Otto Wagner, created distinctive buildings in what came to be known as the Slovenian style. He is enjoying a revival now, and the designs of Suhadolc and of Boštjan Debelak, a generation younger, are partly in homage to that style.

Postmodernism in general appears to have been warmly welcomed, especially in the Croatian capital Zagreb, where there is much new building. Here, Oleg Hržić brazenly mixes many elements, from Egyptian art and archaeology to Memphis, in his furniture for local galleries and private houses. The designs are mostly one-of-a-kind, but he recently had a commission for seven hundred auditorium seats. Now Hržić is confident that the move to a more industrial scale is coming within reach.

Like many Yugoslavs, Hržić studied in Moscow as well as in his native country. The teaching was predominantly in the Beaux-Arts tradition, but the influence of one teacher, who had been one of the pioneers of Russian Constructivism, also rubbed off, although at that time, during the Brezhnev era, Constructivism was still dangerous stuff. The constructed quality of Hržić's furniture is often what characterizes his work amid a sequence of references, quotations, and in-jokes based on everything from Empire styles to De Stijl to pop art.

Hržić's group, Artresor, an affiliation of a sculptor, a painter, two graphic designers, and two architects, was one of the first to be established under new laws passed in 1989 that permit independent consultancy. Ljubljana and Zagreb are the favored cities. There were no early groups setting up in Belgrade.

Hommage à Zig-zag chair
Oleg Hržić
Artresor, 1986

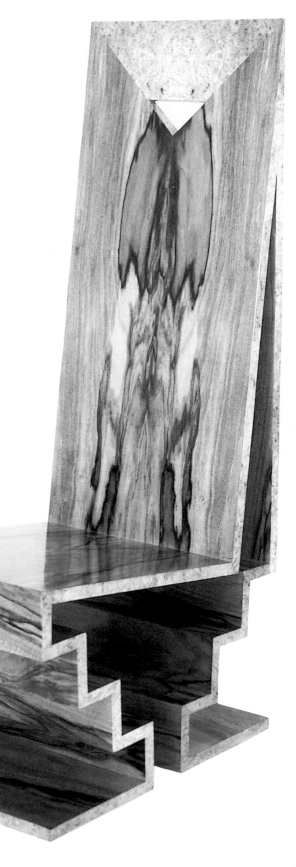

Russia

Arbat Square in Moscow is the most expensive property on the board of the Soviet version of the game "Monopoly" introduced to the country in 1988. It is also the home of the once government-run, but now privatized, Society of Soviet Designers. It would be wrong, however, to deduce from the smart address of this institution that design is accorded any great importance within the Soviet Union as it grows to embrace capitalism.

What design is and should be is itself subject to some confusion during the faltering transition instigated by Soviet President Mikhail Gorbachev's perestroika. According to Dmitri Azrikan, one of a small but growing band of freelance designers, "It must be admitted that there are two trends in design in this country: 'real' design, finding its expression in mass production, and 'professional' design, which mostly remains on paper." There are proponents of both trends, but it will take many more years of glasnost and perestroika before they begin to merge to permit the creation of articles that have a quality people feel proud to call "Soviet." It is quite another matter whether, by that time, the adjective "Soviet" will have any positive connotation itself.

For the moment, it is the former type of design that dominates, as Simon Krupin, another independent designer, explains: "Design in my country has a strict difference from that in a country with a normal economy. Where there is a lack of products of any kind, no matter how bad their design or quality, there will be no producers interested in design. On the other hand, our industry was condemned by government decision to make use of design because 'it should be there.' It is there, okay, but as a mere formality. No wonder the result is often poor in idea, bad in quality, and inappropriate in material and technology."

The blame for this can be laid at the door of the government ministries. It was the centralized economy that decreed that a radio produced in the Latvian capital Riga would be identical to a radio produced in the Armenian capital Yerevan, for example. "The only difference," says Azrikan cynically, "was that the radio produced in Riga was made more carefully." Although Moscow is the country's cultural center, it is also the center of officialdom. As a result, design practice and teaching in Moscow is the most conservative in the country.

Away from Moscow and its ministries, attempts are being made to reflect regional character in an atmosphere of gathering nationalism from the various Soviet republics. Leningrad (now rechristened St. Petersburg), perhaps the most European city in the Soviet Union, looks to German and Italian design for its model. The Baltic republics try to imitate the Scandinavians. There is more oriental luxury in the ceramics, textiles, furniture, and domestic utensils from the Transcaucasian republics. In the heart of the Russian Republic, design teaching at the Sverdlovsk Architectural Institute has taken a lead in the synthesis of Russian Constructivism with current trends in Western design.

With many of the republics assuming varying degrees of independence, the expression of cultural identity is bound to become more important. Finer distinctions will emerge. Estonia, Latvia, and Lithuania are often lumped together as the Baltic republics. Though the three have in common the fact that they played little part in the Bolshevik uprising of 1917, they had very different histories up to that point. Latvia and Estonia were ruled from Sweden in the sixteenth and seventeenth centuries and were later allied with Russian-controlled Finland. Lithuania shares a strong Roman Catholic tradition with neighboring Poland. Estonia and Latvia remain the wealthiest republics in the Union, though they lag well behind the Scandinavian countries with which they choose to compare themselves. Lithuania was a great power in the Middle Ages but fell behind when it was subsumed into the Russian Empire. To the south, the Ottoman influence was strong in Armenia, Georgia, and Azerbaijan until 1914. These differences may grow in importance if and when the republics succeed in building substantial export markets. The label "Made in the USSR" could be regarded with distaste. Branding products according to the republic of their manufacture could well have greater appeal to Western consumers.

Yuri Soloviev expects the new Soviet design first to imitate Western ideas but then gradually to become more locally inspired. The peripatetic Soloviev has long been the figurehead of official Soviet design. A former president of the Society of Soviet Designers and of the International Council of Societies of Industrial Design, he is also a powerful political figure with a seat on the Supreme Soviet. "I believe in national design," says Soloviev. "Our way of living is different from the Western way of living. We shouldn't use other cultures for our products. Our country has many different republics with different clients, each with a great culture. It is foolish to insist that people who live in the southern republics should use the design that is convenient in our Baltic republics."

A cornerstone of Soviet design has been the widely respected USSR Research Institute of Industrial Design. The institute is based in Moscow and has ten regional offices around the country, which offer

Electric razors
Tatiana Samoilova

There is no shortage of inventiveness among a younger generation of designers in the Soviet republics. Clients, customers, and raw materials are, however, in short supply.

Top: Electronic office systems furniture
Studio Azrikan
1990

Bottom: Structura television
Studio Azrikan

Right: Project for an airline booking terminal
Studio Azrikan
Aeroflot, 1989

Portable radio
Vladimir Telyakov

Briz hair dryer
Studio Azrikan

Clock
Tatiana Samoilova

ER-200 express train
Photograph by Yuri
Belindski/Fotokhronika, courtesy
TASS

Ohta concept automobile
Automotor Research
Laboratory, Leningrad, 1988
Photograph by V. Lozovsky/
Fotokhronika, courtesy TASS

*Train design of a former
generation echoes that in the
U.S., the other superpower of
continental proportions, while
more recent automobile
projects show an awareness of
new trends.*

Opposite: Apparel
V. Zaitsev, 1989
Photograph by V. Yatsina/
Fotokhronika, courtesy TASS

*Fashion designs by the "Soviet
Lacroix" are way beyond the
reach of most citizens.*

designers the chance to work under supervision on projects that are more interesting than those available in industry but also less likely to be realized. Deputy director Vladimir Munipov claims his institute, known by its initials, VNIITE, laid the groundwork for perestroika and pioneered ergonomic design within the Soviet Union. But the evidence of the condition of Soviet design from its more outspoken designers suggests that both Munipov and Soloviev are whistling in the dark.

"Monopoly" may have arrived in Soviet stores, but the substitution of capitalism for communism—if, indeed, that is the desirable course—is hardly so simple. It is almost impossible for Westerners to appreciate how alien the idea of a free market of competing products made by different manufacturers for profit can seem to people brought up under a state-run closed economy. There is much discussion now of how to promote the consumption of goods under a free-market system but also of how to reconcile this with the essentially Socialist wish to meet the needs of all in the community irrespective of their means. The Soviet government's aim, stated in 1987, is to double personal wealth by the end of the century and to treble consumer-goods production. But few want to achieve this miracle of capitalism if it means losing the social ideals of communism.

Already, tales abound of the sheer confusion that has struck the thousands of businesses that have been given their freedom but do not know what to do with it. People who were called managers but who in fact were little more than clerks in charge of their quota now have to manage for real. Cooper Woodring, an American designer who toured the Soviet Union on a fact-finding study in 1988, tells the story of an ashtray "factory" that used to get a weekly visit from the official truck that would drop off supplies of the product for local distribution. One day a government official announced that the truck would not be coming any more. Showing initiative rare enough in any country, the factory manager promptly sought out an industrial designer to help him determine what he could and should be making now that he had the freedom to choose. As Woodring tells it, it was the designer who was at a loss in this case, because he, too, was used to being told what to design.

Of more immediate concern are the shortages—of equipment, of materials, and of manpower. Basic high-tech tools such as computers are in desperately short supply. Soloviev estimates that the Soviet Union, with only three major design schools (one in Moscow, one in Leningrad, and the third in the Ukraine) and the ten VNIITE institutes, has one-tenth of the designers it needs. Against this can be set the potential benefit that Soviet designers span a range

of talents, with individuals turning their hands from tractors one day to apparel the next. The Soviet notion of design is both broader and narrower than the Western one: It is broader in that it includes more disciplines; it is narrower because it is seen as a purely aesthetic exercise, largely overlooking issues of safety, convenience, comfort, and affordability—all, it hardly need be said, matters in need of urgent attention.

The few industrial designers who do emerge from the education system face a stark career choice. Work in industry is beset by the lack of current technology, and this is said, in turn, to impair creativity. The VNIITE offices are better equipped, but projects remain mostly theoretical. The third, and increasingly viable, course is to abandon official design and struggle as an independent artist, retaining one's creative freedom but with little or no prospect of finding clients. The industrial designers who choose this path are often graduates of architectural schools rather than those who have passed through VNIITE. The prospects are little better for graphic designers. They are less constrained in their work but until recently faced an array of frugal official tariffs for their services.

Now that designers are better able to set their own agenda, what will be their prescription for the future? Will perestroika —which means reconstruction—lead to a Reconstructivist style? This might seem a naïve visitor's question, but there are indeed signs of such a revival of interest in the art and design of the Russian Constructivists. Alexei Koshchelev, curator of a 1987 exhibition of Soviet design at the Design Center in Stuttgart, Germany, remarked on the prevalence of the colors red, white, and black in the new work. The same colors have surfaced in recent fashion designs, such as a Spring 1990 "Perestroika collection," which take their place alongside the peasant prints, embroidered waistcoats, and long, full skirts that come out of a different cultural tradition.

The repossession by today's young designers of the art of this period has some logic to it. According to Azrikan, "the provincialism of Soviet design today was caused by a long period of isolation of our country both from Western and from Russian culture. For many years Constructivism was officially considered pernicious for the development of 'Socialist' culture and 'Socialist realism.'" Now that Constructivism is no longer proscribed, it becomes the obvious cultural source, while the very fact that it was once proscribed makes it all the more attractive as a symbol of the new creative freedom. Its influence alongside other prerevolutionary styles is apparent in new art and in posters. Graphic designer Lev Evzovich says: "There is no one style of perestroika. There are many different styles, with influences from the West and from the past. The Soviet avant-garde in painting now know Constructivist theory. I don't think that there will be Western 'deconstructivism' but a kind of 'neoconstructivism.'" Others find Constructivism too obvious and too tainted. "It is only a fashionable dress on the corpse of totalitarianism," says Andrew Meschaninov of MAD Studio in Leningrad.

Russian Constructivism centered on one institution, Vkhutemas (an acronym for the Higher Artistic and Technical Studios), which was an approximate equivalent of the Bauhaus and an influence upon it. Running from 1920 until 1934, it was more or less contemporary with the German school but had less opportunity to exert a lasting influence on design practice. During the 1920s, in the aftermath of the Russian Revolution and civil war, industrial skills in the Soviet Union were inferior to those in Germany, and Stalin was more successful in suppressing and containing the Vkhutemas teaching than was Hitler at the Bauhaus.

It seems ironic to find today's designers harking back to Alexander Rodchenko and others whose ideas were developed in collusion with Marxist theory during the bright dawn of the communist era that is now being dismantled. Some Soviet painters are choosing to bypass this period and recall instead the prerevolutionary art of painters such as the Russian-born Marc Chagall. However, it was only when Constructivism became distorted into the orthodoxy of Socialist Realism that it became discredited.

In product design, it is in any case the philosophy behind Constructivism that could prove relevant and not the style that, stripped of its context, is so readily and pointlessly imitated in the West. According to Azrikan, "The most valuable achievement of Vkhutemas was not material objects such as furniture, lamps, clothes, and workers' clubhouses and hostels, but methods of student teaching of art subjects based on deep penetration and understanding of materials used for the creation of this or that construction." The crux of Constructivist philosophy was its analytical treatment of the design process. This was articulated in the equivalence of formal and material components—line, plane, color as well as wood, steel, glass, etc.—whether in two or three dimensions. The approach generated objects that were suited to a variety of purposes and that made the most of modest means. Vladimir Tatlin proposed clothing made up of parts that could be added on or taken away to suit the country's climatic variations. He and Rodchenko pioneered the design of low-cost furniture for self-assembly.

In the 1920s, state industry and private enterprise coexisted. Rodchenko and the poet Vladimir Mayakovski worked together, effectively serving as

Above: Poster
M. Mazrukho
1989
Photograph courtesy Victoria
and Albert Museum

Left: Poster
V. Vdovin
1989
Photograph by V. Koshevoi/
Fotokhronika, courtesy TASS

"Party" poster
Y. Leonov
1990

the advertising agency for the state. But as the decade matured, the communist party regarded the artistic avant-garde with increasing distrust, and the Constructivists' proletarian monuments were duly superseded by Stalin's grandiose architecture. The Constructivists' way of looking at materials and construction has long been absent from design-school curricula.

With glasnost somewhat more advanced than perestroika, it is understandable that this new expression is appearing sooner in fields that do not depend on industrial production. Yet even here, work is of limited relevance to the general population. "In the last few years, there has been considerable progress in graphic and fashion design, including successes at shows in Europe and the United States, but unfortunately, within the USSR these achievements are not put into practice and are unknown to the public," comments Azrikan. Slava Zaitsev, for example, has been called the Soviet Christian Lacroix and has proved a hit in Paris and New York as well as Moscow. Although he claims Cardin, Givenchy, and Balenciaga as inspirations, he, too, makes generous use of Constructivist reds and grays. And while his coats sell for 300 rubles (then $600 at official exchange rates), Zaitsev had the temerity to tell *Paris Match* that Russian women have the means to afford his work.

Recent competitions for posters in celebration of perestroika betray a rather unsuccessful combination of Constructivist nostalgia and ham-handed propagandist narrative, a hand-me-down from more recent memory. An example by V. Vdovin shows a ten-ruble note with the officially discredited Brezhnev's head in place of Lenin's and a bold diagonal banner proclaiming *Corruption* laid over it. Another, by L. Kaushansky, shows a collage of graphic images from the Stalin era being consumed in fire from the dictator's famous pipe with a roll call of executed innocents appearing in the black space left by the fire.

These examples are not inspiring. It is even harder for architects and industrial designers to evoke Russia's heroic past. In 1990 there were less than a score of design studios in Moscow and only a sprinkling in the provincial cities. Yuri Avvakumov is one of a number of young architects who are looking back to Constructivism, as the name of his Agitarch Studio, set up in 1988, implies. He uses elements of that style to provide an ironic commentary on the present-day situation. Educated at Moscow's Architectural Institute, Avvakumov was a leading participant in the "Paper Architecture" movement, a term he coined to describe the conceptual design that he and his frustrated peers produced during the 1980s.

Other posters paradoxically reuse stylistic devices associated with the now discredited communist revolution.

Left: "Sakharov" poster
Boris Efimov
1990

Below: "Cooperation" poster
A. Kondurov
1989

Above: Poster
V. Arseyenkov
1988

Right: "Confrontation" poster
V. Vdovin
1990

Wristwatch
Simon Krupin
VNIITE, 1985

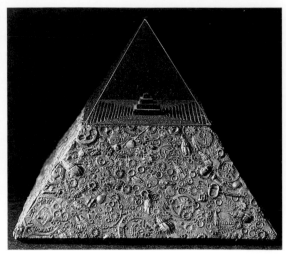

Clock
Simon Krupin
VNIITE, 1986

Far left: Sewing machine
Tatiana Samoilova/Yevgeny
Mongayt

Left: Car radio
Vladimir Telyakov

Far left: Car radio
Vladimir Telyakov

Left: Bracelet
Vladimir Telyakov

*Some designers are beginning
to exploit the aesthetic of the
Soviet military manufacturing
machine in consumer products.*

Simon Krupin established his DA Studio in Leningrad a year later, having mainly worked on projects for VNIITE, aiming to humanize watches and clocks. Krupin seeks to transform the traditionally robust, almost militaristic, accessories into "enigmatic objects, symbols, signs, points of meditation." Vladimir Telyakov, a former radio engineer in Moscow, is keen to bring about a similar meeting of industrial technology and human emotional response with his studies for radios and various portable accessories that have a touchable, chunky articulation to them. Both designers bring out qualities not usually associated with the solid construction of these objects. They have exchanged the negative response to something that looks heavy and militaristic for the positive response to something that appears precious, tactile, and personal, like jewelry. These are theoretical projects, but they are nevertheless instructive for their indication of the possibilities offered as manufacturers begin to switch from military to consumer-goods production.

Dmitri Azrikan is a more traditional designer, making use of contacts at VNIITE and the Society of Soviet Designers. But even good connections have little effect. Studio Azrikan stepped in when Aeroflot, the state airline, backed out of commissioning a new corporate identity from a Western firm, unwilling to pay for the work in hard currency. Azrikan expanded the program to show Aeroflot the possibilities of going beyond a simple image makeover. He devised a semiprivate reservations booth that would make the bureaucratic process of booking a flight more tolerable. But without competition, Aeroflot could see no reason to try so hard to attract customers and aborted the project.

The experience is a bitter reminder of the real world. While Yuri Soloviev, who has seen more than most of Soviet reality, holds out the ultimate prospect for the emergence of national and regional styles, he offers a much more austere vision for the immediate future. Soloviev turns the spotlight on the West and its wastefulness. An average home might have ten loudspeakers spread between its various televisions, radios, and music equipment, he complains. A recent Soviet design integrates all these audio functions and makes do with just the necessary two speakers. A more convoluted example of modular ingenuity can be seen in a VNIITE project for a child's plastic tricycle that comes apart to comprise a series of gardening implements. The Ohta-Nami car, an experimental seven-seater auto designed by D. Parfenov and others at the Prospective Models Laboratory of the Automotive Research Institute in Leningrad, is also reconfigurable, with seats that swivel and a table and bunks that fold away, allowing it to be used as a family bus or as a mobile home.

It is arguable how useful some of these two-in-one designs are, but in spirit they are close to the principles set forth by Tatlin and Rodchenko.

It is here that the past can inform solutions to present difficulties. Constructivism aimed to construct realities. The new realities of lack of money and resources demand a systems approach to design, according to Soloviev, so that goods may be produced using modular assembly to meet the needs of markets young and old, northern and southern, within the huge territory of the Soviet Union.

"Red galley"
Yuri Avvakumov/Sergey Podyomshchikov
1989

Constructivism has inspired projects among a community of paper architects. The movement's precepts could prove of more general use to a design profession confronted with materials shortages and clumsy mass-manufacturing.

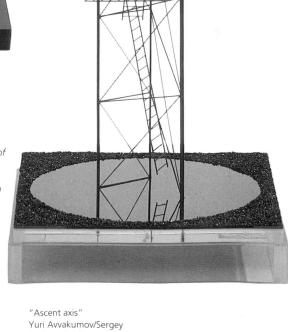

"Ascent axis"
Yuri Avvakumov/Sergey Podyomshchikov
1990

Toothpaste packaging
Colgate Palmolive (Egypt)

Arabic script is often brutally distorted to appear as close as possible to Western companies' identities.

The Egyptian designer who is inclined to sift through the past in search of inspiration suffers an embarrassment of riches. Whereas a European or an American will seldom pause to look back more than a hundred years, the Egyptian cannot escape the weight of fully five thousand years of national cultural history.

The reign of the Pharaohs lasted more than two thousand years, until 341 B.C., but Pharaonic imagery abounds today thanks mainly to the tourist industry. There is a certain amount of sheepish pretense among serious designers when they draw upon such distant sources, but Pharaonic culture does have the virtue of being wholly and exclusively Egyptian. For a country whose people have not had control of their destiny for much of the time since the invasion of Alexander the Great until the present century, there is more relevance in this ancient history than outsiders might at first wish to ascribe to it.

Independent Egypt today must balance several images of itself. On the one hand, Egypt considers itself a foremost member of the "Arab nation," an informal confederation of all Arab states. When it suits, however, Egypt can distance itself from its Arab brothers by invoking its Pharaonic past. For these reasons, suggests Shakwy Abd El-Hafez, who is preparing a doctoral thesis on cultural identity in Egyptian design, "the concept of 'national character' is a favorite one in Egypt. The concept of *qawmi'ya* —it means 'nationalism'—is an elastic one. The nationalism could be understood as Egyptian, or as Arabic, or as Islamic." In key expressions of national identity it is important to make a show of this balance. Hence, Egyptian paper money shows hieroglyphics on one side and Islamic buildings and patterns on the other, and the tomb of the unknown soldier, designed by Samy Rafi, combines Islamic calligraphy with a pyramidal form.

Successive waves of foreign domination brought with them new cultures which are remembered with varying degrees of affection. Arab culture was assimilated and fused with the prevailing Coptic Christian arts. As the Arab influence grew, Coptic motifs from nature were gradually stylized (Islam all but forbids representational designs) to become geometric patterns. The Ottoman influence from more than three centuries of Turkish rule is shunned, but a Napoleonic interlude of just three years has left a lasting fondness for the French decorative arts. The affluent districts of Cairo sport apartment blocks in exuberant Art Nouveau and Art Deco styles. Craftsmen in the workshops in Cairo's Khan El-Khalily bazaar busily fashion ornate gilt furniture in a

style some people mockingly refer to as "Louis Farouk" after the profligate King Farouk who ruled Egypt until Nasser's revolution in 1952.

According to Hafez, "there are two relevant stages in the development of Egyptian art and design." The first period ranges from the end of the nineteenth century until the Second World War and includes Farouk's reign; the second came with the beginning of Nasser's régime. When Gamal Nasser came to power, it was with a dream of Egypt as a triple leader—of Africa, of the Arab countries, and of the Islamic world. In addition, Egypt has, since the visit of Napoleon around the year 1800, felt itself closer in spirit to Europe than have other Arab countries. Yet Egypt's exploitation of its position at the crossroads of three continents has been haphazard. In general, the political influence that Egypt gained during Nasser's rule was not mirrored by any rise of its cultural influence (with the exception of its filmmaking industry, which serves the entire Arab world). In other fields, an exodus of human talent led to a deterioration in cultural life.

The imposition of a planned economy and rapid industrialization impoverished the local artifact culture. In the bazaars, aluminum pots and pans now hang alongside brass ones, the indirect output of a massive Soviet-financed aluminum plant near Luxor. The hammered and patterned brass containers that once were both useful and beautiful are now sold only to tourists. Egyptians buy the cheaper aluminum articles, which no one has thought to embellish. Arabic calligraphy is also at risk. The presence of international brands such as Coca-Cola and Colgate is one factor contributing to this loss of skill. The Arabic versions of these logotypes warp the lettering to resemble as closely as possible the type style chosen for the brand symbols in Roman letters.

Some traditional techniques are being adapted to new markets. The National Art Development Institute of Mashrabeya makes traditional intricate wooden *moucharaby* screens. Once used for doors and windows, in which role they were both functional (excluding excess light) and decorative, they are now purely ornamental, being used for tabletops and other items of furniture. "The patterns are traditional. The rules are standard. The usage is the new thing," says the institute's Nawal El-Messiri. The tradition of geometric inlay work survives, but it does so by making use of new materials, for example strips of white PVC in place of the bone that historically provides a white contrast with dark wood inlays.

The combination of traditional and modern techniques is a matter that preoccupies Mosaad El-Kadi, who established the industrial design department at the Helwan University Faculty of Applied

Moucharaby screens
National Art Development
Institute of Mashrabeya

*Egyptian currency reflects the
wish both to signal membership
of the Arab world and to
indicate faithfulness to a unique
Pharaonic past.*

Vase
Samir el Gundi store

Logotype
Montasser Moneim
Al-Fahd Travel Agent

Telephone prototype
Sayed Abdou

*This telephone makes an
abstraction of the Islamic
crescent moon shape.*

Baby stroller
Montasser Moneim

Arts in Cairo. "We must have a national character like Japanese or German or English design. If only we can take something from the Islamic style and adapt it in a new way," he says.

Egypt has three fine-art schools, but the Faculty of Applied Arts is reputed to be the only design school in the Arab world. It is natural that it should be located in Cairo, traditionally the intellectual hub of the Arab world as well as the most developed manufacturing economy in the region. The school's 1,200 students specialize in interior, textile, and graphic design and photography. But the industrial design department is by far the smallest, reflecting the low demand for designers in local industry.

Despite pressing practical problems, Kadi believes students can be taught to synthesize modern techniques and local design traditions. The Faculty of Applied Arts has few illusions about the difficulty of the task that lies ahead. A recent conference on its campus sought to enlighten industry and show them what designers could do for them. The faculty maintains a studio that, in the absence of many independent design practices, takes on work for commercial clients. All faculty and student work exhibited is on offer to potential clients, and there are plans to open a permanent public design center.

Despite the efforts of the school and of the Ministry of Culture to promote Pharaonic art and Arab culture at various times, there remains, says Hafez, "a big gap between these notions and the reality of design in Egypt." Montasser Moneim, recently returned to Cairo after studying at Art Center Europe in Switzerland, confirms this picture. He found no industrial design consultancies in the city and promptly established a studio "to promote myself as an industrial designer in the proper meaning of the words." He quickly found that clients asked for corporate identity and packaging design, because it was their understanding that anybody calling himself a designer should offer these services. Subcontracted by a large advertising agency, for example, Moneim proposed a new identity for Egyptair based on a student project in which he had adapted the current Horus god figure into the streamlined appearance typical of Art Center work. Reasoning that Singapore Airlines had successfully capitalized on a stereotypical national costume for its female crews, Moneim also suggested flight attendant uniforms adapted straight from costumes depicted in Pharaonic reliefs. The airline accepted a safer proposal, perhaps because the Pharaonic designs proved incompatible with contemporary Arab requirements for modesty in dress. Amr Helmy

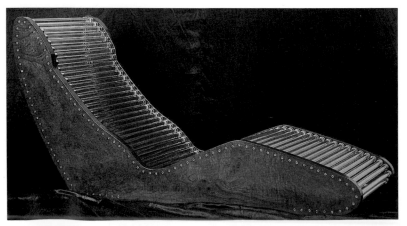

Chaise longue
Montasser Moneim
1990

is a contemporary of Moneim. "I cannot name ten designers in Egypt," he complains, adding that it is perhaps because he and Moneim are from rich families that they can afford the luxury of being designers ahead of their time.

Frustrated by the lack of three-dimensional work in Egypt, Moneim has recently started putting his own furniture designs into production. "There is a problem doing this in Egypt—the quality and finish and the understanding of the workers. They start arguing when you change what they have always done. It's a big problem to make them put aside what they used to do and do something new." Helmy designs and sells kitchen units, working from a studio with two assistants and two Macintosh computers. Like many young people, Helmy and Moneim feel the baroque French style, tainted by Ottoman favor as well as by the patronage of King Farouk, belongs to a previous generation. They want to create work in the modern idiom yet still retain elements of the Egyptian. "This renewal of modern classicism in Europe—Mario Botta does it, though most people don't appreciate it—we must do that here," says Helmy. With this in mind, he recently added a kitchen in the Nubian style to his range. His aim was to treat the various cabinets like the elevations of village houses. The final product is unexpected, but on second thoughts perhaps no more so than the "country style" kitchens sold by European retailers. What is more problematic is the prohibitive cost of these designs to all but the very richest buyers.

A good precedent for what Helmy is doing exists in the architecture of Hassan Fat'hy. Many Arab architects have taken up where Fat'hy left off, with mixed results. The Egyptians Gamal Bakry and Abdel Wahed El Wakil are among his inheritors. Fat'hy's work is much admired outside Egypt, where it is seen as an Egyptian vernacular. To Egyptians, however, Fat'hy's buildings transplant elements of Nubian architecture from the Sudan and Upper Egypt into homes for the rich in the Cairene suburbs. Critics point out that Fat'hy's low-cost housing has been no more successful than the International Style projects he opposed. The value of Fat'hy's ideas is less a matter of the genuineness of his vernacular style than of the combination of appropriate function with traditional form. By using thick-walled mud construction in place of concrete blocks, Fat'hy can better protect his buildings against heat gain. His understanding of the flow of air acquired from Nubian desert buildings also enables him to design cool interiors. The functional improvements do much to validate the appearance of the architecture. In their product and furniture design, Helmy and his peers have yet to achieve this union of function and traditional form.

Above: Arrousa chest
Amr Helmy Designs

Left: Shenbo bookcase
Amr Helmy Designs

Nubian style kitchen
Amr Helmy Designs

Helmy uses elements of Nubian style in fitted kitchens much as Hassan Fat'hy used them in architecture.

India

The first day of Diwali, an important Hindu festival. Frenzied pipes and drums. Truck after orange truck clatters past. Through the kaleidoscopic crowd appears the source of the noise—not pipes these days but a child sitting on the back of one of the trucks, calmly twiddling a synthesizer that has been hooked up to a more-than-adequate loudspeaker.

The colors are even louder. People throw dye, a hot pink explosion with each handful of dust. And, at the Industrial Design Centre in Bombay, even the machine tools in the model shop are splashed with color, consecrated as for many occasions with a pinch of pink, a pinch of black, and an orange chrysanthemum.

Two days later, a Muslim festival. The clamor as before, but now the trucks are all green.

Well over two thousand years ago, India accepted Buddhism into the prevailing Hindu religion, adapting it to its needs and wishes. Much later, Islam arrived on the subcontinent. India accepted that, too. During the artistic renaissance of the Mughal empire, Muslim and Hindu traditions fused to produce a great flowering of the decorative arts. Later still, the British empire ruled the country. Britain did little for the local arts but left behind the English language, the Industrial Revolution, an education system, and a bureaucracy. India accepted them all. "With the Mughals and the British, new things became part of our culture," says designer Suresh Sethi. "India *accepts.*"

When India's second wave of industrialization came in the decades after independence in 1947, it was at the height of the West's dream of a technological future. India did not wish to be left out. At the same time, more and more Indians were growing up in urban surroundings. With a willing government and populace, the Western idea of progress took hold; it was only much later that people stopped to consider what might be at risk from this headlong rush into the future. "Here, where industrialization happened quickly, we have lost the sort of qualities that still provide a cultural distinction between various European products," says Nadkarni Sudhakar, founder of the Industrial Design Centre.

Design was part of the package of development assistance. This created a situation in which, when the time came to revise the design of an original product, that, too, would require an influx of foreign expertise and equipment. An understandable resistance to change arose, the clearest evidence of which is the paucity of car models, mostly of ancient design—the Premier, for example, based on a 1960s' Fiat, and its grander companion, the Ambassador, an even older bulbous British model. Import controls conspired to insulate such antiquated "domestic" products from more contemporary competitors.

Another consequence of technology-led development was that the technology on offer was Western technology and not always appropriate to Indian needs. It became possible to make television sets but not basic articles for agriculture or health care. India's designers say this paradox still holds. Some of them hope for a national design council that would direct funds toward these worthy but uncommercial projects, but the government has so far resisted pressure to set one up, pleading shortage of funds.

The chances that this kind of beneficent design will receive serious attention now appear to be on the wane. During the 1980s, economic growth was running at 8 percent per year. The closed economy is slowly being opened up to permit the import both of finished products and of components for local manufacture. Accompanied by the mushrooming of India's middle class, this has led to a shift in priorities as former Prime Minister Rajiv Gandhi diverted development resources away from heavy industry toward consumer goods. The hand-painted billboards that used to promise alluring new products "Soon" or portrayed them "For information purposes only" are gradually disappearing.

At the moment, many products are made locally using basic components or designs licensed from Western companies. The Tata conglomerate, for example, makes Mercedes-designed trucks in one of its companies and Siemens-designed telephones in another. For both types of product, moves are underway to come up with successors that use local design, technology, and manufacturing. Tooling is often acquired secondhand for an old product with a proven record—a similar approach to that pursued so successfully by Japan several decades ago—because the high cost of bank loans in India limits investment in new manufacturing equipment and at the same time dictates a need to bring products to market as fast as possible.

This is the practical world of Indian design. On the ivory campuses of India's two principal design

Right: Motor scooter
Bajaj

Below: Tatamobile 206 van and SE1210/42 truck
Tata Engineering and Locomotive Company

The Tata conglomerate makes many products adapted from Western models to Indian needs. This truck, for example, has a Punjab-type aluminum load body but a badge very similar to that of Daimler-Benz, with which the manufacturer has links.

Right: Gas stove
S. Balaram
Indian Oil Corporation

Below: Durries
Madhurima Patni
Bhowmick/B.M. Anand/Mahesh
Borse
Development Commissioner,
Handlooms, New Delhi

Logotype
Yeshwant Chaudhary
Design Education Seminar

Logotype
Yeshwant Chaudhary
Dyaneshwar Vidyapeeth

तयाचा वेलु गेला गगनावरी ।

Right: Billboard
The Independent, 1990

*Some designers, such as
Yeshwant Chaudhary, combine
elements of local calligraphy
with Swiss Modernism.
Elsewhere, designs slavishly
follow Western models with
no adaptation.*

Annual report cover with
logotype
Yeshwant Chaudhary
Industrial Credit and Investment
Corporation of India

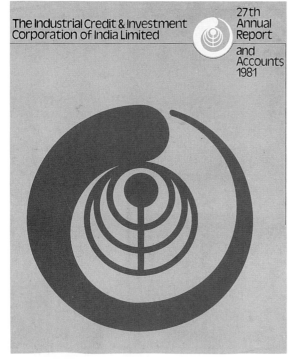

The Industrial Credit & Investment
Corporation of India Limited

27th
Annual
Report
and
Accounts
1981

schools—the Industrial Design Centre, part of Bombay's Indian Institute of Technology, and the National Institute of Design in Ahmedabad—there appears to be some distaste for this expediency but also confusion as to what might represent a suitable alternative. The schools were founded in the 1960s, built in an arcadian late International Style to preach the gospel of international Modernism. Latterly, both schools have come to realize that something was amiss, that perhaps they were betraying their own culture.

No one has undergone this Damascene conversion more abruptly than Kirti Trivedi, a professor at the Industrial Design Centre. Formerly persuaded of the value of universal Modernism, he is now trying—and, by his own admission, often failing—to create products with local identity. In a formal sense, there is little to go on. Trivedi points to the Centre's library, with its lamentable section on Indian arts. But outside there is inspiration—in the colors, in the devices such as decorative framing that are used to give objects significance, and in the complexity of Hindu architecture. On a deeper level, Trivedi believes that certain Hindu religious canons could help form the basis for a distinct design method.

Trivedi's colleague, Raghunath Joshi, has made a start with a thirty-year campaign to revive Hindi calligraphy. In India, a dozen scripts represent the fifteen or more languages spoken by more than 800 million people, and the strong regional traditions behind them are daily reinforced in the thousand or more newspapers published throughout the subcontinent. Joshi hopes to expand the range of typefaces available and to encourage inventive use of the ornate characters as decorative devices in packaging. He remarks: "Indian letterforms can play an important role as images. Our object is to give emphasis to Indian language typography. You can still appreciate the hand lettering on the backs of lorries, but we need a more organized typography." Joshi believes that the letterforms of the classical language of India could be used to print the ancient texts that are still widely read. "We have to preserve our tradition but we cannot ignore contemporary needs," he says. "It's as if you were to reprint the book of Kells; you would not use Optima."

This problem is very different from that of representing a nationwide corporation. Here, the richness of tongues and alphabets becomes an embarrassment. In creating a corporate identity for the Indian Post Office in 1989, Joshi hoped to make use of elements of the Devanagari script. The language issue is a contentious one, however, and because portions of the population use other scripts, his design was rejected in favor of a bland, abstract symbol. "We cannot use letterforms for a corporate identity that

must be understood in fifteen languages," notes graphic designer Sudarshan Dheer with regret. "So we have to use a symbol, but then there is a danger that a time comes when one symbol will look like another."

Joshi, who formerly worked in an advertising agency, has also fought to ensure that advertising campaigns are not just written but also planned in Hindi and not in English: "At present the fashion is to conceive an entire campaign in English, and then it is translated into Hindi where necessary. I proved that the results are much better appreciated if they are conceived in Hindi."

Among the intelligentsia, the common denominator is not the Hindi spoken by nearly half the people of India but the English spoken by one in fifty. (It is a quirk of history that English is the less objectionable lingua franca to the non-Hindi-speaking portion of the population.) Where English is used, the graphic design often echoes that in Britain. Newspapers are often direct copies of similar or identical British

titles, even when this affects their readability. "Our *Times* is a copy of your *Times*. Ours has eight columns because yours has eight columns. Even the Indian-language papers have an eight-column grid even though Hindi requires wider columns," notes Joshi. The *Times of India* was founded 150 years ago during the British colonial period, so its British look can legitimately be said to reinforce its Indian pedigree. What is less clear is why India's *Independent*, established in 1989, should look so like the British *Independent* started only a few years earlier, or why the Indian *Sunday Times* should slavishly have followed a 1990 redesign of the British paper of the same name.

India has room to harbor many such paradoxes. Sheer size and the comparative openness to foreign influence make it possible to sustain vast industrialized cities on the one hand and innumerable rural communities, where traditional crafts are still practiced without artifice, on the other. Craft products may be the result of self-expression here as else-

Above: Fabrics
Shraddha Desai/Aditi Ranjan
Ikat

Far left: Poster
Vikas Satwalekar
NID, 1987

Left: Poster
Pravin Sevak
NID, 1990

Juxtaposition of colors that in Western countries would be called a clash is an element in Indian graphics taken from color combinations in fabric design and dress.

Distinctive symbols can emerge from the union of Western and Indian motifs but when communication is the priority, as in this family-planning information, a more direct pictorial style must be used.

Below: Family-planning visual aids
National Institute of Design
Family Planning Foundation

Right: Hospital corporate identity
Sudarshan Dheer

Below: Corporate identity
Sudarshan Dheer
Aakar Art Gallery

Right: Corporate identity
Sudarshan Dheer
Saheli fashion store

City taxi prototype
K. Srinivasan
1988

*Modernization is the order of the
day in some areas while the
reassertion of traditional patterns
is more important in others. NID
students and faculty cover both
bases.*

Bamboo tongs
M.P. Ranjan/G. Upadhyaya
Department of Industries,
Government of Tripura

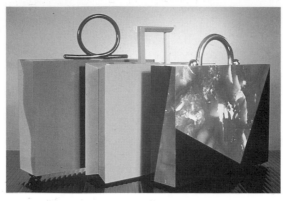

Briefcase line
Kirti Trivedi

*Designed to be made in low
volumes, these briefcases make
use of scraps of laminate for
decoration.*

where but they are not the irrelevant self-indulgence
that they have become in developed countries. In
their separate realms, both industry and handwork
have a sound base, making India perhaps better
placed than any other nation to attempt a synthesis
of craft and design. "It is so interwoven you can
hardly decipher where one ends and the other
begins. Craft was, and is, part of life," says Haku
Shah, a craftsman and theorist in Ahmedabad. "A lot
of craftsmen are innovative—they do design. They
do not just copy. In fact, I'm of the opinion that the
craftsmen may have more to contribute than the
pseudo-designers."

In the preindustrial period during the nineteenth
century, Indian handicrafts were much admired
abroad. The situation today is very different. "Now,"
notes Trivedi, "even with fully imported and highly
sophisticated manufacturing plants, Indians find it
difficult to match the quality of products produced in
those same plants abroad." Shah hopes that the split
between "craft" for luxury knickknacks and
"design" for dull utility goods that usually comes
with industrial progress can be avoided if designers
and craftspeople can be persuaded to collaborate.
Craft is already threatened, says Shah, because of a
lack of appropriate raw materials, failing know-how,
and the growing uselessness of artifacts that is
encouraged by the high demand for tourist sou-
venirs. Chandra Vijai Singh of the National Institute
of Design adds that craftspeople are just as prey as
designers in industry to adverse market forces:
"Ugliness has happened because of our insufficient
sensitivity to craftsmen. The craftsman has the skills
but is tied to the commercial network. His livelihood
depends on marketability. Because of tourism, crafts
are becoming like industrial products with 'quality
control.' Objects are valued on material, not skill.
Much craftsmanship is superficial, and the mediocre
fear that change will reveal them as no craftsmen."
Taking the opposite position from Shah, he adds the
hope that "designers can help add value to these
impoverished crafts."

The designer could help to secure a role for craft
in modern production, agrees Shah, but first he or
she must be prepared to slow down in order to be
able to appreciate the true craftsperson's feel for the
utility of the objects created and the truthfulness to
the materials used in their creation. Shah believes
that "the values that the designer carries should be
set aside during this whole process." The National
Institute of Design includes a "craft documentation"
project to awaken its students to these sensibilities,
but, given everyday business hardships, it seems
unlikely that many commercial designers will take
time to follow this example.

There have been a number of well-publicized

attempts to find a place for craft in modern India. One government initiative was the Golden Eye project of 1985 in which famous designers such as Ettore Sottsass, Frei Otto, and Jack Lenor Larsen were invited to India to collaborate with local craftspeople. The project was not the lasting success it might have been, says one Indian designer, "because of bureaucratic hurdles, not because the designer-craftsman interaction failed." Nevertheless, it was also depressing to see that some designers appeared more interested in plundering raw materials than in trying to get under the skin of local craft techniques and philosophies. Another example of one culture's reluctance really to understand another was seen when a team of Western designers came to study brass-working in a region near Delhi. One of the visitors suggested a geometric design that it was felt would appeal to Western buyers but failed to understand that the craftsman, accustomed to engraving more curvaceous ornamentation, could not easily produce the straight lines and sharp angles required with the tools at his disposal.

Local designers may prove more sensitive to local skills. The European Community is sponsoring a project to assist in the creation of products with export potential made from jute and coir (a fiber made from coconut husks). In response to a slump in the jute sacking market caused by the rise of polyethylene, the Jute Marketing and Development Council gave Indian designers a program to come up with products that use the material, not as a cheap substitute for cotton or an expensive one for the plastic that is replacing it, but in ways that make the most of its natural properties. Results such as the lamp with a woven jute shade by National Institute of Design alumna Elizabeth Jacob marry contemporary technology with the old skills and ensure their export potential by identifying as much with cosmopolitan trends as with local tradition.

Rajeev Sethi, the guiding light behind Golden Eye, has spent the years since that project engaged in a rather different, though no less elaborate, attempt to generate an awareness of the craft techniques that still thrive all over India. At a large private house designed by the noted Indian architect Charles Correa in a fashionable beach resort in suburban Bombay, Sethi has brought together woodworkers, stone carvers, blacksmiths, and ceramists from tribes, villages, and towns across India to cover every surface of what the architect probably intended to be a spacious, white Corbusian interior with carved and inlaid teak and mahogany, sandstone, and mother-of-pearl. No expense has been spared, but this may be the project's failing, for in being moved cross-country and up-market, the craft employed here has been rendered essentially purposeless. Once crafts-

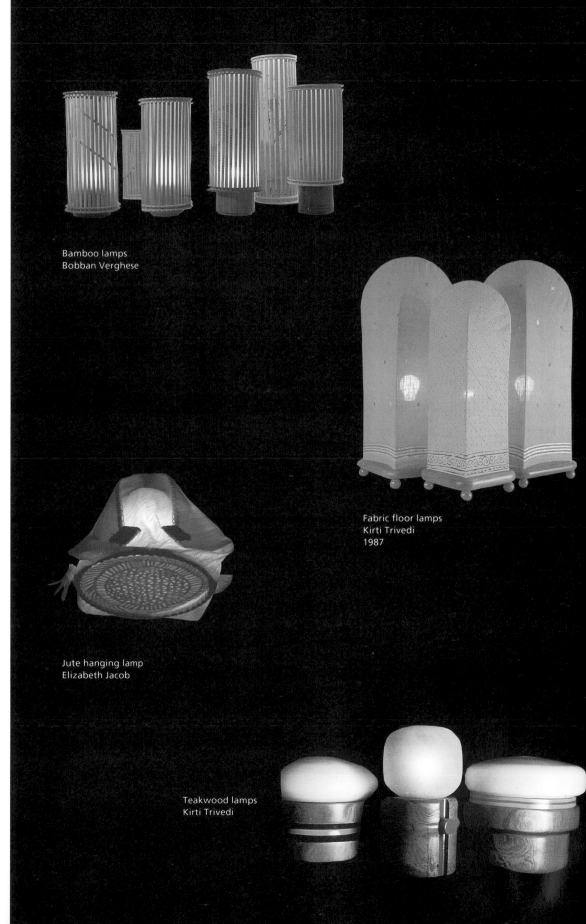

Bamboo lamps
Bobban Verghese

Fabric floor lamps
Kirti Trivedi
1987

Jute hanging lamp
Elizabeth Jacob

Teakwood lamps
Kirti Trivedi

Above and right: Decorated trucks and auto-rickshaw

Below: Auto-rickshaw
B.S. Sringesh

Designers may update forms of familiar objects such as the auto-rickshaw but they cannot easily cater to the range of individual tastes employed when users decorate them.

people are producing for markets separated—whether by distance or wealth—from their own, the meaning quickly disappears from their work.

India's craft tradition may or may not prove a meaningful source of inspiration for the country's designers. There are also more tenuous cultural connections to be made with the rich imagery of Hinduism, the religion of the majority of India's population which, despite its tolerant nature, is a pervasive influence on daily life. Indians accept gods with combined animal and human or male and female characteristics. Exactitude is not the highest priority in the representation of these deities. Realism is less important than the mythology. Some designers believe that this readiness to adopt surreal symbols and use them flexibly and subtly could inform an Indian theory of design. Already, some people see parallels between Hindu iconography and the stylized presentation of drama in the films that have become a colossal industry in Bombay and one of the liveliest media for cultural expression on the Indian subcontinent. While the potential has not yet been formally demonstrated, there is already evidence that those who fail to appreciate this sensibility will suffer. It is seen, according to Kirti Trivedi, when the local population fails to regard the immutable images of foreign corporations with appropriate respect: "When the response is dependent on the form, cultural differences may make the response to a symbol unpredictable. The IBM logotype may evoke the response of cultural imperialism, rather than the positive response it is intended to evoke." IBM was seen by Indians as overweening and was obliged to curtail its business. If its logotype had not been so sacrosanct and had been implemented with variations according to local skills and wishes, it might have been a different story, Trivedi suggests.

At the popular level, a rich decorative tradition already exists in India. As in the United States—another country of long distances—truckers keep their vehicles as proudly as if they were homes (which they often are). Practically every truck and auto-rickshaw is embellished with icons both of gods and goddesses, to ward off evil, and of famous Indian film stars. Lovingly scripted messages adorn the rears of the trucks, and attached to the doors are decorative panels, painted wood in some regions, shiny sheets of metal in others.

The do-it-yourself decoration of Indian trucks may have a connection with the embellishment of Hindu temples, but it is also an extension of a necessity. Truck and auto-rickshaw manufacturers supply a bare chassis with a front cab in order to avoid paying duty on certain categories of vehicle. Local metalworking shops complete the vehicle to the requirements of a company or an individual driver. Though they come fully specified, ordinary cars are sometimes decorated as well, and a large industry has grown up to supply add-on parts. The custom has local roots, but it boomed when manufacturers of the Indian version of a Japanese auto, the Maruti Suzuki, foresaw the demand for a range of attachments to the vehicle.

Articles for the home are often personalized in a similar manner. A radio or stereo might be wrapped in beads or have a cloth cover made for it. Some manufacturers have tried to add local appeal to their products by finding ways to accommodate this custom. At one time, Philips supplied adhesive stickers with its Moving Sound range of personal hi-fi equipment, but people ignored the stickers and went on individualizing the products in their own way. Even radios thoughtfully provided with leather cases were still re-covered with homemade cloth.

Ornamented surfaces are a sign of wealth in India. The visual clutter relays many messages and is not merely the colorful confusion that the foreigner sees. Nadkarni Sudhakar comments: "Here the decoration is really integrated. It goes naturally onto new and old things. In the West, it is used more on traditional things and then it often goes uncomfortably. There is more scope here." At the Industrial Design Centre one of the students' first-year projects is to design a simple plastic vessel. The container is blow-molded so there are few constraints on the form, which makes the problem harder in some ways. The students visit museums and are encouraged to develop traditional forms and decorative motifs. "If you did this sort of thing in Europe, they would immediately take it as kitsch," says Sudhakar.

Kirti Trivedi believes product decoration must deal with the form as well as the surface. He challenges the relevance to India of Euclidean geometric norms by referring to Hindu temple architecture whose complex forms he believes are more closely related to fractal geometry. Ancient *vastu shastra* texts indicate how to build up decorative motifs by recursive and iterative stages similar to those used to generate fractal patterns by computer. A more holistic approach to the entire design process might be taken from the Vedas, liturgical precepts that codify the meanings of objects in Hindu culture. One sutra, the *vastusutra upanishad*, provides an abstract basis for form giving. This might seem far removed from the reality of Indian existence, but it should be remembered that such formulae are more ingrained in Hindu culture than are, for example, Christian laws in the West.

Practicing younger designers are skeptical of Trivedi's idealism. Until recently, Suresh Sethi worked as an industrial designer at Philips's studio in

Ceiling fan
Prashant Ahire

Below: Ceiling fan
Jayprakash Mehta

Ceiling fans in traditional brass and enamel and Sankheda woodcraft style have proved a spectacular export success.

Plastic jugs

Traditional forms are sometimes retained without regard to the use of new materials in manufacturing.

Computer process controller
Suresh Sethi
Kadex

Glider lamps
Suresh Sethi

These lamps attempt to replace traditional representation of gods and goddesses in household objects with a more contemporary myth.

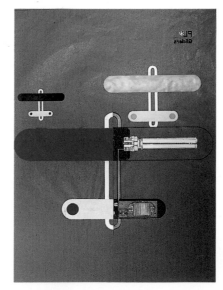

Sunny (above left), Supra (above middle), and Sonata Classic (above) table fans
Abhay Shah Associates
Bajaj Electricals, 1989
Photographs by Preeti Bedi

Water cooler
Dhimant Panchal/
S. Sunder/Mayur Dave
Voltas

Bombay. In that environment, there was no discussion about what constitutes Indian design, far less any abstract philosophizing. Says Sethi: "I thought I was the only one questioning why I should design another Western radio the next day. If there is Indianization, it is only in the process of how to manufacture a product. There was a short time when the graphics were a little more gaudy because of the local color sense, but now it is much more like it is at Philips in Holland."

Sethi's current project is to design a loudspeaker cabinet for the Indian manufacturer Videocon. Freed from the corporate rigors of Philips, could the cabinet not be a brightly colored and decorated box? No, says Sethi. It is the personal element that is important in such decoration, not anything contributed by the manufacturer. Well then, bearing in mind Indians' wish to customize their own products, might it not be possible to supply the speakers as a kit, with a plain wooden speaker box and instructions on how to paint it and perhaps even how to affix the user's own piece of colored silk in place of the usual black synthetic gauze over the front? No again. Not enough people would respond to the implied invitation to "complete" the product. Sethi brings the discussion abruptly down to earth. For this product, meeting people's aspiration for status symbols is more important than aiming to humor some nebulous cultural tradition. The speaker will be a rectangular black box. "Black is an inauspicious color," he comments drily, "but people will buy black because it looks as if it comes from Japan. India *accepts.*"

Abhay Shah has still less time for Trivedi's Indian design. He dismisses it as kitsch. A resolute globalist and an admirer of Frogdesign, he established his industrial design firm, one of the earliest independent groups in the country, in 1986. Abhay Shah Associates comprises three young designers, all graduates of the National Institute of Design, who are making their name without, like many of their peers, having to diversify into graphic and interior design to make ends meet. Shah tells the apocryphal story of two shoe manufacturers who came to assess the Indian market. The first found that everyone went barefoot and saw no market for his product. The second found the same and saw an enormous market. Shah is the second type of person; he has persevered and now advises companies that will listen about product strategy as well as providing product design. "Professional designers here, rather than arguing the ideology of Indianness, should create products for needs and then they would be distinctively Indian," he says. He sees his designs for a range of table and ceiling fans as "global" but was amused to find, while teaching in Paris, that students there found them "ethnic."

As Shah tells it, it took a great deal of persuasion and demonstration to convince the client for the fans, Bajaj Electrical, to go for a full redesign rather than the usual styling exercise. In the end, the high volume of Bajaj's production made it worthwhile to alter the design. Now, some fans that used to have a cast-aluminum base and stem now have an aluminum stem only and a pressed steel base. The saving in materials more than pays for the molds that will produce more sophisticated shapes. The company's top-of-the-range product is a bulbous Braun-like model that was presented to the client in plastic and metallic coated versions. Bajaj managers unanimously opted for the latter. "It is a reinterpretation of what sells. Shiny surfaces and chrome trim are very popular," says Shah. His associate, Arvind Lodaya, adds: "As far as Bajaj goes, I think we have proved that design is cheaper. They were only paying us 10 percent of one month's savings."

Another client, Kirloskar Oil Engines, a diesel engine manufacturer, makes parts for generator sets. When it found that others were buying the components and putting together their own complete generators, Kirloskar took the hint. The company knew of Shah through its advertising agency and asked him for a sleeker, more consumer-friendly casing to compete with the Yamaha and Honda imports that had bitten into its market. This piqued Kirloskar's interest in industrial design. Now Shah is working on bigger generator sets and, with growing mutual understanding, is able to propose functional component changes as well as cosmetic improvements to the casings. It is the classic design success story, recalling Raymond Loewy's experience with the Gestetner company. A slightly more tawdry version of the same tale crops up with the design of a perfume bottle for a third client. "They would ask us to knock off popular bottles," says Lodaya. "They would give us a bottle of Opium or whatever. We had to establish our credentials by first following their constraints, but then we talked them into doing something new."

Suresh Sethi and Abhay Shah Associates are typical of the new order. They can argue over the form that the new Indian design will take in cooperation with clients who for the first time are able to manufacture their own products for their own market without recourse to Western expertise or equipment. The old guard, meanwhile—men such as Sudarshan Dheer, Kirti Trivedi, and Yeshwant Chaudhary, president of the Society of Industrial Designers of India—are approaching the same point but from a different direction, experiencing second thoughts in the hiatus after the passing of international Modernism. They have an additional responsibility. "The older generation must make younger designers more aware of

the identity they are in search of," says Chaudhary. "I am a nationalist but am only now beginning to look into Indian symbology. We are just becoming aware that there needs to be a change of approach that would bring elements of two- and three-dimensional decoration more vigorously into functional design. We have had 150 years of foreign rule, so it will take a few years to escape from it—one of the bad things about Indian culture is that it accepts all incoming forces." Once again, for better or worse, India accepts.

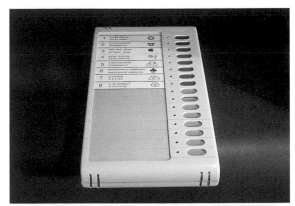

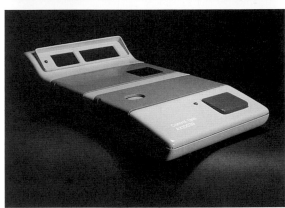

Electronic voting machine ballot unit (above) and control unit (right) A.G. Rao/Ravi Poovaiah Bharat Electronics for the Elections Commission of India, 1988

One hundred fifty thousand of these voting machines were made, unusually of plastic parts, tooled abroad. The design makes allowances for low levels of literacy and the multiplicity of candidates in Indian elections but was not used because its action was not trusted by some politicians.

Tipper barrow
Indesign Consultants
National Tractors Traders

Salora mixer/grinder
Indesign Consultants
Jiwa Appliances

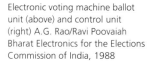

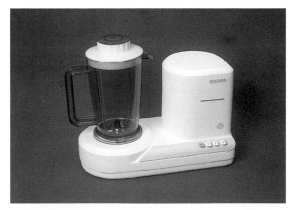

A Singapore Airlines flight into Changi Airport provides an ample hint of the incongruities to come in the prosperous city-state that is modern Singapore. The flight attendants wear sarong *kebayas,* traditional costumes of a sort, and a spectacular marketing success, but designed by French couturier Pierre Balmain. They usher you out into an airport that is conspicuously clean, high-tech, and efficient, a way station to the twenty-first century. The contrast reflects two different aspects of Singapore: its effort to rediscover its traditions on the one hand, and its accelerating race toward a technological future on the other. Despite the apparent contradiction, both are expressions of national policy.

Living in Singapore is like working for a large corporation. Its chief executive officer from independence in 1965 until 1990 was the Prime Minister Lee Kwan Yew. Things tend to be done by government directive—or not done by government laisser-faire. Thus, when the Singapore government announces an initiative on design or on some matter of national culture, there is near certitude that it will produce visible results. The design councils of Europe, America, and Japan can only look on in envy as they wrestle futilely to spread the good word through larger, less pliable, nations.

Were it not for current purposeful attempts to invent vehicles for national cultural expression, it might be possible to see Singapore as a "culture-free" enterprise zone, a sort of globalist's utopia where national characteristics might be transcended in the pursuit of trade and wealth. Such a thing would be a logical extension of Singapore's historical raison d'être as a trading entrepôt. But Singapore is already moving past the stage where this would be attractive. Businesses are conscious that they must add value to locally made products. Meanwhile, there are ever fewer reasons to keep the multinationals in town, and they, too, are moving on to other places in Southeast Asia where labor costs are still low.

One way to add value to manufactured goods is by design, and the Singapore Trade Development Board has included design promotion among its activities since 1984. Having previously made efforts to cut costs and improve productivity, the board pinpointed design after having examined the products of the other countries that it found itself up against at trade fairs abroad. Sannie Abdul, senior manager of design promotion, observes: "We are exposed to multinational corporations which have already taken care of their design. But many local

manufacturers still do not know what design can do for them." Following the model established by Britain's Design Council, the Trade Development Board pays up to three-quarters of a consulting firm's design fee on behalf of first-time clients.

But skepticism remains high for reasons that are deeply ingrained. Singapore's history means that cash is still king. "Singapore being a trading port, quick turnover is essential. They do not know how to use industrial designers," says Michael Gan of the Designers' Association of Singapore. The government has persevered in its attempt to change local attitudes. Singapore has begun a series of star-studded international design forums. In literature accompanying the first of these biennial conferences in 1988, Lee Kwan Yew exhorted: "Today, the term 'Made in Singapore' simply means that the product is made in Singapore. We must make it mean: 'This is of good design and is good value for money.'" Overseas design firms have been offered financial inducements to set up shop in Singapore. So have manufacturers who would undertake to design products locally.

All this professional expertise was intended to provide a high-quality resource on the doorstep of local industry, but there was also the hope that its presence might stimulate local interest in design by osmosis. However, Singaporeans appear to be underwhelmed. Britain's Addison is one of the few design firms to have stayed, but it finds it is asked to do very little industrial design. It fills its time with graphic and packaging design. Hewlett Packard built a research and development center in Singapore, but it, too, ended up doing very little industrial design. Western designers are at pains to point out that the Singapore market remains highly price-sensitive and in general cannot or will not entertain their high-fee services.

Alongside efforts to build an indigenous design profession, Singapore is trying to discover its cultural identity. It is no simple matter. The United States is Singapore's principal export market. Its educational heritage is British. Japan is its role model in business. Driving in from the airport, the road signs are American in appearance, the license plates look British, but the cars are Japanese. Chew Moh Jin of Design Counsel complains of the effect these forces have on young designers: "Perhaps 80 percent of the products in stores here are Japanese. The younger generation are all looking east for ideas. They ignore the nice European products. The media has much to do with this, by their pushing of the Japanese work ethic and management style." The fault lies more with the students than with their educators, according to some practicing designers who critique student projects. Singapore's

Police Life Annual
Quek Hui Har, Design3
Republic of Singapore Police,
1990

The airbrush is a universal tool, but its use here, according to the designer, is in a Singaporean manner .

Packaging
Quek Hui Har, Design3
Kenneth's Easy-Cook, 1989

The photography and typography of this package are British-derived, but the pack border provides an Asian flourish.

Work Improvement Teams
Annual
Quek Hui Har, Design3
Singapore Telecom, 1989

An amateur's logotype on this annual elegantly unites the initials WIT with a visual representation of a team and a hint of local calligraphy.

polytechnics are shortly to disgorge their first design graduates, a generation that has grown up entirely in the cultural vacuum of modern Singapore and that seems to lack the fundamental spirit of inquiry needed create good design.

The cultural context is closely bound up with the economic context. Sannie Abdul hopes to see Singapore as a skill center for the countries of the Association of Southeast Asian Nations, offering not just trade and financial services but also design resources for manufacturers based in Malaysia, Indonesia, Thailand, and Indochina. China itself is the unspoken prize. The vision makes sense. Singapore's only resource is its people, and, in contrast to Korea or Japan, whose huge manufacturing companies employ the majority of designers, it is natural that its designers should form independent firms that would have the flexibility to work for clients of all types throughout the region.

The wish to build a cultural identity is something that has come with a quarter-century of growing prosperity. As Tan Khee Soon of Design3, one of Singapore's older design firms, observes: "In the early years the effort was on engineering and accountancy. We had people from Hong Kong coming and telling us we had no culture—then we began to wake up! In the last four or five years there have been efforts to promote arts and crafts and culture concurrent with the design initiative."

The new prime minister, Goh Chok Tong, has promised that his government will give the arts a higher priority. Given Singapore's record for steering its development, it is likely that this pledge will have more impact than a similar promise made in most other countries. "Being a Singaporean I know that when the government pushes something, it will move," says Yeo Chung Sun of Lawton and Yeo Design Associates, a firm that grew from the residue of a Swedish company's brief tenure in the country after having accepted the government's inducements to set up a Singapore office.

The ingredients for an indigenous culture are many. The majority of Singaporeans are ethnic Chinese, with Malays and Indians making up most of the rest. In the past, these groups have remained discrete. "Each race has its own separate identity," says Tan. "But apparently they are starting to gel. More people now think of themselves as Singaporean first and Chinese or Malaysian or whatever second." Abdul agrees: "We are a new country, but we cannot afford to neglect these things. We have very rich cultures, but each has been kept by its ethnic group. We are slowly merging to a point where we will be able to identify ourselves as one people. It will take some time, but something will emerge."

But Singapore is a country in a hurry. While the administration forces the pace with attempts to synthesize a national style by combining aspects of the costume, dance, and so on of the principal ethnic groups that make up Singapore's population, there are signs of a backlash. Banners on the streets, for example, exhort in both English and Chinese characters: "Say Something in Chinese Today" to people too accustomed to speaking English.

Designers refer wryly to the official effort to create a national costume. Some government ministers have taken to appearing in orchid-print shirts. Such things would be naïve if not downright silly in a larger country, but in Singapore today's wild idea can easily become tomorrow's fact of life. The question for Singapore now is whether an invented identity is necessarily any worse than one arrived at over decades.

Corporate identity
United Overseas Bank Group

*Red is an auspicious color
frequently seen in the logotypes
of banks and public authorities.*

Calendar
Dan Teo Khai Mun
1988

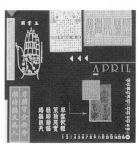

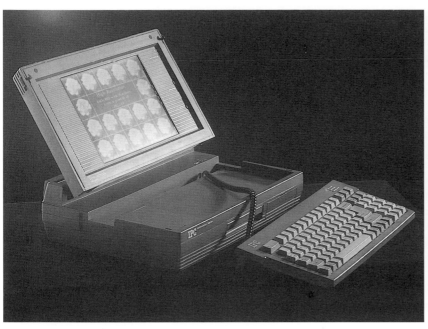

Portable computer
Lawton and Yeo Design
Associates
Essex Electric, 1989

Blood sampling machine
Lawton and Yeo Design
Associates
Diagnostic Biotechnology, 1990

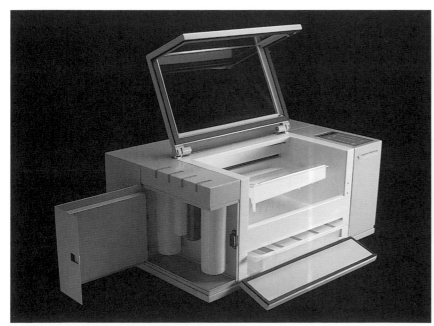

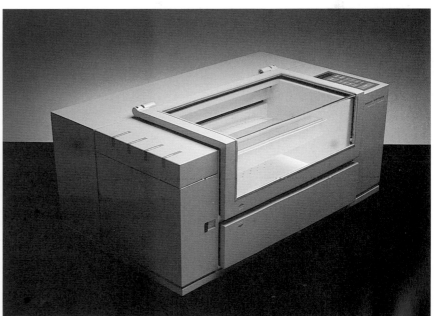

Hong Kong

Every year, one of the many competitions organized by the Hong Kong Trade Development Council is a competition for the design of watches and clocks. And every year, many of the entries—and some of the winners—bear more than a passing resemblance to existing but more expensive watches and clocks from abroad.

In a crowded classroom at the Swire School of Design of Hong Kong Polytechnic, Matthew Turner confronts his students with this observation. One student in the room is the outright winner of the most recent competition. Several runners-up are also present. In keeping with recent tradition their designs, too, are strangely familiar. Why is this? Do the students not feel ashamed? There is silence in the room and a sense of a gulf between the cultures of teacher and students. There are a few sniggers, but there is no embarrassment. For "passing off" is part of Hong Kong life. Sometimes even competition jurors are known not to be averse to a little imitation of their own. The fact is, it simply does *not* occur to people not to do what comes naturally, and copy what has been done before.

Turner has been in Hong Kong long enough that he no longer feels outraged at this. Indeed, as a lecturer in contextual studies, he has been obliged to reconsider the value of originality, that quality that good designers the world over are supposed to strive for. He is not completely alone with his heretical thoughts, however. As the curators of a thought-provoking British Museum exhibition called "Fake?" pointed out, "the modern emphasis on originality is eccentric." Most civilizations revere the continuation of a tradition and the re-creation of its images. Until the twentieth century, European artists were trained by copying their elders. During the Renaissance in Europe an ability to pass off one's work as "antiquities" was deemed admirable.

Yet commentators have long found a "lack of imagination" in Hong Kong. In the nineteenth century, it was the designer and scholar Owen Jones who made the criticism. British designer Rodney Fitch echoed him in a recent review of students' work. It is salutary to remember, however, that it is demand from the West that sustains the copying habit. Turner calls this behavior on the part of the developed world "a subtle form of intellectual protectionism" and adds: "Our monopoly of design taste cannot prevent the success of Asian 'kitsch.'"

Different imitations produce different degrees of offense. One that went too far came from Ken Shimasaki, an American Japanese who has settled in

Tumbler-Like, Bendy, and Home Reminder clocks

Prizewinning student designs from the 1990 Hong Kong International Watch and Clock Fair.

Tino collection stationery
Lee Tak Chi/Lau Yung Mo
Tint International Marketing, 1989

Opposite: "Diving mask" portable cassette player
Lee Tak Chi/Lau Yung Mo
Pollyflame International, 1987

Logotype
Alan Chan Design

Western and Eastern letterforms
are blended with varying
degrees of subtlety in the
creation of Hong Kong
company logotypes.

Right: Logotype
Eddie Lau, Alan Chan Design
Kai Fashions, 1984

Below: Logotype
Alan Chan Design
Pye's Boutique, 1985

Hong Kong. He designed a portable stereo cassette player for an American company that captures the spirit if not the letter of Sony's popular "My First Sony" children's line of products. A lawsuit quickly followed, finding infringement in the red, yellow, and blue colors common to both designs. "No one should have the right to primary colors," protests Shimasaki, who insists he has actually tried to discourage imitation among Hong Kong's design community. "It's pretty much fading out. Taiwan does the knock-offs now."

Set in the wider social and economic context of Hong Kong, it is perhaps easy to see why designers copy. Nobody regards him- or herself as a permanent resident, especially in the years preceding 1997, when Britain's lease on the colony will revert to the Chinese. A forlorn "Hong Kong—my home" campaign is doing nothing to change that feeling. Everybody is here to make a buck and move on. In a city where even buildings have generally covered the costs of their construction after three or four years, it is small wonder that companies demand very quick returns from their often meager investment in product design and manufacture. This distinguishes Hong Kong from any other country, even from Singapore, Taiwan, and South Korea—countries that are often included with Hong Kong under the banner of the Four Dragons because of their cultural or economic links with the People's Republic of China. Hong Kong runs on confidence, but without it it stalls, and there is no doubt that Hong Kong is presently slipping down the Dragons' ranking table.

There is hope that Hong Kong will continue to prosper if events after 1997 turn out for the best. An open China would emerge as the principal source for cheap labor, and Hong Kong would become an important skill resource. "We feel that Hong Kong should become the design service center in Asia." says Tony Sin of the Hong Kong Designers' Association. But against this view is the fact that few Hong Kong Chinese believe that the guarantee negotiated by the British and Chinese governments of a fifty-year transition period will be honored. "After 1997 this place will be the main area for expertise for China—if everybody hasn't left. But if they were given passports, every member of my staff would be off," says one designer.

Despite these misgivings, there is already a powerful and growing commercial connection between Hong Kong and communist China. In more and more operations, financing comes from Hong Kong, but manufacturing happens across the water in the special economic zone, Shenzhen. Often, design and development take place in Hong Kong, but the colony's designers are also reporting a boom in direct inquiries from Chinese companies. The Hong Kong administration refuses to acknowledge that this is the situation, but the fact is that the official border is becoming ever more porous. Shenzhen is coming to seem like an extension of Hong Kong, and the real border is between Shenzhen and "China."

Links with China may mean that the requirement to add value by improving the quality of design that is being felt in Korea and Singapore will not be a powerful factor here. With a vast pool of labor on its doorstep and large potential markets in Eastern Europe, the Soviet Union, and China itself, it is likely that Hong Kong can carry on as it has always done.

(Taiwan's situation is very different. With still less prospect of economic cooperation with China than Hong Kong, Taiwan is forced to add value to its products and create its own brands as Thailand, Malaysia, and other countries undercut it on labor costs. The Taiwan government is playing a leading role and has invited a number of international corporate identity firms, Landor Associates and RSCG Conran Design among them, to advise on ways to present Taiwan and its products in a better light. There is substance behind the image, with accompanying government initiatives to establish research centers to develop indigenous product technology which will sell their findings to companies that could never have undertaken the research themselves. Meanwhile, in Hong Kong there are moves by individual companies and

the Trade Development Council to promote local brand development, but nothing on the same coordinated scale. Patrick Bruce, managing director of RSCG Conran Design, has one client who makes products as an original equipment manufacturer (OEM) for AEG, Philips, and Toastmaster. Now the company is looking to export directly to Europe under its own brand. "Brand development is way beyond the resources of the average Hong Kong company. It's seen as a simple issue that can be resolved by product design alone," says Bruce. He adds that local companies do not acknowledge that a brand takes time and money to establish and that it must be protected once established.)

On the whole, there is little prospect of the maturity and sense of purpose seen in Taiwan coming to Hong Kong. The typical Hong Kong product has more "functions" than functionalism, more novelty than innovation. These are related concepts, but the former word in each pair has a pejorative tone to design purists (perhaps because it is often closer to the truth). It is significant, too, that the latter two words imply that some research has been done on

Packaging
Alan Chan Design
Mandarin Oriental

Logotype
Bossini fashion stores

*Shameless imitation is an aspect
of Hong Kong design that
cannot be ignored.*

Logotype
Hong Kong Hilton Hotel

"Hello Hong Kong" poster
Alan Chan Design
Seibu Department Store, Tokyo,
1987

Signage
Ji-Ping Chang,
RSCG Conran Design
Hong Kong Housing Authority,
1990

*Signage for a housing project is
inspired by tiles seen in
traditional gardens.*

Magazine advertisement
Kan Tai Keung Design
Cheer Group

the way to the new product. Like Taiwan, Hong Kong has thousands of companies each employing only a handful of people. They cannot possibly conduct the sort of research that product innovation requires, and in Hong Kong there is no prospect of government assistance. Hence, the substitution of novelty for innovation.

There are exceptions to the norm. Douglas Tomkin's carefully named Hong Kong Design Innovation is one such company, formed initially as a spin-off from the Polytechnic but now operating effectively as an independent firm. Hong Kong Design Innovation has worked for the police and housing authority, but most of its projects are for export. Tomkin designed Hong Kong's first fax machine after a client came to him several years ago solely for the mechanical engineering, a common misapprehension of local clients who have little idea of what design can do for them. By now the firm has designed three more machines for the same client, including models specifically for Europe and America that reflect demands specific to those markets. The Australian Tomkin has an international perspective that is common enough among the postcolonial class in Hong Kong but is conspicuously lacking among many incurious young Hong Kong natives. He comments: "What becomes clear after a while is that students are going into an industry that is OEM. There isn't any indigenous understanding of the market, which is overseas, or the problems of developing a new product."

This parochialism is perhaps one reason why David Meredith, principal of the Swire School of Design, comes across as a despairing missionary in a city of unrepentant savages. He paints such a black picture of what passes for creativity locally that one wonders why he remains in his job at all. However, he also offers some perceptive new reasons for the low motivation he sees among his students. Most of the Swire School's thirty graduates each year will go to work in factories, where, if they wish to make a respectable living, they will soon move into management. Independent studios cannot afford to reward their designers well enough to keep them. In addition, Meredith believes, because the parents of many students have been poorly educated, they cannot provide the interest and encouragement the students need to develop a sense of vocation.

When those students move into manufacturing industry, their priorities are all too evident in many of the products they make. Ji-Ping Chang, product design director at RSCG Conran Design in Hong Kong, observes: "There are quality, well-resolved objects in terms of design, but if you look at the detail, the fit, and the use of materials, they are not necessarily well made." She refuses to be discour-

aged by this state of affairs, however, adding: "This market is exciting because we are going through an experimental phase. There is a lack of corporate culture, but that lack shows how a company without a past burden can behave. We're in the process of making history."

Corporate culture is not the only culture to be given short shrift by today's Hong Kong manufacturers. Tony Sin, who in addition to his role with the Hong Kong Designers' Association is a curator at the Hong Kong Museum of Science and Technology, and Christopher Chow, chief designer at the Hong Kong Trade Development Council, agree that the several thousand years of Chinese invention and cultural heritage are ill served by current design activity. Says Chow: "The Japanese have excelled by applying their own tradition to modern presentation, but the Chinese have not been doing that successfully."

Ji-Ping Chang has made an attempt to recapture some Chinese spirit in the design of a range of ceramic tiles for use as signage in local housing projects. The most original of four alternative proposals presented to the client, the ceramic pieces are inspired by tiles used in traditional Hong Kong gardens, though the symbols themselves were designed at RSCG Conran's London offices. The tiles could theoretically be made by crafts processes or, if greater uniformity were desirable, they could be silkscreened. The earthy tones of the tiles are the result of using traditional materials and techniques and would perhaps be less intrusive than the primary colors of conventional enameled metal signs. Chang brought similar thinking to bear when leading a local thesis project to design a doll for a Taiwanese toy manufacturer. She directed the students to look at folkloric sources such as Shang dynasty burial dolls instead of Barbie and Ninja Turtle look-alikes. But she has no illusions about the importance of also bringing a contemporary relevance to the dolls: "We would have failed if we had simply reproduced what was done then. You must borrow only the spirit and interpret it in your own way." Ultimately, the success of the project was compromised by the manufacturer's wish to bring the product to market very quickly. The exercise raises the question of whether Taiwan, let alone Hong Kong, will ever pause long enough to allow a richer design culture to come to maturity.

Whether dolls or plastic novelties, it has been toys that have made Hong Kong what it is today. Toys can be made in high volume in small factories. They take up little storage space in the crowded colony. They demand less of a commitment from a manufacturer than consumer durables. Despite often substantial tooling costs, the high-volume manufacture and efficient distribution of many toys allows for a quick turnover of ideas. There is little need for mar-

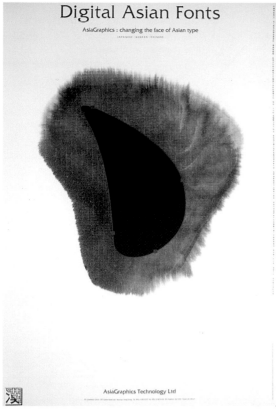

Digital Asian Fonts

AsiaGraphics : changing the face of Asian type

JAPANESE · KOREAN · CHINESE

AsiaGraphics Technology Ltd

Poster
Choi Kai-Yan
Asia Graphics Technology

Chinese calligraphy is threatened as much as traditional typography is in the West by digital technology. Choi Kai-Yan highlights the fact by overlaying part of a digital character over its hand-drawn equivalent.

Poster
Choi Kai-Yan

Telephone
Alex Kwan Chi Kin, Rom Leung
Designer

Cordless fan/hair dryer
Flora Tam Wai Ming

Top: Toaster prototype
Max Cheung, Hong Kong
Design Innovation
Electrical and Electronics, 1987

Some Hong Kong design seems to emulate Western ideas of good taste, but cheap plastics and colorful details still leave them with an almost toylike quality.

Wind-up lantern, middle;
Wind-up radio, bottom
Max Cheung, Hong Kong
Design Innovation
Liwaco Overseas Marketing,
1989

ket research—a toy can come and go from a market and few people will notice. Given these constraints, it is likely that products with a toylike quality, if not toys themselves, will remain a staple of Hong Kong's export market.

A pretend shaver that just buzzes and does nothing else; a combination water pistol and calculator; a cigarette lighter disguised as a minute coffeemaker—butane fills the "coffee pot"; all these are quintessential Hong Kong design. A telephone-as-tomato is the subject of a research project by Matthew Turner. Taska, the company that makes it, used to copy Japanese slim-line phones. When its president hit upon fruit as a way of breaking away from the conformity, he employed first a British, then a Hong Kong designer, to design the tomato telephone. Neither designer understood what he was after. In the end, he had to design it himself. Needless to say, the product was a great success, becoming a best-seller on America's Home Shopping Network.

Ostensibly more adult products sometimes have a toylike spirit too, whether in appearance or in function. A project for an otherwise rather Braun-like toaster by Max Cheung at Hong Kong Design Innovation, for example, has controls just a bit too bright and shiny to be high-style accents. Instead they might have more to do with the designer's familiarity with the process and product of local plastics manufacturers. A distance-measuring device, also by Hong Kong Design Innovation, shows a sense of playfulness in function, using an ultrasonic transducer of the type found in autofocus cameras. Says Douglas Tomkin: "It has all the features that make it ideal for Hong Kong—it's very suitable for high-volume manufacture; it's cheap to ship; it has fairly basic technology in its plastic moldings and electronics; it's got gimmick value; it doesn't require vast investment to set up a production line; and you can get it to the market within six months." The usual pressures did not stop Tomkin from making improvements to the gadget. He improved the accuracy with a funnel-like attachment to collimate the ultrasonic beam; he added a calculator to allow the user to take the displayed dimensions of a room and arrive at other useful data—such as carpet area, quantity of paint required for the walls, even the capacity of a suitable air-conditioner for the space.

This is innovation as well as novelty, functionality as well as "functions." More quintessentially Hong Kong is Lee Tak Chi of Tint International, "suppliers of original design products." Established in the early 1980s as a product design firm, Tint now does its own product development and acts as its own broker, coordinating the activities of suitable manufacturers and marketers for its creations, and working for royalties rather than fixed fees. The shift of emphasis is indicative of the general maturing of the strategies of Hong Kong's entrepreneurs. Lee is a graduate of London's Central School of Art and Design; most of his staff are from the Swire School. Faculty members at either place would probably be slightly shocked to see the quantity, range, and irreverence of these designers' output of company and catalog gifts, stationery, and toys, all for export. "We approach products like an advertising firm," explains Lee. The results can be surprising. An amoeba-shaped desktop calculator for the Dutch company, Marksman, for example, took its cue from the recent trend in European car styling. "No one had tried this style in stationery."

As is often the case in Hong Kong, the design concept of the calculator has not been followed through to great perfection. The product suffers from the need to use off-the-shelf parts in order to maximize volume and profit. It is not well resolved, but the quality of the finished article is adequate for the price tag. With better molds, higher-quality plastics, more sophisticated graphics, and if parts, such as the liquid-crystal display and its clear plastic protective cover, were specially made to fit with the spirit of the overall design, the product could almost be the cult object of a Starck or a Colani. But no. This is cheap and anonymous. This is Hong Kong.

Lee's wackiest product clearly shows the advertising thought process at work. This ultimate object, a "diving-mask" personal stereo, grew out of a brainstorming session that sought to hybridize what has become a commodity product with something utterly unexpected. The diving mask became inevitable when someone had the idea to put a layer of colored water inside the clear plastic mask in front of the cassette holder. Executed in bright yellow plastic, it is a wicked parody of the Sony Sports Walkman. It is not exactly original, but it is not a copy either. It is novel but not innovative. It is Hong Kong design at its best—uncomplicated, unpretentious, marketable fun.

Aerobasic calculator
Lee Tak Chi/Lau Yung Mo
Pollyflame International, 1989

This calculator derives its form from international trends in automobile styling.

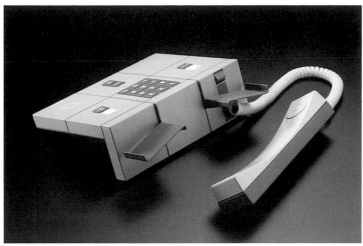

Orio Design 3001 telephone
CSL
Wangi Elec

Ultrasonic measurement device
Max Cheung, Hong Kong
Design Innovation
Seiko Instruments, 1990

*Many Hong Kong products
tread a thin line between
innovation and novelty.*

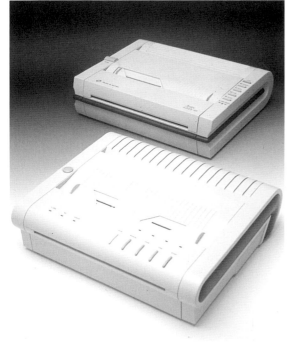

Fax machine
Max Cheung, Hong Kong
Design Innovation
Elec and Eltek, 1989

South Korea's dilemma is this: Economically and commercially, it wishes to emulate Japan. In other respects, however, it wishes to signal its distinction from the country that invaded and imposed its culture forcibly between 1910 and 1945.

For the *chaebol*, the massive conglomerates that dominate South Korea's economy, the former aspiration is the more important. They have grown by imitating the *zaibatsu* (giant corporations) of Japan. When local labor costs were low, they copied the latter's products. Now, as South Koreans reward themselves for decades of powerful economic growth by paying themselves more, they look to the methods of Japan's mature economy as they begin to add value to the goods they create. But for ordinary people, Koreanness is important; consumers buy what their *chaebol* produce out of patriotism as well as for the very good reason that, thanks to tariffs on their imported equivalents, there is little choice.

Thus, there are virtually no Japanese or other foreign vehicles on the streets. Almost everything on wheels is a Hyundai or a Daewoo (though some models may have Japanese engines under the hood). Having grown by building small automobiles more cheaply than anyone else—in short, doing what the Japanese did a decade or two ago—these two companies are now diversifying with new designs, echoing the recent Japanese trend of producing tiny, quirky cars. They are still following in Japan's footsteps but are now much closer on its heels.

Of the *chaebol*, Samsung and Lucky Goldstar, respectively the largest and third largest corporations in South Korea (Hyundai and Daewoo place second and fourth), are the most involved in consumer product manufacture. Like archrivals Sony and Panasonic in their day, the two corporations vie to catch the public's eye with advertisements in unlikely places (on airport luggage carts, for example) that feature the company name more prominently than any product. Both have recently moved to establish formal programs of design management in their consumer-electronics divisions. "The *chaebol* now understand that we need to give our products some national character," comments Han-Yoo Park, director of the Korea Institute of Industrial Design and Packaging. "We can no longer sell our Japanese and German redesigns."

The new attitude means that "redesigns"—

often blatant copies of established designs from elsewhere—may begin to disappear. One Japanese designer recalls being approached repeatedly by one of the *chaebol*, which excused the low design fee on offer by saying that little work would be involved as the company only wanted its new product to be a copy of an existing item "with maybe a few cosmetic changes." The designer turned the company down. This sort of behavior is on the way out. There is a growing mood of self-criticism in the design profession and the design press. As for the sort of products that the *chaebol* make, the new character is likely to be international more than national. South Korea's old-guard designers were educated in Korean schools, often by Japanese. The younger generation, by contrast, has often been educated abroad, particularly in the United States, and is acutely aware of international developments. These designers are already finding themselves in quite senior positions as their companies realize the importance of design to their next economic leap forward. The Korean attitude to returning natives represents one advantage Korea has over Japan. Because it is not an island but has experienced the constant traffic of Mongols, Chinese, and Japanese, Korea is more accepting of foreign influence. A Korean returning from abroad with a foreign education will be given a warmer welcome than a Japanese returning to Japan.

The sheer size of the *chaebol* makes a single design policy an impossibility. The Samsung Electronics Company, based in Suwŏn (two hours' drive from Seoul), with sales of more than $4 billion in 1988 and a work force of 40,000, is just one of more than thirty companies within the Samsung Group and the only one with an autonomous design department. In 1988 it upgraded its product planning and design for consumer electronics and domestic appliances by pulling that function out of the obscurity of research and development and establishing a design department in its own right. Meanwhile, designs for other products, such as telephones, which fall under the province of a different Samsung company in Seoul, continue to emerge from a different business structure, where design is not accorded such a high priority.

Goldstar, the consumer-products company within the Lucky Goldstar group, also runs a design center at its headquarters in Seoul, with some hundred staff designers, comparable in strength to that at Samsung Electronics. In 1990, encouraged by a new, design-aware company president, the general manager of Goldstar's design center, Soon-In Lee,

Right: Poster for peace
Kyung-Hum Kim and Jin-Ku Lee

Poster on the subject of autism
Chang Gwon-Bang

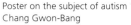

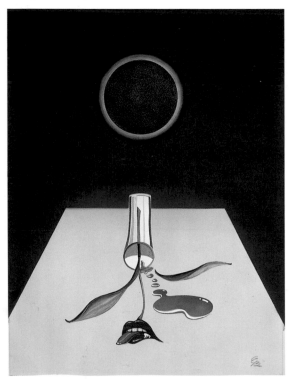

Tourism poster
Lee Bong Sub

*Although Koreans profess a
distaste for color, it does surface
from time to time in high
concentrations both in
contemporary graphic design
and in traditional temple
decoration.*

Samsung camera

*Korea's manufacturing chaebol
admire the design management
of their Japanese competitors.
Their product design is rapidly
coming to equal that of Japan
in quality.*

Illustration for a game
Kyo-Man Kim

Temple colors and patterns

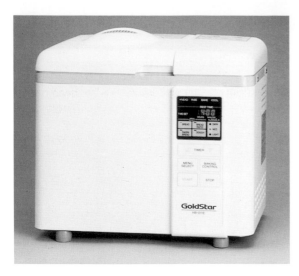

Top: Home bakery
Goldstar Electronics, 1991
Photograph courtesy Goldstar
Electronics International, Inc.

Above: Microwave oven
Goldstar Electronics, 1991
Photograph courtesy Goldstar
Electronics International, Inc.

Air purifier
Tongyang Cement Company

Goldstar employs internationally known design firms to support its in-house design effort. So far, more thought is given to tailoring products for export markets than for domestic consumers.

began introducing a new strategy, based on the supposition that good design could be used to make up some of the ground lost to the Japanese in technology. Lee plans to take his strategy a stage further than has Samsung, decentralizing Goldstar's design activity and establishing design centers in distant markets—something that even Sony is only now beginning to do. Goldstar's subsidiary design center in Dublin, for example, will serve as a base for the collection of European and American market intelligence. Ultimately, designers in Dublin will work in parallel with those in Seoul.

Both Samsung Electronics and Goldstar admire Sony as a model of design management. Jung-Wan Han, Samsung consumer-electronics products design manager, speaks for both Korean companies when he says: "Basically, we cannot overtake the Japanese success in the global market if we simply follow their traditions and setups. The technology we have in Korea is below Japanese standards, but we don't feel our design is much behind theirs." Jae-Hwan Lee, a member of Samsung's design team for refrigerators and air-conditioning equipment, notes that Korean products are beginning to emulate the attention to detail and decorative ideas of the Japanese: "Unfortunately, we are likely to follow their example because they are so successful in the market. Now we feel we need this kind of product, and it's kind of sad."

Like Sony, Samsung Electronics now employs top international design firms such as Frogdesign to help it develop products with global appeal. Goldstar has organized workshops with design managers from Sony and Philips and has commissioned Roberts Weaver, Busse Design, and Fitch RichardsonSmith to help ensure European and American acceptance for their products. There is no thought of a local design style for electronic products where the home market is one accustomed to imports. For domestic appliances, however, it can be a different story. Some Goldstar washing machines have washing motions designed to care for fabrics of the types and dimensions used specifically in Korea. The designs were based on findings from research conducted at a women's university in Seoul. Some new Samsung machines have rounded tops, which Jae-Hwan Lee claims echo the curves of china dishes known as *su-ban,* traditionally used to hold cut flowers. He notes: "We are trying to diversify the design trends based on the minute differences between small regions. In the States, New Yorkers have different tastes from people living in San Francisco; southern Europeans are different from northern Europeans." Jae-Hwan Lee sees these differences between the comparable areas of Korea and Japan as having more to do with the way a product is used than how it looks. He talks

of using fuzzy-logic circuits for electronic control to accommodate these subtle differences in custom and usage. "It's like the difference between the [Korean and Japanese] tea ceremonies," he says.

With the help of their design consultants, both Samsung and Goldstar happily design "European" and "American" products. But, while preferences abroad are detected and ministered to, little thought is given to the equivalent "Korean" product, despite the fact that this product accounts for perhaps 30 percent—the single largest chunk—of all sales. The figure is the same as the percentage of Sony's products that are sold in Japan, a market for which that company is now producing domestic models of its global products that incorporate certain Japanese characteristics. Yet Goldstar's Soon-In Lee can tell the story of how Matsushita's design chief came with a group of young designers from Japan to visit Seoul's National Folklore Museum to see its displays of artifacts, which are older than those in equivalent Japanese collections. The following year, in Tokyo's Akihabara shopping district, Lee found Matsushita products, such as a rice cooker resembling an old food-carrying box, bearing clear Korean overtones. The Japanese came to Korea not to pillage another culture but to learn more about their own. "Philosophy and religious beliefs spread from China through Korea to Japan," explains Han-Yoo Park. "But modern industrial products reverse that flow."

Korea's function as a conduit for Chinese, Mongol, and Japanese influences throughout its Koryo (tenth to fourteenth centuries) and Yi (fifteenth to nineteenth centuries) dynasties and throughout the Japanese colonial period has, of course, introduced shared characteristics, but, as in Japan, periods of insularity have also permitted the culture to evolve relatively independently between upheavals. There are intrinsic similarities, for example in the teaching curricula of design schools in South Korea and Japan, but there are distinguishing features in the work they produce. "There is no Korean or Japanese style in product design," concedes graphic designer Chang Gwon-Bang, "but there are differences in crafts and visual communications that go back to the Yi Dynasty. The difference is that we use less color and purer form. Korea is quite gray. China and Japan use red and gold. Korean architecture is a natural wood color. The people dislike color." Chang exaggerates the case. Buildings, people's everyday dress, and, most obvious of all, the monochrome cars that clutter Seoul's highways, are indeed generally dull, but there are also frequent flashes of color, both traditional (the rainbow *dan-chung* patterns that decorate the temple woodwork) and modern (the synthetically dyed fabrics that make up Korea's *han-bok* costume).

Hyundai Sonata
1990

Koreans are fiercely loyal to local manufacturers but prefer them to emulate Japanese styling trends.

Logotype
San Whan Corporation

Many logotypes work hackneyed variations on the yin-yang symbol seen in the South Korean flag.

Chang Gwon-Bang believes the reticence is in part a reflection of the wish to harmonize with nature, a product of the form of Confucianism adopted by Korea in contrast to the prevailing Buddhism of China. Ceramics grew paler as they traveled from China to Korea, for example, and the celadon pottery for which Korea is famous is much paler than the intense blue Chinese work that was its precursor. "We believe that there is a Korean identity in cultural traditions which is totally different from the Chinese and Japanese," says Chang Sea Young, president of the Space Group of Korea, an architecture and design firm that sought to create work with a local character long before it became fashionable for the large corporations to do so. "But unfortunately a lot was lost during the Japanese occupation from 1910 to 1945." Chang believes that Korean long-term thinking—which he says is even longer than that of the Japanese—will prove useful in overcoming this dislocation: "We started research to try and find a Korean identity, even in product design. I don't think we have a good example at the moment. We are still searching. There will be many false starts, but we don't mind having those false starts because we consider it a long-term thing."

Space Group's facilities include galleries and a theater, which aim to facilitate a cross-fertilization from the fine arts and performing arts, where cultural traditions have perhaps been less disturbed, into design and architecture. Chang does not expect anything tangible to emerge from his studies, but stresses the difference between the Western wish to visualize and the Eastern ability to find a more spiritual dimension: "This is the big difference between Western and Eastern ways of thinking. In Western culture you may think the spirit can be visualized. Here the spirit means something internal. When you see a celadon artifact, if you do not see it with a spiritual eye, maybe you do not see it at all. But if you do see it, it has an excellence which distinguishes it even from the best ceramics in Japan or China."

Yet explicit elements of the national culture do exist. One such is Korea's invented *han-gul* alphabet. *Han-gul* characters are elegant arrangements of circles and lines. They would appear to form the perfect basis for distinctive typographic and logotype designs, but there is little evidence of their creative use. There are, on the other hand, several corporate identities that work unsubtle variations on the yin-yang circular symbol used in the Korean flag.

Like the Space Group, the Korea Institute of Industrial Design and Packaging has undertaken studies of traditional sources in an effort to fulfill its charter to help small- and medium-sized companies make better use of design. But, in general, the impetus does not come from any national cultural policy but is stimulated by commercial imperatives. "A lopsided government policy stressing economic development has brought about a lethargy of culture in our society," laments Cho Young-Jae, dean of the Graduate School of Industrial Arts at Seoul National University, in a recent issue of Korea's *Design Journal.* Large companies have learned the hard way, by watching their foreign competitors. Now, smaller companies are learning by their example.

The result of this cascade effect so far is that design awareness is running well ahead of good practice. One *chaebol*-made telephone is called the Art Phone and proclaims itself one of the company's "Good Design Products." Billboard advertisements flaunt the word *design*. New cars work it into decal slogans emblazoned on their sides. Design awards and exhibitions abound. Everywhere, design is in the air. Having gotten to this stage, the prospects are good that action will increasingly take the place of words. Once again, Korea appears to be following its old rival and foe and becoming every bit as design-conscious as Japan.

Tourist map
Kyoung-Kyum Kim/Chang-Sik Kim

143

Japan

It may be that the future of design is taking shape in an unprepossessing house shrouded by trees in the Shibuya district of Tokyo. It is from here that Naoki Sakai and his Water Studio have unleashed product concepts that are making entire industries rethink the role design has in their business.

The aluminum O Product and plastic O2 cameras for Olympus, the Be-1 and Pao autos for Nissan, the SW-1 motorcycle for Suzuki, and the Asterisk Stage II watch for Seiko are futuristic and retrospective all in one breath. They are the product of a very few, but vivid, imaginations. In Japan of all places, Sakai has cut a path all the way through middle management to talk directly to the top—though no one is quite sure how. There is no truck with market research. And Sakai makes no apology for not really doing any design or engineering either—all that is done by the client. "I make human desires," he says.

Director Juzo Iino is almost as expansive when, referring to Water Studio's work for Olympus, she attempts to explain the firm's philosophy: "We think this camera is different from Canon's and Nikon's cameras because this camera has a fantasy concept. It's funny and cute. The product is in a very important position for Olympus because it gives a sensational message to the market.

"We make fashion. We are not product designers. The design concept is the most important work. It is very creative. When we make a design concept we look all over the world.

"We want to make design very human, for young, funny people, not academic design for old, rich people. We want to make many designs for young people in the world.

"In the product world, future design is very old, we think. But in the fashion market, future design is very fantasy, like Jean-Paul Gaultier."

Water Studio does, in fact, take its lead from the fashion industry. Sakai, a former T-shirt producer, is part fashion designer, part impresario. He calls himself a "life designer." Others have called him a "conceptor." Many of his concepts are produced, like couture, in limited editions. The inspiration for these curiously familiar objects comes from books of historical images and from "memory." Satisfying the whims of young people is a constant refrain of the forty-three-year-old and his staff of sixteen, most of whom are in their twenties. Young people in Japan, says Iino, have grown rich in material possessions, sensuous, "life-styled." "So when they choose a product, they want a fantasy in the product message. This message is our concept."

Are the fin de siècle outpourings of Water Studio evidence of malicious shallowness or merely a candid reflection of the state of design in this over-rich, over-designed environment? Certainly Sakai's designs are not typical of what is happening in Japan, but they are perhaps symptomatic of the new demands of a sophisticated domestic market which has risen rapidly to rival and now to overtake all others.

It was not always thus. There is a Japanese phrase, *hachijutten shugi,* which describes the sort of products with which it was once possible to get by. It means, roughly, "80 percentism" or "good enough." But *hachijutten shugi* is good enough no more. "In the past the public used imperfect but reasonable products, but now they want 100 percent," says Yuichi Yamada, editor of *Design News,* published by the Japan Industrial Design Promotion Organization.

Hachijutten shugi was an unavoidable stage along the road of Japan's development since the end of the Second World War. The Ministry of International Trade and Industry (MITI) coordinated the development and determined the priorities of key industries with a battery of interventionist policies. It was MITI that brought in the technology and quality control that made it possible for one industry after another to overtake longer-established competitors abroad and build Japan's export market. It also sowed the seeds for design to join the armory of Japanese competitiveness. MITI's role is far from over. The ministry designated 1989 a year of redoubled design activity, and it has begun to implement a policy of devolution, establishing design centers in the prefectures in a bid to redress the perceived imbalance between prosperous Tokyo and the country's "rust-belt" regions.

MITI's attentions were lavished first on heavy industries such as shipbuilding and automobile manufacturing. After the Tokyo Olympic Games in 1964, the emphasis shifted to microelectronics technology and consumer-electronics goods. In due course, Japan became dominant in televisions, hi-fis, photographic equipment, and watches. It is only in the most culturally loaded products that Japan has failed to make much headway in export markets—in white goods, kitchen appliances, tableware, and, most notably, furniture.

On the home front, products in these areas remain comparatively immune to change. Some designers believe that the survival of traditionally made products for important rituals such as the tea ceremony and dining in some way compensates for the loss of cultural identity in product types made primarily for export. "The fact that we still have these products excuses what we have in mass production,"

Table, right; stool, below
Shiro Kuramata
Pastoe, 1988

Chaise longue
Toyo Ito
Driade, 1988

Perhaps because of different customs in posture, Japan has been conspicuously weak in the field of furniture manufacture. The few Japanese furniture designers have generally found European clients.

O-Product camera
Water Studio
Olympus, 1988

The newfound willingness by major manufacturers to explore quirky new concepts shows that Japan is emerging as an exciting design innovator.

Pao automobile
Water Studio
Nissan, 1989

S-Cargo automobile
Nissan
Photograph courtesy Design
Museum, London

CDZ-1 compact disk player
Sony

P-Touch personal lettering
system
Hirano Design
Brother Industries

Bottom: AX-110 typewriter
Hirano Design
Brother Industries

says interior designer Shigeru Uchida. Paradoxically, the fact that these two classes of product enjoy this uneasy coexistence may make it less likely than ever that craft skills in the one can be brought to bear on commercial design activities in the other.

It is not lack of resources that prevents some form of union from being achieved between the handwork involved in making ceramic or enameled wooden articles and the advanced manufacturing technology that makes possible high-quality plastic and consumer-electronics products. After all, the consumers are demanding 100 percent and have the cash to pay for it. Rather, the rift is evidence of a sense of disorientation, the result of a severing of cultural roots that was the price paid for Japan's postwar economic growth. The irony is all the greater in that Japan's strength as a manufacturing and trading power has made it the national economy par excellence in the world today and, hence, perhaps the best positioned to put into practice ideas of national identity in design.

Perhaps the best place to witness the modern market in harmony with cultural tradition is in Tokyo's myriad tiny fashion boutiques, restaurants, and clubs. When rich consumers buy high-margin products and services from high-profit retailers, the retailers find themselves passing the excess profits back to the consumers in the form of lavishly designed environments. These spare but expensive places often have a meditative quality that may have something to do with Zen Buddhism. This is certainly the case with Shigeru Uchida's work, which takes some inspiration from the spirit of Japanese arts from before the dawn of the Edo period around 1600. But Uchida readily concedes that this is blended with influences from an education centered on Western aesthetic values. "What concerns me is the relationship of things placed within a space and how people interact. One feels the space," he explains. His placing of line, plane, and volume is intuitive, bearing as much relation to De Stijl and Ludwig Mies van der Rohe's "universal space" as to Zen Buddhist ideas of the balance between the negative and positive spatial forces of yin and yang.

Elsewhere, there is further evidence of cultural dislocation in the quest for novelty. The baroque postmodernism of the British architect Nigel Coates and the buildings of Philippe Starck, which resemble giant products, provide contrasting examples. It is interesting to note, however, that the hunger for the consumption of celebrity has not thrown up a Japanese hero. There is one set of values for and within the global market, another for Japan and the Japanese whose national character still does not encourage excessive individualism.

This applies as much to industries as to people.

It is one reason why five of every six Japanese designers works in-house. Independent practitioners remain a tiny minority, albeit one growing in numbers and influence. Toyota, for example, employs approximately six hundred designers. Despite these legions, most corporations do little innovative design. It has been said that Japan has succeeded in coming first because its industries are so good at coming second. There is much truth in this. For every Sony or Nissan—the principal innovators in their respective markets—there is a host of manufacturers who follow their lead and who make up the bulk of the market. Yet these companies have just as much need of a design policy as their conspicuous role models. Hirano Design has helped Toshiba, Hitachi, and Brother refine their design strategies. Tetsuyuki Hirano believes that Hitachi, for example, presents a more complex problem than Sony, which, though a design leader, is a comparatively small and sharply focused company. Hitachi must coordinate design activity across divisions producing a wide range of industrial and consumer products. Do not expect any of these companies to pioneer "Japanese" design, warns Hirano. The Japanese civilization has not contributed greatly to the preindustrial shaping of any of the artifacts that they now find themselves manufacturing. They see no other path forward than that of globalism.

Yet in recent years products have emerged from Japan that would not have emerged from any other country. In these cases, it is invention rather than design that springs from a unique set of national characteristics. Necessity is the mother of invention, and the Japanese have some particular necessities. Not the least of these is the need to print and transmit messages in the kanji alphabet. The difficulty of manipulating these characters led directly to the development of the facsimile machine. Some commentators also believe that the Walkman is a product of the wish of the Japanese to achieve a hermetic isolation from their fellows whenever possible.

The celebrated spark of imagination that led to the creation of the Walkman may not be repeatable. Even Sony appears to have lost some of its will to innovate. It prefers to reinforce the perceived worth of the Sony brand with safer products and has sent signals that design has become a less important ingredient to its success by absorbing its design department within "merchandising." Those companies that are good at coming second are still less confident. Independent designers perceive a general malaise and of course feel that they offer the best remedy. Their existence only really became a fact of industrial life in the late 1980s, and they are confident that their share of the action will grow—if, that is, their role is not usurped by concept boutiques like Water Studio.

Nijo-Daime "So" prefabricated
tea-room
Shigeru Uchida
Gallery Ma, 1989

Below: Paper showroom
Shigeru Uchida
Aoyama Mihoncho, 1989
Photograph by Nacasa &
Partners

*The contemplative quality of
Uchida's designs have their root
in Zen tradition.*

In their anonymous way, the vast majority of Japanese industrial designers who work in-house for the big manufacturers are also picking up and discarding trend after trend in pursuit of the novelty that the market demands. Yamada recites the litany—pastel colors, seen most notably in audio products from Sharp, touchy-feely "action surfaces," and now "bio-colors," not just the predictable subtle shades of nature but also, for example, the insectlike green iridescence of the Nissan Sylvia. "A few years ago, pink was a trend, but now the baby colors are becoming out of date. It was a metaphor for the happiness of our lives. Maybe we have become happy so we don't need it any more," Yamada suggests archly. He adds: "Pursuing high-quality products is the current trend so the colors become richer and darker. The Japanese recognize that heavy, dark colors and materials have a higher value."

More naturalism has also been introduced in product form. This development is most obvious in upscale consumer-electronics products, with increasingly "organic" shapes being found in personal stereos and cameras especially. Some believe that this trend reflects the greater use during product development of computer-aided design systems, which make it easier to realize complex shapes. On the other hand, one of the most influential of the new biomorphic products, the Sony headphones designed by Luigi Colani, was sculpted by hand. Whatever the nature of the creative act involved in fashioning these products, there is also a competitive justification for their presence. Free of the confines of the sharp-edged rectangle, there is theoretically greater opportunity to differentiate rival goods (though it is odd to find that for all this there is still remarkable uniformity among them in the stores). Nevertheless, manufacturers seem happy to be led down the organic garden path. If the use of computer-aided design equipment is indeed facilitating this development, then it is one that seems bound to continue.

Japan is also exhibiting a trend toward larger products. This overturns a long-standing expectation that everything Japanese is geared for ever-greater miniaturization and flies in the face of the reality of the ever-present squeeze on domestic space. "Such large products—for example, larger refrigerators, washing machines, televisions—are not necessary for us, but they are a metaphor for affluence," says Yamada. Cars, too, are growing larger. Luxury models such as the Nissan Infiniti are becoming the rule; the tiny Sakai models, only available in limited editions, very much the cultish exception. Some of this upward drift in the size of products can be attributed

to the values of a new generation, brought up in a greatly Americanized Japan, which believes in the display of status. The parents of this generation had less desire for such show and customarily stored products that were not in use.

The innate Japanese quality of products, if it exists at all, does not come from factors such as size, shape, and color. These are variables open to manipulation by companies that are happy to satisfy the transient whims of the market. According to industrial designer Kozo Sato, what these manufacturers create is solely the product of diligent market research and certainly not a sign of the sort of cultural self-confidence shared by producer and consumer in Italy. What, then, are the elusive ingredients of Japaneseness? According to Masato Isaka of the GK design firm, they are a sense of simplicity, compactness, and fine detailing—"more with less" and "less is more." A recent personal audio system for Yamaha, one of GK's oldest clients, exemplifies these qualities with its subtle controls and placid façade. For some, the gray suedelike plastic echoes the dour colors of the Edo period in Japanese art. "The Japanese care about details," comments Tetsuyuki Hirano. "They always look at a product in its small aspects [whereas] the Germans still think of the total concept." In Germany a product is well detailed because it is seen as a logical extension of its functionalism; in Japan it is well detailed in order that it be beautiful to look at. This is 100 percentism.

Some designers believe that this level of finesse in product design and manufacture is bound up with a long history of craft. Not so, says Sato, who credits current successes more to postwar learning from the United States and Germany: "The Bauhaus had a cultural context as an art movement. We took their movement but without adding our cultural context. This is a problem now, but at the time it was not important." The cultural discontinuity of the postwar years compounds the discontinuity introduced with the Meiji Restoration during the last half of the nineteenth century when the arts and artifacts of the preceding Edo period were largely forgotten or destroyed.

It is significant that the corporations—such as Sony and Honda—that are recognized as Japan's design leaders are ones that grew up after the Second World War. It is not their priority to resuscitate a style of design rooted in Japanese history. The arts that flourished in a Japan that shut itself off from the world appear to have little relevance to the cultural evolution of today's successful international trading power. "People ask why don't we use Kyoto and Nara [capital cities during the centuries before the Meiji Restoration when Japan was shut off from

Right: Komako Sake bottle
GK Graphics
Kikkoman Corporation, 1985

Kozo Sato, principal of one of the new young independent design firms that are now springing up in Japan, has made reference to traditional craft techniques and artifacts in his work.

Top: CD player
Kozo Design Studio
Pioneer Electronic Corporation, 1990

Above: Multiple-media information terminal
Kozo Design Studio
1984

Astarte line audio equipment
GK
Yamaha Corporation, 1989

Above: "Mishima" film set
Eiko Ishioka

Left: "M. Butterfly" stage set
Eiko Ishioka

Eiko Ishioka's stage and graphic designs find a middle ground with a Japanese spirit that is nevertheless comprehensible abroad.

JAPAN

Poster
Ikko Tanaka, 1986

Graphic design styles polarize sharply between the florid work of Tadanori Yokoo at one extreme and the cool simplicity of Ikko Tanaka on the other.

"Garuda" poster
Tadanori Yokoo
Garuda Performa[...]
Company, 1990

Electric fan heater
Toshiba Corporation, 1989

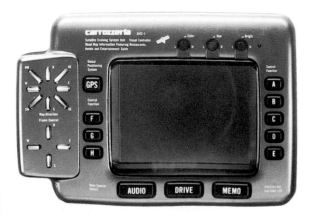

Car information system
Pioneer Electronic Corporation,
1989

the outside world] as sources," says Sato. "But this is not exciting for the Japanese. We made many fine things then, but with no outside criticism or awareness of their value."

Despite these misgivings, there have been various attempts to design products that are explicitly Japanese. Sato's own project for a flat-screen personal computer uses the colors of traditional confectionery in place of the crude primary colors of the lights and highlights on most terminals. The body of the machine rejects the conventional pale gray in favor of a mottled dark-greenish shade. With this color and with its profile of an ogee curve, the keyboard resembles a traditional Japanese pantile.

A study for a Pioneer compact-disc player by Sato is one of a number of recent designs to use black lacquerwork or a simulation of lacquer in highly polished plastic to evoke the Japanese craft tradition. The lacquer effect on Sato's compact-disc player is limited to the control panel. The same is true in the Nissan Infiniti, where the instruments are mounted on a lacquerwork dashboard. A recent Sony compact-disc audio system was also packaged in a "hand-crafted cabinet in piano black lacquer." The lacquerwork seems appropriate because the system looks more like a freestanding unit of furniture than a conventional piece of hi-fi equipment. The Pioneer and Nissan designs use lacquer where a wood surface might be expected. These things can be taken too far, however. Sato recalls once seeing a "lacquerwork" telephone, and that, he says, was pure kitsch.

Masayoshi Tsuchiya, a designer within the audio group in the Sony design department, claims a more tenuous Japanese character for the WM-109, one of the company's hundreds of models of Walkman personal stereo sets. Tsuchiya took the idea for a black-and-white Walkman from a striking fashion photograph, and then, casting around for a suitable finish for the product, was struck by the appearance of a ceramic chopstick holder. The double-painted metal of the final product tries to capture the brittle blue-whiteness of the porcelain.

While there have been still more self-conscious attempts to convey a Japanese quality among the corporate identities of exporting companies, appearances are deceptive. "About half of the corporate identity programs in Japan are done by American companies," claims graphic designer Ikko Tanaka. Among the better recent examples are programs for Minolta by Saul Bass and for Nissan by Chermayeff and Geismar. The American designers are making further inroads, thanks more to their professionalism in presentation and implementation than to the quality of their image making, which can strike the Japanese as too literal-minded.

Top: Logotype
Yusaka Kamekura
NTT Corporation

Bottom: Corporate identity
GK Graphics
Cosmo Oil Company, 1986

Some indigenous corporate identity work has a definite Japanese quality, but many companies look to U.S. design firms for their symbols.

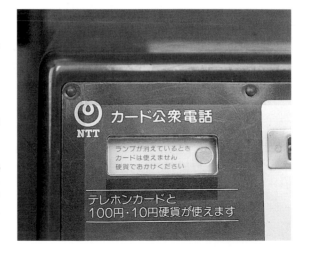

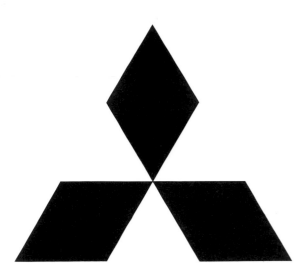

Logotype
Mitsubishi Corporation

Logotype
Sumitomo Bank

Less modish logotypes such as those of Mitsubishi and Sumitomo bank are based on family crest symbols.

Many of Japan's best-known logotypes are simply the company names in a Western typeface modified by the addition of what might be called samurai serifs—Canon, Aiwa, Akai, and NEC are examples of the genre. All these companies are well known overseas, and the perception of their Japaneseness created by using this device can have done them little harm. Although many of these identities date from just after the war, the American Landor Associates continued the tradition with its recent corporate identity for Japan Airlines. The previous symbol, a circular motif of a red crane with wings outspread, was based on a medieval family crest, and heraldry remains the foundation for many of Japan's more durable symbols, including, for example, the triangular motif of Mitsubishi.

In general, the best of Japanese graphic design is less tainted by modern foreign influence. The link with the art of the Edo period of the seventeenth and eighteenth centuries is evident in the precise linearity and two-dimensionality of many compositions. (Representation of shadow and perspective in Japanese art did not emerge until the end of the nineteenth century, far later than in Western art.) Many modern posters contain clear references to the watercolor and ukiyoe woodblock printing techniques of the Edo period in their use of gradations of tone and blocks of uniform color. The readiness to use calligraphy as part of a design also stems from the custom of integrating written and pictorial matter in traditional prints. "There is a Japanese style in graphic design," says Tanaka. "In general it has a flatness. As a whole, it can also be said that preciseness of craftsmanship in design is another quality. This might be an influence from the size of the land we have. If you look at our design from afar, it may not have punch, but if you look closely you see a precision in the design and printing." Tanaka suggests that Japanese graphic design is very nearly the opposite of that in Poland or France, for example, where an expressionistic impact counts for much. In these countries, communication is direct, blunt, sometimes startling, but in Japan it is more often oblique. "Japan is a homogeneous society, and until the seventeenth century it was a closed country, so means of communication are not straightforward and bold." This is well demonstrated today in television advertising that would baffle Western audiences. Some locally conceived corporate identities, such as that for Cosmo gas stations by GK or for the NTT telephone company by Yusaka Kamekura, also have a distinctively elliptical quality.

With the fall of the Edo shogunate in 1868, Japan began to exchange ideas with the outside world. The reciprocal influences of Japanese and Western cultures have been apparent ever since. The Meiji era broadened the color sensibility, adding bright new colors to the somber range favored before. In recent years, California pop culture, fluorescent colors, and Japanese aesthetics have traveled back and forth across the Pacific, enlivening both cultures, just as once European Art Nouveau once took inspiration from Japan. Ikko Tanaka stands aloof from these recent developments, although, like Shigeru Uchida, he has been influenced by classic Modernism. The psychedelic, baroque, and frequently bizarre work of his peers, Tadanori Yokoo and Eiko Ishioka, is more the product of these recent cultural confusions, as are the covers of many Japanese magazines and comic books. Tanaka suggests that the difference between the two styles is that between florid Buddhism and ascetic Shintoism. Others may disagree, but what is certain is that both are inherently Japanese.

Corporate identity
Landor Associates
Japan Airlines, 1989

The lettering used by many Japanese corporations doing business overseas sport what might be called "samurai serifs," an unsubtle reference to traditional calligraphy.

ECII telephone
Ecco Design
1990

At the New Jersey–bound entrance to the Holland Tunnel in Manhattan is a hazard-striped barrier strung across the road warning of a height limit ahead. Necessary information, to be sure, but the sign just after it is far more telling. It reads: "We Mean It." Americans have never been able to take information graphics with the seriousness of the easily led northern Europeans. Much more characteristic is the sign—an official one—that reads: "Don't Even Think of Parking Here."

Like these signs, American design at its best is all about communicating, and doing so with pragmatism and humor. The United States has never had much time for the monotheisms of the Bauhaus, Ulm, and the Swiss graphic design schools. "We are not a homogeneous nation. One ideology would simply be un-American," says Paula Scher, a New York partner of Pentagram. "The common thread is wit, humor, parody, self-mockery, and the lampooning of dogma and tradition. The heart of American design is anti-elitism. Americans are anti-elitists and anti-ismists. This happens to be the finest aspect of our national personality."

The roots of this anti-elitism lie in America's attitude to its democracy—the one thing about the country that cannot be mocked. Over the centuries people have emigrated to America prepared, if not actually desperate, to leave their history behind them. Since the Declaration of Independence in 1776, the United States has encouraged individuality at the expense of any collective cultural identity. The immigrant groups willingly subjected themselves and their identities to the alloying heat of the American melting pot. The low degree of respect accorded to tradition today applies in all walks of American life, whether that tradition relates to immigrant cultures or to American culture created by those cultures once they settled. "I think the term 'eclectic' expresses the feeling that one gets from viewing American design in general," says Tom Hardy, design manager of IBM. "Democracy (individualism) and immigration (the mix of cultures) are key links in this landscape."

This is not to say that certain traditions have not had their impact on the United States. But their influence is due more to the character of certain individuals than to a collective assimilation of a culture. Swiss Modernism influenced graphic design in the United States because of the teaching of Herbert Bayer and others who moved to the country. "The Swiss grid is the underpinning of American corporate graphics, and Paul Rand is the biggest king of Swiss design in the world," says Los Angeles-based graphic designer

April Greiman. Stripped of the moral self-righteousness it exerted in Europe, it became in America merely another style, put to good use only by a few and travestied by the rest. The same happened with the architecture of the Modern movement in Europe, imported to the United States by Henry-Russell Hitchcock and Philip Johnson as the International Style, the title of their 1932 exhibition at the Museum of Modern Art in New York. Up to a point, it happened again when the Bauhaus was expelled from Germany and attempted to reconstitute itself in Chicago.

These influences were primarily visual. More innately American were the literary strands in graphic design. The period between the two world wars saw a flowering of advertising copywriting that found its match in graphic design. Much of the humor on display here stems from the Jewish culture. "Herb Lubalin and then Lou Dorfsman made type talk," says Steven Heller, an art director with the New York Times and the author of many works on graphic design. "They liked playing with language because they came out of a tradition where language was played with." Although American copywriting is not what it once was, the inventive arrangement of letters and words to humorous effect remains a theme of American graphic design today, nowhere more so than in the work of Tibor Kalman's New York design firm, M & Co.

Perhaps the most memorable example of such design is the "I ♥ NY" symbol Milton Glaser devised for New York State tourism promotion. Glaser's illustrative work with Push Pin Studios was also seen as distinctly American. "It was a kind of antidote to Swiss design and to a general view of Modernism as being the basis for all design activities. It was defined by its antithesis to Modernist philosophy," says Glaser. "It dealt with issues of irony and complexity and corruption rather than purity and so on."

In product design, the virtues of democracy and individuality have not been so liberating. They did sow the seed for the notion that utility products should be available to the maximum number, which in turn saw to it that the United States was where the modern profession of industrial designer came into being. However, these same ideals that placed the principles of choice, quality, convenience, and inventiveness before people in due course also gave rise to planned obsolescence, gadgetry, and gimmickry, and, paradoxically, perpetuated the low level of design awareness that is now a contributor to America's comparative lack of competitiveness in the international trade in manufactured goods.

This low level of design awareness began with a lack of stylishness. Without the courts and aristocracies of European countries, America directed its at-

Lassie Come Home kennel
Smart Design, 1989

Jefferson chair
Niels Diffrient

American products often have slopes and bevels where international competitors will use simple geometric forms.

Spectra camera, electronic control "pro" version
Henry Dreyfuss Associates
Polaroid Corporation, 1990

tention toward the practical rather than the decorative. This drive, combined with the individual spirit, encouraged the emergence of conspicuous inventors such as Henry Ford and Thomas Edison. These figures seem rare today as the growing pressures of consumerism have replaced genuine innovation with a ceaseless tide of poorly conceived novelty products advertised in airline catalogs and on cable television. Yet these are no less American than their predecessors. According to Tucker Viemeister of Smart Design, "Americans are always looking for ways to make life easier, which leads to all kinds of inventions, from contraptions to peel an apple, to gizmos to copy the pages of a book, to remote controllers to open their garage doors. But the function is always more important than the look of the device. That it actually works is the final judge."

A strong sense of the practical is also evident in the solid foundations that were laid for the modern disciplines of human factors engineering and industrial design, both of which largely took shape as professions in the United States in the years before the Second World War. The legacy of the pioneering human factors work of Henry Dreyfuss and others is seen today in the products created by his and other firms. Oxo's Good Grips kitchen gadgets by Davin Stowell and others at Smart Design are said in product literature to "demonstrate that ergonomics aren't just for automobiles and medical equipment." The tools—can openers, corers, even a pizza wheel—have large-diameter handles with an elastomer coating and special finger grips. Though intended especially for people who might have difficulty operating conventional tools, Good Grips avoid the stigma of appearing as if they have been designed for these groups. "They were designed to aid users of all abilities. People with special needs should not have to search for special products. Although the bigger handles are a requirement for some disabilities, they are more comfortable for everyone," says Viemeister.

Henry Dreyfuss Associates' Spectra camera for Polaroid contains a nest of intricate mechanics that enable it to produce its instant photographs. The need to minimize the body size and make the camera easy to hold led to the complex but compact shape, which is a far cry from the European ideal of pure geometric form. "Utilizing natural draft angles helped us reduce the final apparent size of the camera and make it more comfortable to hold," says its designer, Jim Ryan. Don Genaro, senior partner of Henry Dreyfuss Associates, believes that good human factors, an emphasis on a product's clarity of purpose, and an effort to eliminate ambiguities in appearance that might otherwise impair function remain dominant in the best American product

design today.

"The Puritan ethic drives our need for simple, functional, engineered, economical design," says Viemeister. "The idea is not to fuss over it—easy, no big deal, casual. As a people we just want to relax." This is evident in the comfortable cashmere fashions of New York designer Donna Karan as well as in the continuing popularity of jeans. It is seen in furniture, from the Barcalounger at one end of the social scale to the (functionally equivalent) Eames lounge chair and ottoman at the other. The latter comes from Herman Miller, a firm whose Dutch Protestant origins are still much in evidence. Herman Miller occupies the same corner of the same state—Michigan—as several of America's other furniture manufacturers, including Steelcase, the nation's largest. Between them, these firms have used engineering and ergonomics to advance office furniture design to the point where American leadership in the field is incontestable. The Puritan spirit, common across much of the design profession and a powerful force in industries such as these, serves to shut out more radical or decadent designers in a manner that would be unthinkable in Italy, for example. These people find themselves all but excluded from the manufacturing process. As a result, say Godley-Schwan, a Brooklyn duo of furniture designers, "the more innovative design is seen more often as one-of-a-kind pieces. Marketing of the more innovative design is more isolated, existing for a small market primarily through galleries or specialized showrooms." With disciplinary boundaries so sharply drawn, this design is quickly categorized as art and ghettoized to appropriate parts of town.

The early heroes of the design profession were versatile men who were not so hasty with narrow definitions. Raymond Loewy became an industrial designer after a career in advertising. Dreyfuss and Norman Bel Geddes came out of the theatrical profession. Charles Eames pioneered the application of new technologies in the making of furniture but also managed to make films and architecture. However, this polymath spirit, as American as Jefferson, was gradually eradicated as the design profession matured. Today and to a limited degree, only a very few figures, such as Emilio Ambasz and Massimo Vignelli, adhere to this tradition.

For the majority, however, it pays to cut a quieter figure. Marketing and engineering considerations still dominate manufacturers' decision-making processes. Products must be designed to be efficiently made in the factory and profitable in the market, says Eric Chan of ECCO Design. He notes that "this pragmatic approach is very deep in the corporate culture and has a great impact on design decisions." Despite their flamboyant ways, the founding fathers

Apparel
Donna Karan
Fall 1991

*Casual comfort is a criterion
in American fashion design.*

Dancer cabinets, left; Terrain
cabinet, right
Godley-Schwan, 1990

*Godley-Schwan find that there
is little dialogue between the
avant-garde and the giants of
American furniture manufacture
as there would be in, say, Italy.*

Communications station set
Ecco Design
Nynex Corporation, 1989

*An advance in product
ergonomics is exploited for
stylistic purposes in Eric Chan's
communications equipment
for Nynex.*

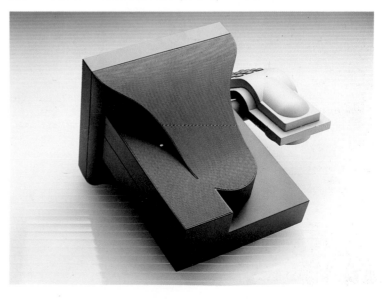

Good Grips kitchen tools
Smart Design
Oxo, 1990

The best American product design does not compromise when it comes to ergonomics, but neither does ergonomics become the mantra it is in some northern European design.

Billboard
April Greiman
Walker Art Center, 1990

of American design did their bit to inculcate the notion that the future of the profession lay in cooperation with manufacturing industry.

A more complex world demanded greater specialization, and in common with other professions design gradually segmented into specialties with little exchange of ideas between them. There are now signs that some people are recognizing a need to reverse this trend, if not as individuals then as companies. Some of the new generation, such as Smart Design, purposely bring related design disciplines under one roof. In California, Frogdesign, IDEO, and others are broadening their capabilities by merging with other design firms or by bringing in people with talents in new areas.

In Genaro's view, the evolution of the industrial design profession has happened in such a way that the United States today offers a microcosm of the design scene worldwide: "We who practice industrial design in the U.S. have a unique situation wherein the markets served offer a rich variety geographically, climatically, and culturally. It all adds up to global market conditions within the very borders of the U.S. The resultant absence of a 'nationalistic' cultural design identity, in the strict sense, is therefore understandable." Genaro goes further, observing that even with all this diversity to call upon and with every known material and manufacturing process at their disposal, American designers have nevertheless concluded that their role is to create products that transcend cultural context.

There are hints in this argument of other familiar American attitudes. There is the preoccupation with their own huge country that outsiders take as xenophobia and isolationism. There is also a determined form of culturelessness, related to the disregard for cultural traditions, whereby regional differences are suppressed in favor of anodyne solutions that are acceptable to all. Some designers believe that these attitudes must now be overcome if American design is to recover some of the esteem it once enjoyed. "The U. S. is a parochial country. It's because we're so big. Our bigness has not only been our success, it's probably going to be our downfall," says Deane Richardson of Fitch RichardsonSmith. "Isolationism is reflected in American products," adds Gerard Furbershaw of Lunar Design. "You see these products that would never sell any place else in the world because they are so ugly."

While there is indeed no cohesive identity the way there is in some smaller countries, this is not to say that American designers necessarily succeed in creating products that transcend their cultural contexts. The potential for difference is shown in a comparison of the products of IBM and Apple Computer. The former represent the first age of American de-

sign patronage, the old, the East Coast, pragmatic form. The latter represents the new age, the West Coast, and dogmatic form. Both corporations have a demanding credo. To join either would seem to be a little like entering a monastery, the only difference being that the IBM faith is Presbyterian whereas Apple is charismatic.

Apple Computer is based in Cupertino, California. Alongside it, up and down Silicon Valley and stretching beyond it in an arc that runs from Arizona out to the southern California coast and north to Portland and Seattle, are many of the second generation of American industrial design firms, the successors to Walter Dorwin Teague, Dreyfuss, Geddes, and Loewy. California now manufactures more than any other state in the Union. It has a stronger base of innovation, more international trade, and a thriving service sector, making it fertile territory for both graphic and product design. These qualities make California even more prone to seek self-renewal than other states, but more open to foreign influences as well. "Californians tend to look anywhere and everywhere for influences to help them reinvent their life-style and surroundings," says Jeff Smith of Lunar Design, a Palo Alto product design firm. "Easterners seem to take more cues from the past and are less inventive in spirit."

Much of California's population was not born in the state but migrated to it from other parts of the country or from other parts of the world. April Greiman, who is regarded as having spearheaded the "New Wave" in graphic design, is a New Yorker with an education from Kansas and Switzerland. Bill Moggridge, who heads IDEO, and Hartmut Esslinger of Frogdesign came from England and Germany, respectively. Henk Elenga, a Dutch designer running what is semi-seriously referred to as the Hard Werken LA Desk, also made the transition: "I thought this would be a nice desert to come to—physically and mentally—and it is." It is, of course, not uncommon for Europeans to make this rather snooty observation about America in general and California in particular. But there *is* both culture and cultural history here. The latter, though not long by Old World standards, is no less genuine for that. Moggridge believes that the apparent culturelessness of the place, the endless process of willfully sweeping aside what has gone before, whether in technology, history, or the arts, *is* the culture. It could not be transplanted or even very easily imagined anywhere else.

Greiman and others claim their location gives their work a spiritual dimension that is missing elsewhere. They also enjoy new sources of inspiration from around the Pacific shores and especially from Japan. In general, designers such as Michael

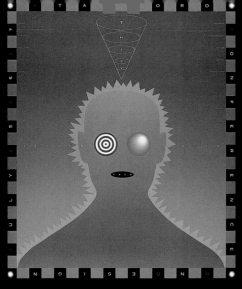

A group of graphic designers, all seemingly called Michael, have done much to characterize a San Francisco "look."

Above: Poster
Michael Vanderbyl

Right: Logotype
Michael Vanderbyl

Below: Poster
Michael Vanderbyl

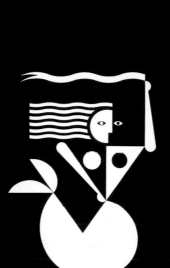

Above: Poster
Michael Mabry/Peter Soe
AIGA New York

Above right: Magazine illustration
Michael Mabry/Matthew Drace
S.F. Focus Magazine

Right: Golden Shears award
Michael Mabry/Jeff Pilotte/Matthew Drace
S.F. Focus Magazine and Absolut Vodka

Left: Poster
Michael Manwaring, 1990
Photograph by Michael Datoli

Above: Identification signage
Michael Manwaring
San Jose Redevelopment Agency, 1990

Right: Poster
Michael Manwaring, 1990

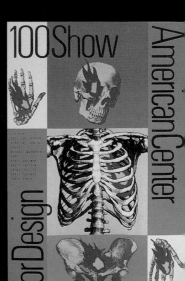

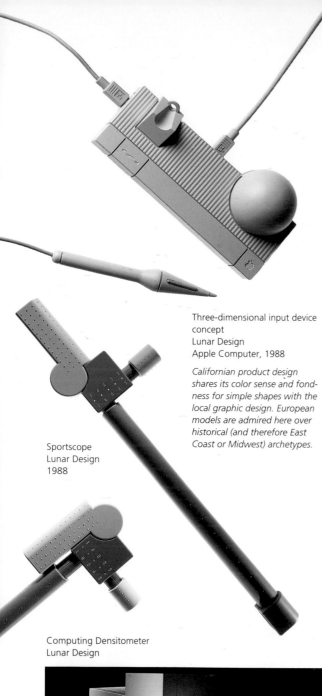

Three-dimensional input device concept
Lunar Design
Apple Computer, 1988

Californian product design shares its color sense and fondness for simple shapes with the local graphic design. European models are admired here over historical (and therefore East Coast or Midwest) archetypes.

Sportscope
Lunar Design
1988

Computing Densitometer
Lunar Design

Vanderbyl, Michael Manwaring, and Michael Mabry in San Francisco as well as April Greiman in Los Angeles use color with more confidence than other American designers. This is due partly to the local light and climate but also to the influence of the different color palettes that are customarily used in Mexico and Japan.

The transpacific liaison is not entirely a new thing. Some of the Eameses' work took its cue from Japanese design, for example. But it is worth remembering that Japan and the rest of Asia are considerably farther away from California than is any part of the United States. The Pacific Rim influence can be attributed to the quest for novelty and new friendships as much as any practical cause. Of the latter, strong and increasing trade ties are important. Californians buy proportionally more Japanese cars than other Americans. This is partly because they feel closer to Japan, but it is also an indicator of a national trend, for California is a bellwether of American taste.

California has been exploited as a sort of lifestyle workshop in the creation of a number of recent design successes. Mountain bikes were born in California as were automobiles such as the Nissan Pulsar and the Mazda Miata. The Miata, also known as the MX-5, is a reworking of the traditional British or Italian sports car, various models of which are much favored in the state. The initial design was done in the state by Mazda. Perhaps the most noticeable California influence is in "sports" fashions, a field that the San Francisco company Esprit has done much to make its own. Acutely conscious of the power of design in selling clothes that promised to bestow a certain life-style, Esprit founders Doug and Susie Tompkins made use of unusually effective architecture, graphic design, and packaging to sell a mediocre product.

The business of industrial design in California is far less relaxed. Spurred by the sense of excitement of working in the front line of technological development for companies that are often bitter rivals, industrial designers have responded by rejecting the happy-go-lucky appearance traditional to many products and tightening up the formal language of their design. "Americans have seen that seemingly obvious pragmatic axioms of design, such as generous draft angles and coarse textures to hide blemishes, are often detrimental to product aesthetics," comments Lunar Design's Jeff Smith. Apple Computer blazed the trail for case moldings with zero angles of draft, but the most severe statement in the new language comes from the anthracite black cube computer by Frogdesign for Next, the company Steven Jobs set up when he left Apple.

There is a marked agreement among the top

Valley firms on the nature of the formal refinement that has taken place. This is probably because client companies, ever watchful of what their rivals are doing, are keen to conform to the prevailing style. But it is also undoubtedly due in large measure to the fact that so many of the Valley firms are so closely interrelated. It began in 1979 when Bill Moggridge established ID Two as a companion office to Moggridge Associates in London. The Englishman gained a German rival when Hartmut Esslinger opened a Frogdesign office in the Valley a few years later. Since then, Mike Nuttall, another Briton, left ID Two to set up Matrix Product Design. (More recently, ID Two, Nuttall's company, and David Kelley Design, a respected local design and engineering firm, have joined forces as IDEO.) Another new group, Interform, started with a German principal from Frogdesign and another from GVO, a long-established design firm in the area. Lunar Design in turn grew out of Interform. More recently, new groups have sprung up as young designers who have learned the ropes at Frogdesign and IDEO's antecedents go their own ways. Through all this, it is notable that the Anglo-Saxon hegemony is largely unbroken. Some of the newest groups are trying to break away from the rules of good form that have become the local orthodoxy, but in general it is remarkable how strong this school has become, not just in the Valley but also at Fischerdesign in Arizona, Patton Design in Costa Mesa (in southern California), Ziba Design in Oregon, and Technology Design in Seattle, which share with their northern California cousins a preoccupation with platonic form straight out of the tradition of European Modernism.

Apple Computer remains the local paradigm. As the company has grown, it has commissioned several of the local design firms—an arrangement that has profited both parties. In 1990 the company changed its design policy and began to set up an in-house design department under Robert Brunner, a former principal of Lunar Design, one of the groups to enjoy Apple's patronage. Brunner, of course, hopes that his will be more adventurous than the average American corporate design department. He cites Braun among his models. The Anglo-Saxon hegemony seems assured.

If there is a more inherently American design, it is perhaps that from the rust-belt that stretches from Chicago to New York. The decline of industry here may have forced a reappraisal of the role of the industrial designer. Design schools, such as the Cranbrook Academy of Art in Michigan and that of Ohio State University, have investigated new design languages, quickly known by the unhappy buzzwords "product semantics," that could be used to appropriate elements from the American product tradition.

Voyager headset
Fitch RichardsonSmith
Texas Instruments

One of the most inventive regions for design now is the former "rust-belt," home of Fitch RichardsonSmith and many new design firms.

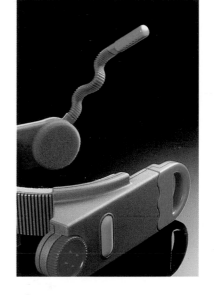

Logotype
Thirst
Lyric Opera of Chicago, 1989

The use of letter forms to create a pictorial image has long been a favored technique in American graphic design.

Esprit showroom
Michael Vanderbyl

Poster
Thirst
Details, 1990

Other work recalls the distinctively American design of the 1940s and 1950s.

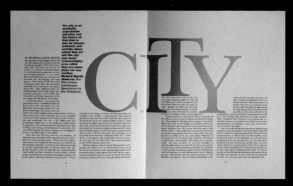

New York designers often find the work of their Californian colleagues colorful, polished—and banal. Their work on the other hand is brash and witty, supposedly favoring context over style.

Above: Graphic identity
Drenttel Doyle Partners
World Financial Center,
1988–90

Above right and right:
Exhibition catalog
Drenttel Doyle Partners
Olympia and York, 1990

Left: Corporate literature
M & Co.
Knoll International, 1990

Below: Stationery
M & Co.

There was once
a company named Knoll.
Its reputation rested
on museum-quality
furniture.

That company is
no longer relevant.

A few design firms have found the region to have advantages. "The rust-belt has gone through most of its transition," observes Deane Richardson of Fitch RichardsonSmith who has constructed at his base in Columbus, Ohio, a large firm that brings fresh disciplines to bear on design problems. "Human factors has evolved into what we call information design, a field made up of cognitive psychologists, experimental psychologists, and writers, probably journalism majors who have a computer science minor." Richardson's staff comprises designers from the local and national schools and graduates of these other disciplines drawn from nearby Carnegie-Mellon University.

The Cranbrook ideas have found their clearest expression in projects by the Chicago-based group Design Logic, a collaboration between Martin Thaler, a graduate of London's Royal College of Art, and Cranbrook alumnus David Gresham, who is now design director of Fitch RichardsonSmith, after a brief sojourn as principal of Details, a New York group that produces office accessories for Steelcase. Some of Design Logic's early work, such as a telephone-answering machine produced as a study for Dictaphone, reacts against Euclidean conventions by quoting from the American vernacular. The machine looks like a U.S. Mailbox, even down to an echo of its cheap corrugated aluminum construction. When it records a message a liquid-crystal display panel indicates the fact, just as a mailman will flip up the red flag of a mailbox to show that a letter is waiting.

Similar ideas have informed graphic design teaching at the school, which draws on sources both American and European. "If Cranbrook teaching has any identifiable external root," says David Frej, a recent graduate now running his own graphic design studio, Influx, also in Chicago, "it is in vernacular graphic, typographic, product, and architectural forms that exist here or 'over there.'" It is perhaps no coincidence that Robert Venturi also works in this most truly American stretch of the country. The intellectualized vernacular architecture that he creates bears parallels with the creations of the Cranbrook and Ohio State thinking in product design and the witty East Coast graphics work of groups such as M & Co.

Venturi has built comparatively little although his writings have been extremely influential. Likewise, little design has entered the mainstream that expresses vernacular origins. It, too, may prove more important to theory than to practice. The question now is whether American industry can see the potential on its doorstep to use designers to revitalize its industry, cut the nation's trade deficit, and, by creating products of this sort, conjure up some of the excitement of earlier eras in American design.

Robert Venturi and Denise Scott-Brown gave architecture pause for thought with their reference to vernacular sources. It remains to be seen whether Design Logic and others can produce the same effect among manufacturers.

Below: Telephone answering machine prototype
Design Logic
Dictaphone, 1987

Inset: U.S. Mail box

Chairs
Venturi, Rauch and Scott-Brown
Knoll International

Poster
Influx
Details, 1990

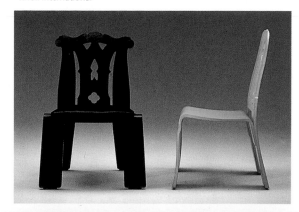

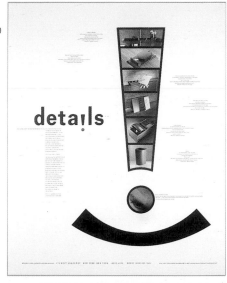

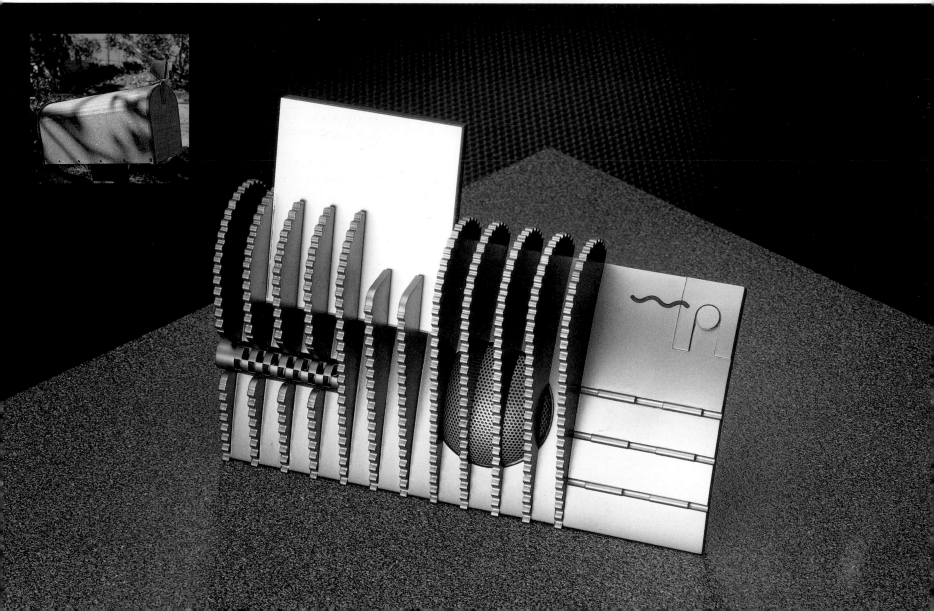

Canada

In the heat of the separatist summer of 1990, one might have expected that Quebec, more than any other province in Canada, would provide testimony to its uniqueness. But Quebec's designers were bemused. Their work had no identity, they said. They were happy to describe the elements of French or German cultural identity in design, they noted the emergence of *la chanson québecois,* new folk song, they saw local qualities in the advertising, but of their own work, *rien à dire.* "It's against our will to find a Quebecois style," says Frédéric Metz, director of the design center of the Université du Québec à Montréal. "Even my most separatist student just wants to do good graphic design."

The Meech Lake accord, which would have recognized Quebec, which is home to a quarter of Canada's population, as a distinct society, was quashed in June 1990 by some other provinces which thought Quebec no more deserving of special treatment than they were themselves. However, the issues of independence and provincial and national identity are sure to remain in the news, putting Quebec and Canada in the unusual company of Lithuania and the Soviet Union, Slovenia and Yugoslavia, and Kashmir and India.

Unlike these places, Canada and its provinces are well accustomed to democracy and enjoy a high standard of living. What they lack is a sense of history. Though the region was settled by the French as early as the sixteenth century, it is common even for the Quebecois to complain of the cultural poverty that stems from the newness of their land. Certainly Canada, a quickly and thinly populated half-continent, has little sense of national identity. The government has always advocated a multicultural society, in contrast to the melting-pot assimilation encouraged in the United States. As a result, what little sense of identity there is centers on a person's province. "Is there a Canadian identity?" asks François Dallaire, a graphic designer in Montreal. "You should ask *that* of English Canada! That's a political issue. If we ask somebody here what is Canada, the answer is Quebec."

Quebec has long been in love with the idea of independence, which surfaced as a political issue during the 1960s. The difference now is that Quebec is a dynamic, powerful, high-tech "state" with the economic wherewithal to make its way in the world. Formerly dominant anglophone businesses have been driven out and replaced by French-speaking ones. Both Canada and the United States are apprehensive. If Quebec were to declare

independence from greater Canada, it might give the other provinces ideas. Newfoundland, in particular, with a population predominantly descended from the west of England and Ireland, might wish to secede or even, it has been suggested, become a state of the American Union. If it can happen in Canada, why not in the United States? An independent Spanish-speaking bloc? California? It looks as if North America could diverge toward a condition of loose confederation with little more than a free-trade deal to bind the whole together, as the countries of the European Community converge toward precisely the same thing.

The difficulty of illustrating Canadian culture is made plain by François Dallegret who designed street furniture and graphics for the Vancouver Expo in 1986, taking motifs of nationhood such as the teepee and the maple leaf as his sources. "Everything was exploded and patchworked, says Dallegret, a Parisian who came to Montreal twenty years ago. "It was a way of going back a bit and looking at ourselves through our symbols—those that we have, which don't amount to much—and playing with them. It was a very toylike approach to the subject which suited its temporary purpose."

Less trivial expressions of identity will necessarily focus on individual provinces, but even in the case of vociferous Quebec, it seems premature to expect very much. Says Dallegret: "We're all hoping it will emerge sometime. But we are in a part of the world that is pretty young, so I think we have to take any chance we can to invent a form of identity."

The raw material for this invention is the French culture. Although Quebec developed economically largely under British rule, it was the French who made the greater cultural impression. The Catholic church has been a powerful influence. Montreal's citizens have probably always been more fashionably dressed and better fed than any others in North America. Its houses and apartment blocks look French, even if the skyscrapers look American.

As in France, Quebec's industries bear evidence of a heavy government hand at the tiller. As in France, great prestige attaches to the energy, telecommunications, and transportation industries. In the 1960s, for example, Quebec "nationalized" its electricity companies, leading to the creation of Hydro-Quebec. Jean Morin's design company, Axion, created a durable logotype for the utility, intended to make it familiar not only to the Quebecois but also to New Englanders who imported its energy.

In 1980, the people of Quebec voted against independence for the province, but since then French-speaking population growth has slowed, and the Quebecois feel that new waves of immigrants, and the influence of English-speaking Canadians

Corporate identity
Gagnon/Valkus
Hydro-Québec, 1966

Postage stamps
Axion
Canada Post Corporation,
1985

Poster
Frédéric Metz
Bretelle, Université du
Québec à Montréal, 1988

*Graphic design in French-
speaking Canada shows more
affection for European than
for American styles.*

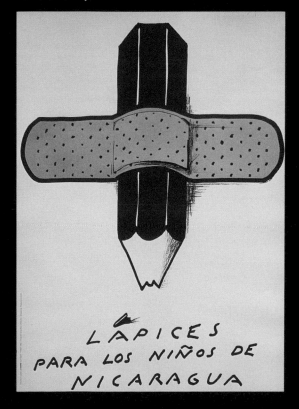

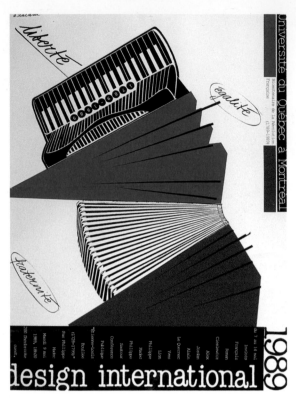

Poster
Alfred Halasa
Bretelle, Université du Québec
à Montréal, 1989

Poster
Alfred Halasa
Bretelle, Université du Québec
à Montréal, 1990

threaten their culture. The response has been to prop up the French language. Road names are a curious hybrid of Anglo-Saxon names and French descriptions—Axion is on rue Sherbrooke ouest, formerly West Sherbrooke Street. Advertising that once emanated mainly from agencies in Toronto is now devised locally, making much use of French wordplay, in celebration of linguistic distinctiveness but also perhaps to put down monolingual anglophones who have the nerve to live in Quebec.

There are also tiny visual clues to what is going on. Signs based on pictograms are perhaps more prevalent here. They short-circuit the bilingual longhand and sidestep the politics. Lowercase type wins favor, not just because it is the orthodoxy of the Swiss international style but because it allows French accents to be shown. "It's a question of language," says Dallaire. "There was a lot of uppercase a few years ago, but a lot of people didn't know where to put the accents. Now the language laws demand that the accents be there."

While some take measures to preserve aspects of French culture, others make efforts to dissuade those who would homogenize things. When Dallaire was approached by an Ontario container company planning to expand its operations into neighboring Quebec, the client naïvely wanted to reflect its greater reach by exploiting the Canadian national symbol in its logo. "They wanted a maple-leaf motif," says Dallaire, "but I said that would not be a good idea here."

Outside the commercial sphere, the parallels with France quickly break down. Quebec had no French aristocracy and hence has far less feeling for the decorative arts and more unashamed commercialism. "In France, I think they are still cautious about putting [commercial considerations] before excellence," says Dallegret, who divides his time between studios in Paris and Montreal. "The French still worry about style and quality. Here, quality is sometimes just wiped out. Here, money is what they bear in mind."

An indirect result of this is that Quebec's design schools are not all they might be. In graphics, Swiss Modernism had an even greater impact here than it did further south in the United States. And the best Canadian designers have often gone to the United States, Switzerland, France, or Britain to finish their educations. Morin's work, for example, still bears the imprint of his time in Zurich. It clearly works as well in anglophone Toronto (and in New York and San Francisco) as in francophone Montreal—there are Axion studios in all four cities.

The elements of Quebecois graphic design are thus a Swiss-inspired crispness in composition and typography and an austere approach to color. "Six months of the year here it's white. There's snow everywhere, so people don't use a lot of color. Here, people are afraid of color like the Swiss are afraid of color," explains Dallaire, who does his best to conquer this fear in his own work. These ingredients are not especially Quebecois, Canadian, or even French. But what is perhaps most important of all is that they are quite definitely not American. Morin's corporate identity for Bell Canada, for example, simply uses the letters of the name immaculately spaced and set in a subtle Berthold cut. The strong type on its own is sufficient to create the logotype and to distinguish it from that of any American telephone company. And that, after all, is the main thing in a country where remaining distinct from the United States is the real battle.

Corporate identity
Jean Morin
Bell Canada, 1976

Logotype
François Dallaire
Wachiya gift shops, 1988

Right: Gift boxes
François Dallaire
Le Rouet boutiques, 1986

Far right: Poster
François Dallaire
Telefilm Canada, 1989

*Crisp typography further
distinguishes Quebec graphic
design from the untidy
eclecticism found in the United
States.*

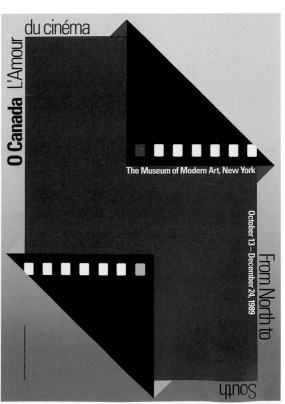

Globalists

IBM

IBM is many people's idea of a global corporation. It has one principal product type, and it has a monolithic presence impressed worldwide by its products, graphics, and even by many of its buildings. The business has historically been run from the headquarters town of Armonk, New York. Aspects of the company's appearance are kept under equally tight control from nearby Stamford, Connecticut, where Corporate Communications has its offices.

The IBM Design Program has been part of Corporate Communications since 1956. Its manager, Tom Hardy, explains the apparent paradox of a global corporation with central control: "Although corporate headquarters is in the United States, our Design Program is a global function with fifteen Design Centers worldwide, developing the industrial design solutions of our product line."

The IBM Design Program covers industrial design, graphic design, exhibit design, and architecture. Graphic interface design has recently been given equal status on this list. In addition, a Strategic Design function operates out of Stamford, initiating advanced design concepts for each segment of the product line. Hardy is directly responsible for all areas except architecture, which is handled by a separate real estate department. The Stamford hub disseminates standards and guidelines in the remaining four areas, coordinates the activities of the larger design centers in Britain, Germany, France, Japan, and the United States, and reviews the design results of other units elsewhere. "Worldwide market needs (for example, language and ergonomic requirements) are factored into a basic design concept that is marketed worldwide," says Hardy, "while unique local needs are handled as a custom design by the responsible local Design Center."

IBM is practicing what it has long preached. In the words of the former chief executive, Thomas J. Watson, Jr., the man who was responsible for consolidating IBM's position as a design leader during the 1950s and 1960s and who made the maxim "Good design is good business" his own, the corporation is now "centralizing by decentralizing." It is not only in design that IBM is doing this; the company has also established new centers for particular areas of business activity away from Armonk.

The design centers are located where hardware and software are developed. Central coordination of their activities has recently been made much easier by the acquisition of a Sony high-resolution color image transmission system, the first of its kind in operation globally by a corporation's design function.

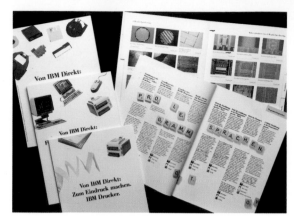

IBM Germany catalogs
1989

PS/1 computer packaging
Paul Rand
1989

IBM has sought to maintain a unified design image through graphics and packaging as well as product design.

Design program folder
Paul Rand
1984

Above: PC Convertible portable
computer
Richard Sapper
1986

*The German-born, Milan-based
designer Richard Sapper has
responsibility for giving IBM
products a stronger visual
presence that will appeal to
global markets.*

Left: 7575 computer-driven
robot
1986

The system, a Digital Information Handler 2000, facilitates the product design process, for example by enabling a designer to call up a library image of an existing product and picture it alongside a current proposal. It also speeds the proposal review. Images can be telephoned to Hardy's office in Stamford, Connecticut, and, using the system's ability to annotate, marked up with comments and suggested revisions and returned in next to no time. Full-scale models are always required, but now travel by designers or shipment of a three-dimensional model is rarely needed in order to communicate a basic concept or resolve some design detail.

The Design Program exercises concurrence rights on all products that come out of the fifteen centers worldwide. This is vital for the preservation of the company's design language. IBM may not reach the peaks of excellence sometimes achieved by Apple Computer or Olivetti, but it does remain less prone to occasional lapses of design judgment. IBM has a justification for conservatism in that it has a broader range of products to market than either of these rivals. IBM feels it must maintain the congruence between its products not only for the sake of keeping up corporate appearances but also because many of them may be connected to form larger systems. The electronic compatibility is signified by using a consistent visual language.

For these and other reasons, IBM does the vast bulk of its design in-house. Close control is vital. Even before the arrival of the Sony image-handling system, the process of product development was highly labile. As Hardy puts it: "Keeping pace with development dynamics has always been important. However, given shorter product design cycles and decentralization, it is imperative that we maintain internal teams of skilled professionals for efficiency and coherence."

This is not to say that, like most large companies, IBM does not feel the need to bring the fresh minds of outsiders to bear on its design problems. It was Watson who appointed Eliot Noyes as IBM's first consultant designer. The relationship was personal, close, and for life. So has been the relationship with Paul Rand, the graphic designer brought in under the Noyes aegis who devised the IBM logotype still in use today. Only architecture was slightly different. Here, Noyes kept his own running list of the world's top architects who were commissioned as occasion arose.

The fidelity of the consultant relationship has been maintained since then. Richard Sapper was appointed in 1980, three years after Noyes's death. The difference today is that Sapper, best known for his Tizio lamp for Artemide and tabletop products for Alessi, is a German living in Italy, not, like Noyes, an

American living in Connecticut. Sapper's main job is periodically to undertake a specific design assignment as a way of establishing new principles and directions for IBM's overall product range. The IBM PC Convertible was his first opus for the company. According to Hardy, it has only been very recently that Sapper's influence has begun to spill over into the products at large.

The appointment of a European to this important post encourages speculation about the formal direction IBM plans to take. Sapper is known for designs that are strong in elevation, whereas IBM products have generally shown evidence of America's pragmatic attitude to form giving. When his influence has filtered through the entire range of products, it is quite possible that the IBM design language will be more like that of Apple (codified by a German) or Olivetti (codified by Italians).

IBM is especially conscious of competition from Apple in the critical area of interface design. Having lost ground to the upstart company with the friendly, icon-based software, IBM is taking decisive steps to catch up. Edward Tufte, a professor at Yale University and author of the seminal books, *The Visual Display of Quantitative Information* and *Envisioning Information*, is IBM's consultant in this field, on a par with Rand and Sapper in theirs. Initially employed to tidy up IBM's operator manuals, Tufte is now working with Norman Cox, a Dallas-based designer who was one of the team that pioneered the display layouts for the Xerox Star work station, to improve IBM's use of color, typography, and icons on computer screens.

The design appointments of the 1980s make it clear that IBM is conscious that the competition is also using design as a strategic tool and equally clear that it does not intend to let the situation rest. The 1990s could show the corporation in a new light.

Lift/Tilt/Swivel display stand
1990

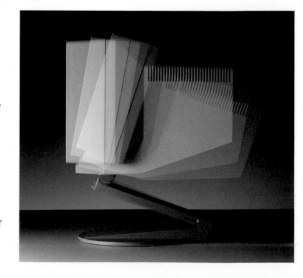

Above: PS/2 Model 70 portable computer
1988

Below: Desktop laser printer
1989

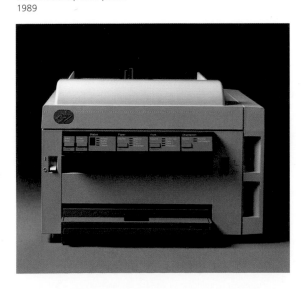

Philips

It is perhaps remarkable that Philips has managed to carve out a reputation for design leadership at all. Unlike IBM or Sony, it makes a very broad range of products, from personal stereos to lighting fixtures to medical imaging apparatus. In its way, it is far more like the diversified corporations Matsushita or Toshiba, companies whose design management models are seldom greatly admired.

Philips is Europe's largest electronics company and the only company in the world that can now rival the Japanese in terms of both quantity and quality of its production in this field. The Philips brand of global design took shape during the 1980s under its then Managing Director of Corporate Industrial Design, Robert Blaich, who was previously director of design at the American furniture manufacturer Herman Miller. Given the range of goods that Philips makes, any design policy must to some extent strive to be all things to all people. This is indeed the case, with a unified visual language enforced in some areas but not in others. "I'm not interested in homogenization," says Blaich. "I'm interested in harmonization. People often ask me: 'Do you have one image of what all Philips products should be?' And of course I haven't because we're making things from small hand-held products—pocket memos, radio recorders, LCD products—up to big body scanners and medical systems. So you can't have one basic philosophy."

At one level Philips design is not without the puritanism that stems from its hundred-year history and northern European location in Eindhoven. Its kitchen appliances are in the same vein as those made by Braun. Its medical equipment demands simple, functional lines. These products look the way they do thanks to the program of harmonization that Philips has brought to bear across these lines.

In other sectors, Philips has shed its austere image to create aggressively styled fashion products in an attempt to capture markets delineated not by geography but by age groups. The most spectacular appeal has been to the youth market with the Moving Sound range of audio equipment. Brought out in successive "collections," these portable cassette players and boom-boxes used color and graphics as a fashion accessory rather than as an indicator of function or brand. One collection was bright yellow; another made use of fluorescent Aztec-style motifs. The Roller Radio, a bold assemblage of rounded forms designed by Graham Hinde, a young designer recruited from Kingston Polytechnic in London, was another success. A series of streamlined

Discoverer TV children's televisions
1990

matte-black ghetto-blasters studded with light-emitting diode indicators and looking like the dashboard of the Batmobile were equally distinctive.

For a more mature group of global consumers, Philips has evolved a design language based on the recent fashion for "product semantics." One proposal for additions to its top-of-the-line Matchline televisions and hi-fis comprises a number of audio units that stack vertically. Each has a wavy front panel that suggests it belongs with the others. Individual units have "semantic" features—flutelike key controls on the preamplifier, for example. Despite these features, the units have a dignified black appearance that does not set them too far apart from people's expectations of conventional audio and video equipment in the same price bracket.

The wish to harmonize in some areas and yet also to make products that are responsive to the demands of fashion reveals the struggle taking place as Philips tries to change the habits of a corporate lifetime. It desperately needs to speed up the product development cycle, both in order to compete more effectively with the Japanese and to reap the benefit of its considerable reputation for technological innovation.

To anybody who is familiar with the full spectrum of Philips products (and it is important to remember that most consumers have no reason to be), the company's design philosophy seems at best eclectic and at worst hopelessly confused. Certainly it is not monolithic like that of Braun or the Danish manufacturer Bang and Olufsen, of which Philips acquired a quarter share during 1990. (*The Economist* slyly suggested that it did so in order to learn about design.)

Philips operates in more than 100 countries, it manufactures in 60 or more, and it has designers in 21 of them, in addition to the Corporate Industrial Design department in Eindhoven with 130 staff, most of them designers. Philips is known under its own name worldwide but also has a score of brand names, including Pye in Britain, and Norelco, Magnavox, and Sylvania in the United States. There are, in addition, the products of Marantz, which is the name given to the Philips premium hi-fi brand, and Grundig, a sister company in Germany that maintains its own design program. The brands have different geographic spheres of influence and cater to different segments of their respective markets. Sometimes they even compete against other "Philips" products.

The design management structure that Robert Blaich has constructed is a complex matrix of centralized and decentralized activities. It stems in part from the thinking of Thomas J. Watson, Jr., of IBM. "Watson said that to be decentralized, you first have

Clamshell LCD color television
1990

*At its most sophisticated,
Philips' design is
indistinguishable from the best
design of its Japanese
compeitors.*

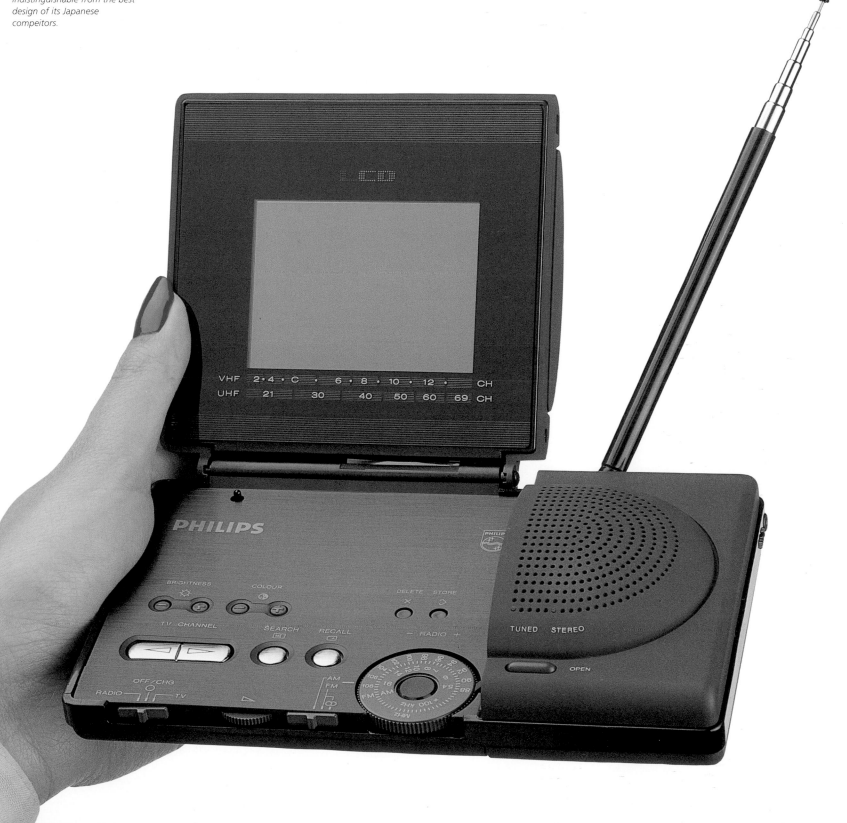

Rota 90 Shavers
1990

to centralize," explains Blaich. "I did that in design at Philips. Now we have satellite operations all around the world, but we're designing global products."

Overall strategy is directed from the Netherlands where individual design managers are in charge of areas such as audio, domestic appliances, and lighting. Unit managers under them are responsible for a team of designers who work in specific product areas such as shavers. "Decentralized" designers work in International Production Centers in Singapore, Hong Kong, Vienna, and elsewhere. In consumer products there are, in addition, fully fledged design managers in Tokyo and Knoxville, Tennessee, which, alongside Eindhoven, make up the Triad structure espoused by Kenichi Ohmae. In some of these production centers, there are senior designers who have considerable responsibility for design, development, production, and marketing. They design products, not in a "local for local" market sense as was the case until the 1970s, but with reference to and guidance from Eindhoven. At other Philips sites, small groups are placed in factories simply to ensure design quality control.

In the case of the Moving Sound line, Eindhoven set the tone for the line and designed the graphics and packaging, but designers in Vienna, Hong Kong, and Singapore worked up the individual product concepts. Some successes, however, appear to have come about almost despite the design management structure. The triumph of the Roller Radio is acknowledged by Philips, but the fact that it is anomalous within the scheme of things—it was a student project before that student joined Philips—goes without comment. The Tracer shaver originated in Japan. Following the Japanese trend for miniaturization, Philips's designers in Tokyo devised a unit with two rather than three rotating heads that would suit the light beard growth of the local population for whom the product was at that stage solely intended. Blaich saw the potential for the new shaver for young people in the global market. The Japanese product was "globalized" by largely superficial means. "Using the basic design we added bright colors, graphics, and a life-style packaging which transformed the shaver, targeted to the Japanese market, to the enormously successful Tracer series for young people worldwide," says Blaich. "Market tests in Australia confirmed its appeal, and the Tracer and its successive generations have been a hit in all parts of the world." Although these examples did not come about in a way described by the design management model, they do perhaps demonstrate a useful flexibility of response.

A test of Blaich's policy came in 1991 with the launch, in Philips's centenary year, of a special range of home-entertainment equipment. Called the Philips

Collection, the products sport a coherent design language, expressed in detailing, colors, graphics, and packaging; the Collection also represents the first time that different Product Divisions have worked together. Philips plans to add new items to the Collection each year.

Blaich numbers twenty-three nationalities among his design staff and insists that the cross-fertilization of cultural experience and values is both an advantage for the creation of global products and an essential factor in the successful management of global design at Philips. He sees the issue of globalization not only from the viewpoint of a multinational manufacturer but also, in his role as past president of the International Council of Societies for Industrial Design, as the representative of ordinary designers everywhere.

On his travels Blaich has found that industrial designers in many countries want to bring "local content" to their work. He counsels small companies and government agencies on the potential for regionalism in their design. But for Philips it is a different story. In India, for example, at the twelve-person design studio that Philips then maintained in Bombay until the late 1980s, they said they wanted to design their own television sets. But neither Blaich nor the Indians themselves could decide what would comprise local content. Were the televisions to look like temples or elephants, asked Blaich facetiously. Were they to have patterned surfaces, and if so, should the decoration be of Hindu or Muslim inspiration? Blaich notes: "You would find that you would have a lot of patterns because the patterns acceptable in the south of India are not acceptable in the north. But what we found is that the man in the street wants a television set just like the people have in Tokyo. They just meant that they as Indians wanted to design it." It is acceptable, indeed desirable, in India and elsewhere, for technology products to have a First World appearance because ownership of such products signifies an aspiration to join that world. "You might say this is homogenization," says Blaich, "but people will accept certain products as 'high technology.' They will put them in their living rooms no matter what the furniture or the surroundings. We used to design products for India thinking that the mentality was different. I disagreed with that. Today in India—or in Brazil as another example of a closed economy—our products are the same as they are here."

Given this experience, it is hard to see how cross-cultural exchange is proving advantageous in the creation of global products unless it is simply to gauge the lowest common denominator that will be acceptable to all cultures. Indeed, there is evidence to suggest that the tide is flowing in the opposite

Philips has sought to find a distinctive voice with designs that use retro styling, product semantics, and other effects.

Above: Easy Line clock radio 1991

Left: Moving Sound stereo/radio/cassette recorder 1990

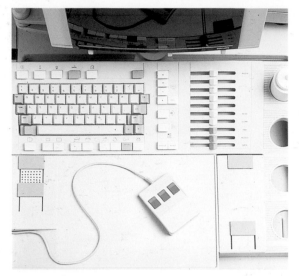

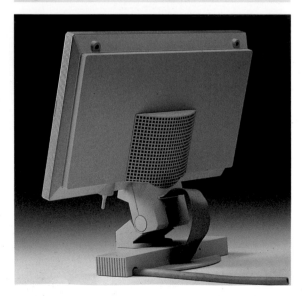

direction. Successive years' brochures for Norelco, for example, show an evolution of coffee makers under the local brand name as they drop a two-tone appearance in favor of "contemporary white" or "charcoal gray." Some Norelco products still suggest their American origins—air cleaners still sport wood-grain surfaces; some of the coffee makers come out of molds quite different from the parallel-sided, 90-degree draft molds used for the Philips models now shown alongside them in the same brochure. Their days are clearly numbered, however. Wood grain and chrome are now beyond the pale, says Blaich. "We are trying to get away from that. We still have a hangover from some of those things. I've finally got rid of it at Magnavox, and that was a battle." The design of the Magnavox line is now a collaboration between Eindhoven and Knoxville. At Norelco, Philips made the decision to relocate manufacturing and hence the design activity. "Bob wants to do global design," says one ex-Norelco designer, "but he wants to do everything in Holland and ship it all over the world."

The strong editorial control is evident in the pre-emption of new, as well as the eradication of old, expressions of local identity. Japanese products for local consumption frequently sport bizarre graphics that Westerners are at a loss to understand. Blaich balked when his designers did the same for Philips's coffee makers: "My Japanese designers came up with some ideas—funny shapes and colors and really crazy things—that were so bad by our standards that we had to say no." The reason for turning them down was that the product would lose any export appeal. Nevertheless, some Philips products for Japan do now pay lip service to local preferences with the addition of some decorative color.

Blaich believes there is no role for such decoration in the output of a manufacturer such as Philips, but he does not agree that all cultural differences should be ironed out: "Where I see the potential for cultural differences is where the product is more personalized. Coffee makers are an example. People drink coffee differently in every part of the world." Coffee makers should cope with the variation by brewing coffee to the appropriate degree in the appropriate quantities. The accommodation stops with function, however. It does not extend to form or ornament: "From a cultural point of view, we have adapted ourselves to the coffee-drinking habits of those countries, but we have designed products that are all in the same form language, saying this is Philips, this is the way Philips sees design."

Above: Personal pager
1991

Left, top: Integris V examination
and viewing console
1990

Middle: LCD thin-screen
computer monitor and
keyboard
1990

Bottom: LCD thin-screen
computer monitor
1990

Opposite:
Café Gourmet coffee maker
1989

Sony

A document from the Sony Design Center establishes the corporation as a leader in globalization in uncompromising terms. It prescribes a course of three "pills" for the transformation from multinational to global corporation: "Offer standardised products worldwide; close communication network worldwide; world cultural integration." This document dates from 1988, but there is already evidence that the reality of Sony's global policy may be considerably more subtle than these words suggest.

Sony's technical goal has long been to create products that are more compact than their predecessors. In this respect, Sony is like many other Japanese corporations, except that it tends to make products that are even smaller and better than its rivals', and it tends to bring them out sooner. It has no fear of being first while most Japanese manufacturers are happier to follow a leader. All else being equal, the most compact model on the market of certain types of product will have the cachet of *appearing to be* the latest (in addition to any new uses that its compactness may give it). It is in its ability to satisfy this universal wish that Sony can be said to make global products.

The product that exemplifies Sony's success is, of course, the Walkman. Since its introduction in 1979, Sony designers have created 300 Walkman models. Fifty new ones emerge each year—a Walkman a week. Over the years, there has been a broadening both in the price range and in the range of functions offered. From the initiation of the product planning process, Sony aims its Walkmen at many specific markets identified by price, age, lifestyle, and geography. The range of models now on offer ensures the widest possible market acceptance. In one sense, this variety serves to consolidate the Walkman's position as the ultimate global product, but in another it suggests a very different direction for future developments.

The story of one particular Walkman, the WM-109, designed by Masayoshi Tsuchiya at Sony, perhaps hints at things to come. As the catalog of case studies from the 1989 Triad Design project exhibition organized by the Boston-based Design Management Institute tells it, "Tsuchiya began to look for a new finish that would express the sophistication he wanted to portray. Walking through Shibuya, a chic shopping district in Tokyo, he saw a white ceramic flounder-shaped chopstick holder with exactly the quality he was looking for. The depth and hard coolness of the ceramic finish had just the high-class yet simple feel and look he wanted." The result was a

global product executed in a Japanese style.

Although it is uncertain whether buyers of the WM-109—a model destined solely for the domestic market—knew of the local nature of its inspiration, the product is reported to have lasted some three years in a market where the usual lifetime is six months. The story of the WM-109 is indicative of a general policy in favor of adding value to products such as the later-generation Walkmen where sheer novelty has worn off. This is especially true of those models aimed at the wealthy and demanding domestic market. But the means by which value was added in this case cannot readily be enshrined in any design policy.

It is not by chance that Sony, a comparatively small company compared to its rivals in the Japanese consumer-electronics industry, has become a paragon of globalism. Sony was founded just after the Second World War and has always been more Western-oriented and Western-influenced than its competitors, as it signified when it chose its present, easily pronounced name. Sony has also earned an enviable reputation for innovation, with the Trinitron television, the Watchman flat-screen television, and Betacam video equipment joining the Walkman in its pantheon of technological achievement.

The Sony Design Center employs approximately 120 designers. Despite continual growth in their numbers over the years, these designers are responsible for more designs per head now than ever before. In general, they are given a degree of autonomy that is uncommon in Japanese corporations. An individual designer, not a design manager, will present an idea not only to sales and engineering but also to top management. In theory, even a newcomer to the Design Center could play a leading role in the creative reports that are given at regular intervals to senior staff who may occasionally include chief executive Norio Ohga or Akio Morita, Sony's chairman and cofounder. Ohga and Morita have the courage of their convictions and it is not unknown for them to overturn a timid middle-management decision. This was notoriously the case with the Walkman.

The impression today, however, is that such a feat could only be repeated with difficulty. The Design Center has recently been absorbed within the merchandising function, a seeming reversal of the usual flow in corporations whereby the design department wins greater autonomy from marketing. There is an increasing tendency to stress the sanctity of the Sony name, which, staff proudly point out, came second only to Coca-Cola in a 1990 survey of international brand recognition by Landor Associates. "Design management should be a very important term, but *image* management is even more important," says Hideo Watanabe, senior general manager

Top: CCD Handycam TR55

Above: GV-U5 video cassette recorder

The universal wish for ever more compact products gives Sony's designs a global appeal.

MDR-1F510K infrared
headphones and modulator

WM-109 Walkman

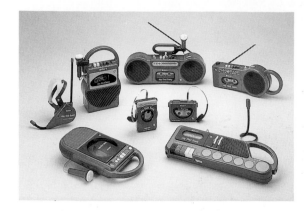

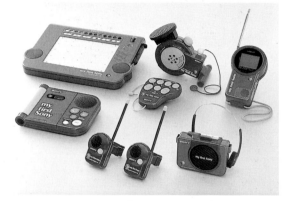

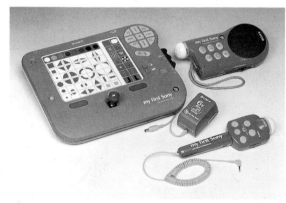

My First Sony children's audio equipment, 1988 (top), 1989 (middle), and 1990 (bottom)

As the My First Sony line has evolved, its cachet has decreased from trendsetter to commodity.

of what is now longwindedly called the Merchandising and Product Communication Strategy Group.

The renaming should not be taken as a sign that Sony is downgrading its design activity but rather as a vote of confidence in the talents of its designers, who are increasingly expected to act as marketers and strategists. (The renaming is in some ways a reversion to former practice; the Design Center was once known as the PP Center, PP generally taken to denote *product planning*, but also, with deliberate ambiguity, *product presentation* or *proposal and promotion*.) As it is now constituted, Watanabe's group comprises two industrial design departments, a number of other design departments, as well as a new systems products planning department, a "global industrial design center," and a "trends research center." During the 1980s Sony's head of design, Yasuo Kuroki, has pursued a policy of centralization, encouraging more discussion between groups responsible for different product lines and permitting tighter control of the Sony image. The aim now is to improve further the coordination of corporate identity between product, packaging, and advertising activities.

Sony uses a simple diagram to explain the product planning process. A three-layered pyramid is labeled *S* at the apex, *A* in the middle, and *B* at the base. The width of the triangle at a given level can be taken as a measure of market volume, the height as a measure of added value or perceived quality. S-type products are "star" or "special" designs that contribute to the creation of a new Sony image. A-type products connote "ability" or "awareness" and are those that best express the Sony style. B-type means "bread and butter" or "business" and applies to high-volume and low-priced products where the goal is maximum profit. When it came out, the Walkman was an S-type product; now most Walkmen are Bs. The My First Sony products for children are also slipping down the pyramid, from S to B.

The pyramid is interesting because it reveals two types of global design: the special sort that appeals to a wide market because it is unique, and the basic sort that is used for low-cost commodity products. The A-type products in between the two extremes tend to be the most "Sonyish" and are the most suited to the Japanese market. As Watanabe told the Japanese magazine *Design News:* "There are things which people want to buy because everyone else has one, and there are other things people do *not* want to buy because everyone else has them. I told Mr Kuroki that in order to expand our business, we should investigate why this happens. We should not only cling to our aim of high-quality products. . . . We tried to express the charm of Sony product tech-

nology with our designs and suggested to our engineers what we thought would be attractive products. The idea has been reflected ever since in our general activities in the Design Center."

There have been lapses of judgment in the effort to make technology charming. The appointment of a European celebrity designer, Luigi Colani, to design a pair of headphones adorned with his signature proved a bridge too far. The headphones are today described with an ironic smile not as a star product but as "stardust," a flash in the pan. Sony concedes that commissioning Colani was a mistake. The company maintains, however, that the aim of the exercise was for Sony's in-house designers to learn from Colani's techniques, and in this respect it is said to have succeeded. However, the product lived on to refute Sony's policy of using only in-house designers. The incident has done nothing to reinforce positive associations with the Sony name and is unlikely to be repeated.

While Sony frequently sets the pace in product development with its technological breakthroughs, the Colani incident shows a wish not to miss out on wider trends in design. "At the Design Center we are always looking at trends in fashion—costume, theater, movies—as well as for an expression of our strategy that runs ahead of fashion," says Matami Yamaguchi, general manager of the Merchandising and Product Communication Strategy Group. "We are thinking, for instance, of adding design offices in Milan, Paris, and London in the search for new trends from the cultural viewpoint." The first steps came in the summer of 1989 when Masayoshi Tsuchiya moved to Milan to serve as the Sony design center's "special representative in Europe."

Sony is building on Kuroki's policy of centraliza-

DD-1 Executive Block portable computer terminal

tion, which has now reached the point where, as at Philips, a calculated decentralization is the order of the day. "We are going to disperse many designers to improve exchange of opinions between local and center," says Watanabe. These centers will be not where the market lies, as might once have been the case, but where there are ideas to be gleaned. Designers will rotate between such cities as Barcelona, New York, and San Francisco, sending back design concepts for sifting by Watanabe and his colleagues in Tokyo. Design development of the more promising leads will then take place in Tokyo or by collaboration between Tokyo and the proposing satellite office. The shift is that recommended by Kenichi Ohmae as the final step along the corporate evolutionary path to globalism.

Establishing the structure of what Akio Morita calls "global localization" may take time. European top management is only gradually being won around to the idea. Once it is in place, however, the possibilities appear limitless. Although the static structure—the physical spread and location of design offices—sounds similar to that of Philips and IBM, the dynamics of the way they will be used appears to be very different. "From the design policy standpoint, we have two reasons in favor of global localization," explains Watanabe. "One is that local opinion should be surveyed, communicating to collect local design opinions and coordinating them at the center for global products. The second is that if we have many local design centers we can choose the strategy. If an Italian designer develops an Italian design, it should not be sold just in Italy but also in Japan and the United States. But if local opinion is expressed too strongly, it might damage the corporate image."

CDZ1 music system

This design made obvious reference to Japanese enamelwork but was reportedly not a commercial success because it offered an inappropriate range of functions.

PTC-500 palmtop computer

Frogdesign

Here's Hartmut Esslinger, the founder of Frogdesign, giving a speech in 1989 on "Design: The Global Language": "The design of the 1990s will be freedom from dogma. Design in the 1990s will be more than design. Design is quality of life. Design is life-style. Design is poetry. Identity will be the buzzword of the 1990s. Where everybody does the same, the few with personality want to express themselves by cultural statements." In the 1950s, he notes, "Italy was inspiring, Germany reinvented functionalism." In the 1960s, Japan was following the United States and neglecting its own roots. . . . These are comments that acknowledge national cultures. There would not seem to be much that is "global" here.

Yet a year before, Esslinger told *Newsweek*: "There are 600 million in Western Europe, the United States and Japan. And the young people in their 20s, 30s and even 40s are more similar than different. They wear the same clothes and listen to the same music. . . . You can't be a regional or national designer anymore."

In his eagerness to convey his enthusiam for his profession, Esslinger may occasionally contradict himself. He may speak mystical rubbish, but he designs beautiful things. At its best, Frogdesign's work comes as close as anyone's to achieving a universal appeal through form. Some products, such as the Next Computer System, exemplify the ideal of Platonism. Steven Jobs, who founded Next after having been edged out of Apple Computer, demanded that his new company's first product be a cube, but Esslinger made sure it was not quite a cube, just as the columns of a Greek temple are bowed slightly in order that they appear parallel-sided. Other designs, such as the bright-red showerheads for German manufacturer Hansgrohe, are freer in their handling of color and form, yet they

achieve a similar rightness.

Frogdesign believes that its computer-aided design technology and model-making equipment allow it to create forms that would be impossible to attain by other means. Whatever the method, the results present the acceptable face of globalism. Nothing in Frogdesign's American or Japanese portfolio leads one to believe otherwise. The Sony Profeel televisions, the Challenge luggage for Louis Vuitton, the cool sophistication of the Apple computers—all these are the impedimenta of the well-heeled gentry in the global village.

Some German conservatives plainly resent Frogdesign's fun-loving passage to fame and fortune. The resentment is mutual. As Esslinger wrote in a catalog for a 1988 exhibition of Frogdesign's work: "We refused to let ourselves be exploited and preferred to starve, rather than accept the design dogma as coined by the school of Ulm [the school that turned Esslinger down in the 1960s]."

Interestingly, products for German clients such as Villeroy and Boch, Zeiss, and furniture manufacturer König and Neurath appear more typically German, a fact that underlines the general kinship of the "globalist style" to that country's design values. And like many foreigners, Friedrich Frenkler, who heads Frogdesign's office in Tokyo, finds Japanese culture inspiring and believes that the Japanese should reconsider it as a source of inspiration rather than follow the example of other countries. But it is uncertain whether Frogdesign's products for mainly national markets from any or all of its offices will now begin to reflect the wish to create "cultural statements." Says Esslinger: "Designs by our group in Germany and by our small group in Japan and the fairly large group in America are kind of different, but I think this depends mostly on the people who work there."

Frogdesign started in Altensteig, a small town in the Black Forest, in 1969. It opened an office in Silicon Valley in 1983 and one in Tokyo in 1987. Approximately sixty people work in the three offices. Esslinger is a great fan of Kenichi Ohmae's Triad theory which argues that a base in each of Europe, America, and Japan is de rigueur for any company with worldwide ambitions. Having pitched camp in these three places, Ohmae argues, a company should use its spread to present itself as equidistant from all its clients. This is quite patently not the case for Frogdesign in California, for example, which is less than five miles down the road from Apple Computer, its first and then most important American client. Some believe that Frogdesign is kept in California mainly by the promise of more work from Steve Jobs. Its base in Japan has likewise much to do with

Next computer, 1989

Magic pots and pans
Fissler, 1988

Egg cooker
AEG, 1985

German notions of gute Form
*are often closely related to
global design values.*

Scanman, mouse, and
thumbball
Logitech, 1989

Yamaha and Sony. Altensteig, meanwhile, is Esslinger's hometown, and the sight of the company's office here quickly dispenses with the cosmopolitan image. This is no Neuschwanstein of design but a nondescript house on a hilltop country lane on the outskirts of town.

In some ways, however, Frogdesign does exemplify Ohmae's globalism. Unlike other firms operating in more than one country, Frogdesign employs a mix of Americans, Europeans, and Asians (though there are too few Asians in the Tokyo office and too many Germans in Altensteig) and regularly moves designers between its three sites. It encourages rivalry between them.

The firm also takes pains to ensure that it maintains a high profile in the international design scene. In addition to running informal, internal competitions between its offices, Frogdesign has inaugurated an international competition for design students, the winners of which sometimes come to work at the company. It takes out glossy, color advertisements on the back covers of, among other publications, Japan's *Axis* and Germany's *Form*. The advertisements take the form of mannered full-page photographs of Frogdesign products and projects, some of them taken by Helmut Newton.

These antics have alienated some in the design community and have probably scared off some potential clients. Some point out that, for all the brouhaha, comparatively few products seem to emerge from the Frogdesign studios. But the overall effect of Frogdesign's presence has undoubtedly been to the good of the profession. It demands high fees for itself but pushes other designers to demand high fees as well in order that they may do better work.

Frogdesign's success revolves around the personality of its creator and has little to do with its international structure. It is not a truly global company. This, however, may be about to change. A Taiwan office opened in 1990. Others are reportedly planned for New York, the Far East, and, in 1992, Europe.

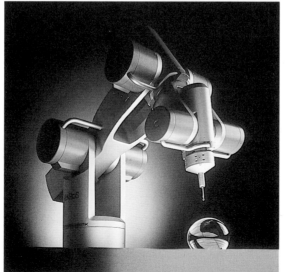

Above: Car telephone
AEG Telefunken, 1983

Left: Robot equipment
Bodenseewerke, 1986

Frogdesign has become the dominant global design firm through a combination of excellent form-giving and bravura self-promotion of its operation in the three Triad centers.

GK

Other than Frogdesign, Japan's GK is the only design firm to have bases in all three of the world's Triad regions. Kenji Ekuan cofounded GK Industrial Design Associates in Tokyo in 1957. The firm grew rapidly along with the rest of Japan through the heady years of the Tokyo Olympic Games and the Osaka Expo to the point where it now has a dozen spin-off companies and nearly three hundred staff in all. These include GK Graphics, GK Sekkei, responsible for environmental and interior design and architecture, and other groups devoted to transportation and heavy mechanical equipment design, in addition to the original product design group now known simply as GK Incorporated. The group once even had its own shop in the Shibuya district of Tokyo.

GK's rise is tied to one early client, Yamaha. Since the 1950s, GK has designed Yamaha's motorcycles as well as pianos and synthesizers, outboard motors, and home audio equipment. Other important clients include Fujitsu, Singer, and Maruishi Cycle Industries. In 1972 and 1988 GK opened regional offices in Kyoto and Hiroshima to take on work mainly for local clients. Compared to the scale of its Japanese operation, GK's international outposts are quite modest. The firm's early interest in activating a network to gather international market information led in 1967 to the establishment of GK Design International in Torrance, California. Today this office has around a dozen staff. An office in Amsterdam, added in 1986, has just half that number. Known under the name Global Design, this office is headed by Loek van der Sande, formerly with Total Design and, like Robert Blaich of Philips and Kenji Ekuan, a past president of the International Council of Societies for Industrial Design.

The offices collaborate on an as-needed basis. If a Japanese manufacturer wants to develop a product for the European market, Global Design undertakes the requisite research. In the case of a recent project for a television, the concept design also came from Amsterdam. For Yamaha motorcycles the overall concept originates in Tokyo, but in the case of models intended for the European and American markets, the Amsterdam and Torrance offices collaborate with designers in Tokyo to ensure that the final designs have the appropriate character.

There is less globe-hopping at GK than at Frogdesign. Designers are only rarely rotated between Triad offices. GK also believes it is unlike Frogdesign in that it does not impose its own style on its clients' products and thus is not global in any

formal or ideological sense. Perhaps more pertinent to GK's successful operation than its global reach is the interdisciplinary reach it achieves by means of its various satellite offices scattered through Tokyo. As GK's literature fulsomely explains: "In the ever diversifying and more internationally developed market environment as we step into the 1990s, no client's needs can be satisfied by any single professional field. Today, the GK Group . . . is maximizing its unique organization and varied skills by taking a dynamic approach to coordinating all the multi-disciplinary design professionals within the group to induce greater capabilities for solving clients' problems. At the same time, GK seeks to service society by fulfilling its strong philosophical commitment to bring harmony of 'soul and material things' in the age of advanced technology and information society."

The mystical turn of phrase comes principally from Kenji Ekuan. Although he once trained to become a Buddhist monk, Ekuan is today a peripatetic player on the stage of world design. At the time of GK's foundation Ekuan spent two years at California's Art Center College of Design, but he has never lost the spiritual touch, and he now combines the life of an outgoing globalist with moments of purely Japanese introspection.

When clients request, as they occasionally do, that their products be designed in a Japanese style, GK takes this to mean that they wish for meticulous detailing and a simplicity in the interpretation. Ekuan explained it thus to an international design conference held in 1988 in Singapore: "Complex simplicity is at the center of Japan's design concepts, and it includes the elements of compactness, adaptability, transformation, and purity. This is most elegantly demonstrated in the *ichirinzashi* or the single blossom arrangement. The art of Japanese flower arrangement attempts to portray the world of nature in a single flower. . . . This same aesthetic approach runs through all of Japan's traditional arts and even modern, state-of-the-art industrial products." Perhaps the best example of this spirit in GK's recent work is the AST series of CD players for Yamaha. The CD player itself is a rectangular gray box of unusually placid proportions. The panels that accept cassettes or compact discs lie flush with the player's matte plastic surface. Opening them becomes almost an invasion of privacy and heightens the sense of ceremony associated with using the product.

More clearly traditionalist examples of GK's Japanese work exist, foremost among them being the Kikkoman soy sauce bottle designed by Kenji Ekuan as long ago as 1961 and still in use many millions of bottles later. A more recent example is the

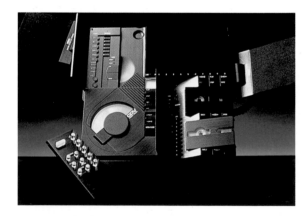

Avot personal audio device proposal
Yamaha Corporation, 1987

Kenji Ekuan draws an analogy between product design and the Japanese art of flower-arranging in describing a national ideal of "complex simplicity."

Simple-2 telephone
Fujitsu, 1986

Morpho motorcycle prototype
Yamaha Motorcycle Company,
1989

Soy sauce dispenser
Kikkoman Corporation, 1961

Corporate identity
Cosmo Oil Company, 1986

Although its products for Yamaha are internationally admired, GK can also design in a more local idiom when called upon to do so.

undulating wheat liquor *(shochu)* bottle designed in 1985. Eating and drinking are among the most ritualized of activities, and the special consideration given to the design of these containers enhances the ritual. The shape of the *shochu* bottle has even been said to amount to an invitation to one party to pour a drink for another party, a useful attribute in Japan where it is not done to pour one's own drink.

GK believes that the requirement for products of complex simplicity, which arose from living conditions characteristic of the cramped islands of Japan will come to be a defining characteristic of global design. As populations grow and psychological distances shrink, the constraints of Japan will become the constraints of the world. "Twenty or thirty years ago, the international scene was just the European scene. Now the international style is no longer only European. In a few years the Japanese style will be recognized as the new global style," believes Masato Isaka, supervising director of planning and design.

In an effort to anticipate ways in which cultural attributes might find physical expression, GK has recently set up a group to explore this part of the creative process. Researchers at the grandly titled Institute of Doguology (*dogu* is a versatile word meaning "tool(s)" or "appliance(s)" or "equipment") aim to examine the ways in which objects are put to use, not only in the immediate context that is covered by the field of ergonomics but also in the wider context of contemporary social and cultural behavior. They hope to interpolate between the history of modern products, many of which were introduced to Japan from the West, and any parallel to them that may exist in Japan's earlier culture. For example, the type of bed made up with sheets was introduced from the West. But there was no ready-made Japanese custom regarding the way the bedclothes would be used and no one thought to import knowledge of Western habits. The Japanese make the bulk of the world's televisions but, because their own tradition of home furnishing is different from that in the West, they perhaps do not appreciate the origin of television styling in wooden cabinets. Nobody knows what a television that emerged from the Japanese culture, where rooms are not cluttered with cabinets, would look like. This acquired knowledge of the cultural history of certain product types will in turn permit GK designers to create products that have a more genuine Japanese (or other) character.

Institute of Doguology researchers, who are as likely to be art historians as designers, are concentrating on the study of tools such as household electrical appliances that many people believe are somehow "culture-free." Such goods are

both modern and commonplace. They reflect everyday life in the countries in which they are used. One study concerns the paraphernalia associated with tea drinking, a custom that varies greatly between the countries in which it is practiced. "Throughout the world there are different *dogu* for the preparation, serving, and drinking of tea," explains researcher Keiko Ihara. "The unique *dogu* and manners of the various cultures were born from the difference in types of tea leaves, in ways of drinking, in the water used, and in the heart expressed by the one serving the tea. These are all so varied that it is hard to believe that they all originated in the same purpose of simply percolating and drinking tea. The shapes of the various types of tea *dogu* are truly frank expressions of the common sense and life-style of the cultures from which they come." Chief researcher Shinsuke Fukushima adds that the British electric kettle, for example, which began life as an article closely related to the preparation of tea, has been largely superseded by the jug kettle, which has moved away from this image (perhaps towards an echo of more sophisticated, "continental" coffee pots?) yet has still proved successful. The comparable item in Japan, where tea is prepared differently, is more like a Thermos bottle, and it too has undergone a number of stylistic changes that may have failed to appreciate the cultural roots of the product type.

Though it might at first seem marginal to the more immediate concerns of the marketplace, this research is not merely window dressing to disguise the rampant ambition of a corporation hell-bent on globalization. As Kenji Ekuan told the Singapore conference: "There are a number of underlying aspects which affect a nation's way of creating things but [which] are often overlooked or unrecognized. I believe it is worthwhile to explore them, for a nation's culture is a 'patent without a patent.' It is a patent that cannot be registered anywhere—yet it contains all the secrets of that nation's methods and ways of creating things.

"In this age of international design, a product that has a distinctive cultural flavor will increasingly become important from the standpoint of global marketing. Every local or regional culture has the potential to be globally appreciated."

Beveltech SG27B bicycle
Maruishi Cycle Industries, 1990

Security system controller
Secom Company, 1989

Monami sewing machine
Singer Nikko Company, 1986

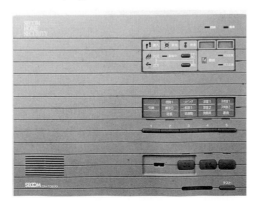

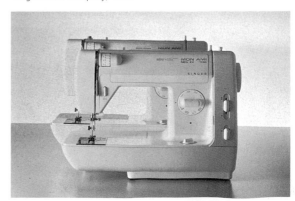

Intimations of variety

How may designs be created that consciously embody and express national or regional cultural identity? One thing is certain. They will not emerge in any enduring form from a system of production that turns its back on the realities of contemporary manufacturing, marketing, and distribution. It is hazardous to suggest that "critical regionalist" architecture could come about in this way; it would be instant oblivion for regionalist design to attempt to follow this course.

Those who reject contemporary technology and resist the current nature of consumer demand will suffer the wrath of the market. By excluding technological advantage in order to protect cultural content, a manufacturer, however well-meaning, risks creating products that are more expensive, less reliable, less efficient, and less competitive. And any belief, explicitly stated or implicitly held, that the market for a product with a certain cultural content should be restricted to consumers within that culture would prove equally disastrous. Luddite, exclusivist, or protectionist attitudes are incompatible with the belief that products can reflect their cultures of origin *and by doing so retain or enhance their competitiveness.*

If products with cultural content are to be created independent of nationalist political sentiment, then one must accept that the cultural content to some degree becomes a tradeable commodity. This is already the case. Many cars reflect aspects of the national cultures of the people who nominally create them (notwithstanding the fact that the styling is often done by a designer from another country and that components are often imported). These cultural aspects may be traded: The television advertisement for the Rover 800 Series Fastback, a sporty sedan made in Britain (some of which have Honda engines), features two Germans driving around Stuttgart talking about the car in German with English subtitles. At the end of the commercial, the driver stops outside the Staatsgalerie, a famous postmodern building by James Stirling, and says admiringly, *"Britischer Architekt,"* concisely highlighting the manufacturer's aim to market the car as "British" to the Germans and "German" to the British. For many products, the local cultural content will become a means of adding value not only for members of the culture in question but also for other cultures. Only for certain products will predominantly local cultural content go hand in hand with local manufacture and local consumption.

Cultural content is traditionally guaranteed in products that are made by craftspeople. In many areas craft has become a largely irrelevant indulgence, but in certain others it has shown a remarkable resilience to the march of technology and in some cases has shown that it can survive happily alongside it. The Italian furniture industry is a good example, combining as it does a high degree of mechanization with craft techniques and an adventurous attitude to design. This industry remains highly competitive and shows no sign of surrendering its commitment to craft processes in preparation for the harsher environment of the single European market after 1992. If anything, these manufacturers are keen to affirm their commitment to a method that has proved spectacularly successful so far.

It is in high-technology consumer products that cultural content perhaps has the greatest potential. This is the area in which craft workmanship has been most thoroughly eradicated, and yet it is here that the need is greatest now to add value and variety to objects that have become boringly similar. Automobiles, consumer-electronics products, kitchen appliances—the staples of the global multinationals—are the products most often seen as being "culture-free" and the ones most in need of differentiation and personalization.

Here, technology, having exacerbated the problem, could perhaps help provide a solution. One technological answer may lie with flexible manufacturing systems. Such systems have taken a long time to reach a workable maturity and are still far from perfect or all-capable. It would be foolish to pretend that these difficulties do not exist or that flexible manufacturing offers a panacea. Nevertheless, the creation of products that reflect cultural characteristics is a task that seems ideally suited to flexible manufacturing, the creative potential of which seems scarcely to have been explored to date.

A flexible manufacturing system (FMS, alternatively known as automated manufacturing technology—AMT) comprises a set of automated assembly machines that are compatible with one another. Using them, a part for manufacture can be passed along a production line under the control of a central computer. Ideally, a product may be assembled from its components in a single continuous, unmanned process. An FMS computer may send instructions to change individual parts of a product in order to create many variants of a basic type without interrupting the production process.

The promise of such systems has occasioned some bold claims on behalf of FMS. According to Tom Forrester in his book *High-Tech Society,* "the savings and productivity gains made possible by FMS can be phenomenal, because a single, all-embracing system can replace several conventional machining lines. FMS yields enormous savings on labor—most assembly work in factories is still labor-intensive. It also saves on plant space and further decreases capital requirements by dramatically reducing the amount of work-in-progress and stock inventory. Product quality is better, so wastage and rectification costs are reduced. Plant utilization is improved because the machines can be kept running most of the time and reprogrammed quickly. Reduced lead-times also enable the manufacturer to react much more swiftly to market trends. Flexible manufacturing systems therefore represent not just a new technology, but an entirely new way of thinking.

"Economists refer to these advantages of flexible automation as 'economies of scope,' as opposed to 'economies of scale.' Under old-fashioned 'hard' automation or mass-production, the greatest savings were realized only with large-scale plants and long production runs. The FMS revolution makes similar economies possible at a wide range of scales. Economies of scope break all the rules of traditional manufacturing. There is no long trip down the learning curve; and entrepreneurial newcomers from unheard-of places can enter the field as never before and swiftly overcome less agile older producers or nations. This is the reality of international competition in the age of FMS."[1]

Not quite, perhaps. FMS is still extremely expensive. It can be hard to specify, hard to install, and hard to keep running. Sophisticated software is needed to ensure that each individual unit of the system plays its part, for if one stage fails, the whole system must stop. For now, FMS is paradoxically an expensive toy for the largest manufacturers best able to invest in new technology, whereas it should ultimately offer the greatest potential to medium-size companies. According to an industry journal, "More than 60 percent of manufacturing industry in Europe is devoted to small and medium batch production in which the product variety is often high. Technologies such as CAD/CAM, robotics and FMS were thought to provide answers to problems involving flexibility. The unpalatable truth is that in many cases they have not fulfilled their promise and in some cases they have proved to be an expensive disaster."[2]

Corporations such as General Motors, Ford, and John Deere have been among the leaders in installing flexible manufacturing systems in the United States. In Japan, Nissan uses an FMS to make its S-Cargo delivery truck, a latter-day Citroen 2CV, switching its production line at short notice to configure versions suitable for bakeries, florists, and other specialty users.[3]

Flexible manufacturing currently demands a reduction in the complexity of many parts in order that machine vision systems can see them and robot manipulators can grip them and orient them correctly for assembly. This has spawned a new discipline called "design for assembly" or DFA. It has not only proved to be a headache to simplify parts to the required degree, but that simplification in its turn has sometimes led to products whose unfamiliar appearance puts their marketability at risk. As the book, *Flexible Manufacturing*, points out, "The redesigning of products required after analysis is so extensive that many people shrink from it. It doesn't fit into their image of the near future of their own product."[4] All in all, then, flexible manufacturing systems are not always as flexible as they are portrayed.

These difficulties go a long way toward explaining the low uptake of FMS among manufacturers of all kinds. What they do not explain is why there has been so little creative thinking, not about what FMS can and cannot do but about what it could and should do. Where FMS has not been seen as a panacea, it has been presented in decidedly uninspiring terms. The following remarks, by Robert H. Hayes, a professor of management at the Harvard Business School, are regrettably typical: "To the extent that better design makes it possible to compress a product's manufacturing throughput time, for example, delivery lead times can be reduced without increasing inventories. This makes possible the development of just-in-time relationships with customers. Equally important, however, is product development time. When management innovations that affect the way the whole company works together combine with new technologies like Computer-Aided Design, Computer-Aided Engineering, Robotic Assembly, and Flexible Manufacturing Systems, the amount of time required to create and implement new designs can be drastically reduced (up to two-thirds)."[5]

But this is where the thinking usually stops. What happens when the time comes that everyone competing in a given sector has taken this step? There is little discussion in the FMS literature[6] on exactly *what* FMS should be put to work to do, in response either to market demands or, more cleverly, to a company's intuition about what it thinks consumers might appreciate. Argument centers, understandably perhaps given the teething troubles, on the problems of computer interface and control. Actual or potential benefits are described almost exclusively in terms of the day-to-day economics of production. Experts in the field confirm that FMS is widely seen as a tool to react to moves by competitors rather than as a way of preempting them by shaping people's expectations and making real things they can scarcely visualize at present. Typical comments observe that "the FMS culture is totally reactive. They respond to someone else's decision on form and shape and material. I'm afraid the dialogue isn't there"; and that "FMS is driven by manufacturing people who just think about making. Design to them is just CAD. They make the wrong products

1. Tom Forester, *High-Tech Society* (Blackwell, 1987).

2. C. B. Besant, "Flexibility in Manufacturing," *International Journal of Advanced Manufacturing Technology* (May 1989): 121.

3. "About Time," *The Economist* (August 11, 1990): 68.

4. P. T. Bolwijn et al., *Flexible Manufacturing* (Elsevier, 1986).

5. Robert H. Hayes, "Design: The Emerging Competitive Battleground" in *Designing for Product Success: Essays and Case Studies from the TRIAD Design Project Exhibit* (Boston: Design Management Institute, 1989).

6. For example, *International Journal of Flexible Manufacturing Systems, Journal of Manufacturing Systems, Assembly Automation, Proceedings of the International Conferences on Flexible Manufacturing Systems, Proceedings of the CIRP Seminars on Manufacturing Systems.*

fast and efficiently."[7] In extreme cases, the lack of dialogue between companies' product design and manufacturing divisions has engendered a fear that installing a FMS might even limit future flexibility rather than increase it.

Clearly, the old credos of Henry Ford and F. W. Taylor for the management of mechanized production no longer apply. It has fallen to the design community to illustrate the potential of FMS and speculate on what such systems might usefully be harnessed to produce. But while management thinking has been unnecessarily blinkered, design speculation has been overoptimistic. There has often been little understanding of the real limitations of FMS and related production technologies, although the basic vision has been clear. As long ago as 1957, before the term FMS was even coined, the design researcher John Chris Jones wrote: "One can imagine the manufacture of domestic goods from minute identical units that would be assembled into a complex whole by the automatic addition of units side by side. Each product could differ from the next without any interruption of the process. Such a system might be sufficiently flexible to allow for the variation of successive products to suit the personal requirements of particular users. . . . But against these intimations of variety we must set the many contemporary and expert prophesies that automation will mean fewer design changes and more uniform products than we have at the moment."[8] And so indeed it has proved. To the extent that it is in use today, automated manufacturing does seem to have made things less varied. Only in the last decade, with products such as the Swatch watch and the Sony Walkman, has the promise of variety begun to be honored. It has taken the technology the intervening thirty years to catch up.

There are now a few examples of FMS used to create varied ranges of consumer products. In Japan, the National Bicycle Industrial Company, a subsidiary of Matsushita, uses a flexible manufacturing system to create Panasonic brand models with more than 11 million permutations. The manufacturing process starts when a customer places an order at a Panasonic cycle store. The specification includes anthropometric data and design preferences. The manufacturer has taken steps to ensure a careful balance between high technology and tradition, however. "The process is not highly automated" explains an article in Fortune, "The factory looks a little like a traditional workshop, with craftspeople hand-wiring gears and silk-screening the customer's name on the frame with the same care that would be given to the finest kimono or lacquerware."[9] The impression of craftsmanship is deliberately heightened by the company's policy of making customers wait two weeks for a bicycle that takes a few hours to make.

Others see potential for FMS in areas of manufacturing that have traditionally been even more labor-intensive. Researchers at North Carolina State University, which is located in the heartland of traditional American furniture manufacturing, believe that their industry could benefit from FMS. "The furniture industry is unusual in that conventional economic analysis may present a strong case for flexible automation," they argue. "Flexible automation may also present certain segments of the furniture industry with a strategic opportunity. Most case-good (non-upholstered) furniture is produced in suites (style groupings), based on forecasted quantities for finished goods inventory. Flexible systems . . . can support individual-item and sold-order production. The subsequent reduction in finished goods inventories and manufacturing lead times would provide significant competitive advantages."[10]

For medium-size manufacturers of things such as bicycles and furniture, where there is a clear case for some customization, there is a role for FMS. But it is instructive to note that the manufacturing process here is not fully automated and that some handwork is perhaps necessary and probably desirable in the finished article. Automated manufacturing technology and craft need not be mutually exclusive; both can contribute to the creation of products that reflect the values of different cultures.

For many smaller manufacturers the inescapable conclusion at present is that FMS is not for them. In smaller companies, the manual worker is still often the most efficient flexible manufacturing system.[11] In general, FMS does not appear to be appropriate (yet) in many industries where the greater flexibility and reliability of human labor outweigh the benefits of twenty-four-hour production and reduced labor costs. It may become so when the costs of the technology involved—robot manipulators, machine vision systems, and artificial-intelligence computers—fall sufficiently. It is also possible that some flexible manufacturing systems may not be under proprietary ownership of one company but that time could be bought on facilities operated by an independent FMS "shop," just as graphic designers often rent time on computer-graphics hardware or as publishers have always gone to printers rather than keep their own presses. A 1989 article in The Economist summarized the state of play and hinted at the potential for design: "Nobody quite knows where all this is leading; but it has the makings of a revolution. In principle, modular and flexible manufacturing should increase competition by lowering the huge costs of entry into mass-market businesses. Furthermore, they should shift the emphasis away from production skills (which anyone can have) towards ideas, flair and sensitivity to what customers might and do want."[12]

7. Stuart Pugh, University of Strathclyde; John Davies and Graham Thompson, UMIST; and Rory Chase, IFS Publications; interviews with the author, January 1991.

8. John Christopher Jones, "Automation and Design," Design 104 (1957).

9. Susan Moffat, "Japan's New Personalized Production," Fortune (October 22, 1990).

10. C. Thomas Culbreth, Russell E. King, and Ezat T. Sanii, "A Flexible Manufacturing System for Furniture Production," Manufacturing Review (December 1989): 257.

11. J. Miller and S. Grocock, "Flexible Assembly Needs in Smaller Companies" in Developments in Automated Assembly, ed. A. Pugh (IFS Publications/Springer Verlag, 1988).

12. "Design It Yourself," The Economist (July 29, 1989): 14.

Even where FMS is in operation, there is as yet little sign of any flair that arises directly from the resources offered by the system. Even companies like Sony and ETA, the part of the Swiss SMH Group that makes Swatch watches, do not appear to have made the most of their robotic assembly lines, despite their reputations for design leadership.

The Sony Walkman is made only in Japan, at two FMS-equipped factories. All models use two basic cassette mechanisms. Circuitry differs according to whether the model is to be one with or without radio, recording, and auto-reverse functions. On top of these seven or eight basic variants, it is then possible to choose the styling from a variety of metal or plastic casings, colors, finishes, and graphics.

The WM-109 Walkman, supposedly of Japanese inspiration, has already proved its value with a shelf life some five times greater than most Walkmen. One can equally imagine a Walkman type of product "in the British style," perhaps with a polished pewter casing and walnut side panels, or a French Walkman like the velvet, gilt, and diamanté design proposed by Frédéric Thevenon at Les Ateliers. If these suggestions seem a little parodic, they could undoubtedly be made more persuasive in proportion to the design time that was given to the problem.

Swatch has demonstrated the potential for culturally based variation at a trivial level. Its Fall/Winter 1990 collection included models in a "Versailles" range called "Stucchi," "Louis Louis," and "Brode d'Or," and a complementary "Medieval" pair of a man's and a woman's watch called "Tristan" and "Isolde," as well as designs of more contemporary inspiration. As their names imply, these watches pillage graphic designs from different periods of history and from different nations.

When it launched its first watches in 1983, Swatch had cut the number of parts in each one by half, to fifty-one. An injection-molded baseplate shell serves as the mounting plate for machined components and includes elements for holding them in place. Assembly takes place in a single process rather than in the two stages of conventional watch manufacture.

This allows Swatch to bring out new models each season, varying the faces, straps, hands, and body of the basic watch. Swatch keeps tabs on trends in design by means of a Design Lab in Milan headed by Matteo Thun, a former Memphis designer, who serves as an art director of a small team coordinating the activities of freelance designers all over the world. The company has recently expanded into manufacturing telephones designed along the same fashion-led principles as the watches and has ambitions to launch a Swatch car in the mid-1990s combining, in the company's words, "innovative design, fun, striking design, and tremendous value for money."

Despite these achievements, Swatch's flexibility is still comparatively limited. There is no variation of the basic shape of individual parts. With a few exceptions, only color and pattern are varied from one season to the next. Swatch has sold 70 million watches to date. It brings out another thirty or so new models every six months based on designs that have been selected from the three hundred proposals submitted annually from designers around the world in response to the program handed out by the Design Lab. These take eighteen months to pass from the final design selection to production. With 10 million sales annually, this means that the run for each individual model averages about 150,000 units. The time to production and the total number of watches from a complete production run are both greater than FMS experts envision for a truly flexible manufacturing system. To continue with the Swatch example, there were thirty-six models in the Fall/Winter 1990 range. Each had a pair of straps, a sets of hands, a face, and a shell that was unique to that model. If Swatch were to take flexibility to the limit, it could create 1,679,616 (thirty-six to the power of four) unique designs. (Actually to follow the exercise through might be ill-advised because the parts were not designed to be complementary for assembly in this way, but the point is made.)

As with other manufacturers of consumer products that make use of one or other form of FMS, Swatch creates dozens of variations but thousands of repetitions and not, as FMS promises, the other way around. A study of flexible manufacturing systems in use in Japan and the United States published in the *Harvard Business Review* found that the average number of different articles made by an FMS in Japan was ninety-three, not an astonishingly high figure, while that in the United States was just ten. The American machines produced correspondingly more of each variant, while the Japanese produced fewer. "With few exceptions, the flexible manufacturing systems installed in the United States show an astonishing lack of flexibility. In many cases, they perform worse than the conventional technology they replace. The technology itself is not to blame; it is management that makes the difference. Compared with Japanese systems, those in U.S. plants produce an order-of-magnitude less variety of parts."[13]

Imaginative management holds the key to the effective use of FMS, but this quality seems to be remarkable by its absence in general practice. Sony uses FMS for its Walkman production but does not appear to wish to use it to increase the variety of these products. The corporation's design chiefs admit that they have both the design and manufacturing

13. Ramchandran Jaikumar, "Postindustrial Manufacturing," *Harvard Business Review* (November–December 1986): 69.

resources to create, say, Walkmen that reflect the attributes of selected national cultures. The principal difficulty in making an "Italian" or an "American" Walkman, for example, would be to choose the materials and the design.[14]

Such a move is both technically possible and strategically well matched to Sony's stated aim to continue adding value to its products. Yet it appears that Sony will not be the first company to introduce a range of products differentiated by design that takes account of cultural differences. Sony's designers feel that such a development could not avoid being retrogressive and nostalgic. They fear that it would erode the image of the Sony brand. It is not uncommon for major manufacturers to experience cold feet at this stage. Having acknowledged the interest among consumers for products that reflect national and cultural differences and having pointed out the potential for FMS to be used to enable the creation of such products, the design critic John Thackara is nevertheless forced to remark: "This tendency in marketing and technology is a problem for the global multinationals for whom selling high-quality, high value-added products to affluent consumers is no substitute for the mass production upon which they were reared."[15]

Yet it is a truism—admittedly one often belied by appearances—that manufacturers seek to differentiate their products from those of their rivals in order to remain competitive. It is true, too, that many companies are, like Sony, seeking to "add value" to products whose fundamental nature and function are by now well understood by consumers. That there is a market for such products has been well demonstrated by Sony Walkmen, Swatch watches, Alessi tableware, and many other objects that have made design such a visible profession during the 1980s. It has also been demonstrated at a different level by the continuing popularity, despite the efforts of the evangelists of "good design," of "kitsch" objects with more overt embellishment that claim to appeal to particular cultures.

These observations would appear to invite further and more discriminating use of design in the creation of products for local and international markets alike. The acknowledgment and expression of cultural identity provides one means for design to achieve its commercial end of providing differentiation and appeal in the market. It is clear that many designers themselves are concerned with reflecting their cultures in their work, and that in many cases this concern is on the increase. This feeling is harbored by designers in developing countries who see their cultures threatened by outside forces, but also by those in developed countries. Cultural values are clearly expressed in the design from some countries.

Such expression is being actively encouraged in others.

Many designers, however, are hesitant to pursue this course unequivocally, worried that their conscious attempts to reflect cultural identity might be seen as artificial or in poor taste. They may take encouragement from those in other creative fields. Architects in particular have long sought to design buildings that are appropriate not only to their immediate surroundings but also to the wider cultural-historical context. Some of the finest buildings of this century are those that best meet this aim. In the very different art of classical music, some leading composers have also made careers on their declared preoccupation not only with the preservation of national music but also with the renewal and reinterpretation of these traditions in their own work. Both creative professions have overcome the self-doubt currently felt by designers. They have shown that it is possible to avoid the association of their work with "unhealthy" political nationalisms and instead to effect a benign but nevertheless significant celebration of national cultures.

In many cases, the resources are already in place for designers in large firms and in corporate design centers to begin to follow the example set by artists in other fields. Studios frequently employ designers from many countries. This is especially the case in the larger corporations and design firms, including those that profess the cause of "global design." As these organizations establish satellite design centers in countries other than their own, they increase their potential to create products that have new meaning to particular cultures. With sophisticated image- and data-transmission equipment, these offices can communicate design ideas faster and more effectively than ever before. Designers in an office in one country could collaborate with designers in a main studio to superimpose a native's perception of his or her own culture on the received, perhaps stereotypical, view of that same culture held by outsiders. Such an approach would help to guarantee a degree of authenticity on the one hand and broad market appeal on the other.

Whatever the method adopted, it is, of course, important that the pursuit of cultural identity in design does not take place at the expense of the criteria that always confront designers—the need to assure functionality and manufacturability, to control costs, and to bear in mind the requirements of the target market. This said, there are no fundamental obstacles preventing designers and the companies for which they work from adopting this new course. All that remains is for them to find the will to do so.

14. Matami Yamaguchi, General Manager, Merchandising and Product Communication Strategy Group, Sony Corporation; interview with the author, October 1990.

15. John Thackara, "Beyond the Object in Design" in *Design after Modernism,* ed. John Thackara (Thames and Hudson, 1988).

Select bibliography

The purpose of this brief bibliography is to single out one title for each country, where available, that characterizes contemporary design in that country. These books are recent, critical, and cover several design disciplines. There are in addition many exhibition catalogs, promotional yearbooks, professional directories, and journal supplements that provide portfolios of activity in particular fields of design within these countries.

Germany
Erlhoff, Michael. *Designed in Germany*. Munich: Prestel, 1990.

Netherlands
Staal, Gert and Hester Wolters, eds. *Holland in Vorm 1945–1987* (Dutch Design). Gravenhage: Stichting Holland in Vorm, 1987.

Denmark
Bernsen, Jens and Susanne Schenstrøm, eds. *100+3 Great Danish Industrial Designs*. Copenhagen: Danish Designråd, 1985.

Great Britain
Huygen, Frederique. *British Design: Image and Identity*. London: Thames and Hudson, 1989.

France
Rouard, Margo and Françoise Jollant-Kneebone, eds. *Design Français 1960–1990 Trois Décennies*. Paris: Agence pour la Promotion de la Création Industrielle/ Syros Alternatives, 1987.

Spain
Julier, Guy. *New Spanish Design*. New York: Rizzoli International Publications, 1991.

Italy
Sparke, Penny. *Italian Design 1987 to the Present*. London: Thames and Hudson, 1988.

Hungary
Néray, Katalin, ed. *Örökség: Tárgy és környezetkultúra Magyarországon 1945–1985* (Heritage: Design and Manmade Environment in Hungary). Budapest: Budapest Design Center/ Mücsarnok, 1985.

India
Munshi, K., A.G Rao, Kirti Trivedi, G.G. Ray, S. Nadkarni, U.A. Athavankar, Ravi Poovaiah, Mickety Patel, and R.K. Joshi. *IDC 20 Years 1969–1989: Selected Papers*. Bombay: Industrial Design Centre/Indian Institute of Technology, 1989.

Japan
Sparke, Penny. *Japanese Design*. London: Michael Joseph, 1987.

United States
Aldersey-Williams, Hugh. *New American Design*. New York: Rizzoli International Publications, 1988.

Canada
Day, Peter and Linda Lewis. *Art in Everyday Life: Observations on Contemporary Canadian Design*. Toronto: Ummerhill Press/The Power Plant, 1988.

Index